EXPOSED

BEHEADINGS, SLAVERY, AND THE
HELLISH REALITY OF RADICAL ISLAM

ERICK STAKELBECK

REGNERY
PUBLISHING
A Division of Salem Media Group

Regnery® is a registered trademark of Salem Communications Holding Corporation

Library of Congress Cataloging-in-Publication Data

Stakelbeck, Erick.
 ISIS Exposed : beheadings, slavery, and the hellish reality of radical Islam / Erick Stakelbeck.
    pages cm
  ISBN 978-1-62157-377-7 (hardback)
 1. IS (Organization) 2. Terrorism--Religious aspects--Islam. 3. Security, International. 4. Middle East--Politics and government--1945- I. Title.
  HV6431.S687 2015
  956.05′4--dc23
                          2015003260

Published in the United States by
Regnery Publishing
A Division of Salem Media Group
300 New Jersey Ave NW
Washington, DC 20001
www.Regnery.com

Manufactured in the United States of America

10 9 8 7 6 5 4 3 2 1

Books are available in quantity for promotional or premium use. For information on discounts and terms, please visit our website: www.Regnery.com.

Distributed to the trade by
Perseus Distribution
250 West 57th Street
New York, NY 10107

*To my mom, Agnes. Thank you for a lifetime
of love, patience, support, and understanding and
for teaching me to trust in the Lord.*

CONTENTS

PROLOGUE

THE ISLAMIC STATE OF MINNESOTA

"WELCOME TO LITTLE MOGADISHU."

I motioned out the car window toward a steady procession of Somali women covered in Islamic garb walking up and down the street, carrying shopping bags.

"This must be it," my cameraman, Ian, agreed.

We pulled over to get the lay of the land. Groups of men congregated outside a gritty strip of Somali-owned businesses on one side of the street, while Riverside Plaza, a densely packed cluster of high-rise apartment buildings populated mainly by low-income immigrants from Somalia, occupied the other side.

As Ian and I strolled the streets of Cedar-Riverside—or "Little Mogadishu," as it's known to locals—capturing footage for a series of TV reports, I wondered how many Minnesotans realized that this neighborhood in the shadow of downtown Minneapolis was the "center of the nation's largest concentration of Somalis."[1] Or that the Twin Cities, Minneapolis and neighboring St. Paul, were home to over a hundred thousand Somalis,[2] more than any metropolitan area in North America.

More important, I wondered how many Americans knew that these two cities nestled in the frozen tundra of the upper Midwest, in a prosperous state that annually ranks among the nation's best for quality of life, had become the number one terrorist breeding ground in the United States— beating out New York, Chicago, Los Angeles, and even Dearborn, Michigan, home to the country's largest Arab-American population and a known hotbed of support for the terror group Hezbollah.[3]

Frosty Minneapolis–St. Paul holds the dubious distinction of being America's Jihad Central—thanks in no small part to its large Somali immigrant communities in neighborhoods like Little Mogadishu, which have proven fertile ground for terrorist recruiters.

Since 2007, dozens of young Somali men and women from the Twin Cities have used their U.S. passports to travel overseas and join Islamic terrorist organizations. The first wave departed for Somalia to join the al Qaeda–linked group al-Shabaab. Most never returned home, and some have been confirmed dead—including a Minneapolis man named Shirwa Ahmed who became the first successful American suicide bomber when he blew himself up as part of a coordinated attack in northern Somalia that killed thirty people in October 2008.[4]

The destination of choice for aspiring *mujahideen* (holy warriors) from Minnesota changed around 2012, as the Syrian Civil War became the prime magnet for jihadists around the world. One organization in particular has captured their imagination—and allegiance—in an unprecedented way: the Islamic State of Iraq and al-Sham, or ISIS. Also sometimes referred to as ISIL—or the Islamic State of Iraq and the Levant—and by the Arabic moniker "Daesh," the terror group originally grew out of an al Qaeda franchise that had fought against U.S. forces in Iraq. Employing a lethal mix of brutal violence, battlefield prowess, fanatical ideology, and social media savvy, ISIS blazed its way across large swathes of Syria and

Iraq in rapid and stunning fashion on its way to declaring a caliphate, or Islamic State. As we'll see throughout this book, ISIS may be the most powerful terrorist movement in history, boasting tens of thousands of foot soldiers (and countless more sympathizers) and threatening not only the Middle East but also the United States and Europe in ways that are profound and unprecedented.

Look no further than Minneapolis and St. Paul. As of this writing, at least fifteen residents of the Twin Cities reportedly have traveled to the Middle East to join ISIS.[5] All but one of these American terrorists—a thirty-three-year-old African American convert named Douglas McCain who was killed fighting alongside the group in Syria in August 2014—were of Somali descent.[6]

The list includes Abdirahmaan Muhumed, a twenty-nine-year-old Minneapolis resident who died in the same battle as McCain.[7] Before leaving Minnesota to join ISIS, Muhumed, who was the father of nine children, worked at Minneapolis-St. Paul International Airport, where he cleaned jetliners for Delta Air Lines. Muhumed reportedly "had unfettered access to jetliners at the airport, which handles 90,000 passengers a day. He also had access to the tarmac and special security clearance to other parts of the airport."[8] How nice. If Muhumed was able to obtain not only a job but security clearances at a major American airport, one wonders how many more aspiring ISIS terrorists have been able to do the same.

As I sat at an outdoor café in the shadow of Little Mogadishu with Bob Fletcher, who for sixteen years served as sheriff of Ramsey County, which includes the city of St. Paul, he explained how terror recruiters have made inroads into the local Somali community. Fletcher retired from the St. Paul police force in 2013 and now heads the Center for Somalia History Studies, where he works with Somali community leaders to counter Islamic radicalization in their neighborhoods. He told me that the emergence of ISIS and its declaration of a new caliphate in the heart of the Middle East has been a game changer:

What's happened is that since July of 2012, we haven't had any kids leave to go join al-Shabaab, but we have had several leave now to go join ISIS. And the reason is that ISIS controls land; they control cities. They are in a position to be able to recruit differently than al-Shabaab. Al-Shabaab, all they have to promise is, "come join us in the jungles while we ambush and plot our terrorist attacks." But what ISIS is selling now is the opportunity to build something, to build a new society, and that is very, very exciting for a lot of kids, to be a part of something new and special—to have some sense of self-worth.[9]

In June 2014, a twenty-year-old man and a nineteen-year-old woman—both Somali Americans who attended the Al Farooq Youth & Family Center mosque in the Minneapolis suburb of Bloomington—disappeared. They are now thought to be in Syria.[10]

Interestingly enough, the same mosque was also frequented by an Egyptian-American radical named Amir Meshal who allegedly preached jihad to young Somalis there. Meshal was no stranger to Somalia, a fact that may have helped him in his interactions with young Somali-Americans at Al Farooq. In 2007, he was arrested and questioned by counterterrorism agents in Kenya and "accused of having received weapons training in an Al-Qaida camp and of serving as a translator for the terrorist group's leaders in Somalia."[11] The charges against Meshal were eventually dropped, and he seems to have kept a low profile until resurfacing in Minnesota sporting a BMW and plenty of cash—according to his reputation around the Al Farooq mosque.

Whether the two missing young people came under Meshal's influence is unclear; once the mosque's leadership learned of his "extremist views," it contacted local police and obtained a no-trespassing order essentially banning him from Al Farooq; and, as of this writing, Meshal's whereabouts are unknown. Whether he was working as a terror recruiter or not (some have even speculated that he may have been an FBI mole), Meshal's alleged activities at Al Farooq show, at the very least, how a charismatic radical can influence impressionable young minds.[12]

In his intensive work with the Somali community, former Ramsey County sheriff Fletcher has heard story after story of how young Twin Cities Somalis were lured to jihad overseas, to Syria and elsewhere. He provided me a fascinating—and chilling—firsthand glimpse of how the terrorist recruitment process works for ISIS and other Islamic terror groups on American soil:

> There is no question that the Internet is one of the primary mediums to get a kid hooked…it is the gateway drug. But there needs to be some real people on the ground that reinforce what they are hearing on the Internet. There needs to be a person that touches them on a personal level…what I refer to as "The Guide." There is going to be a person that physically gets in touch with these kids, and helps facilitate that travel [to the Islamic State].… [Recruits] need to procure travel documents; they need to raise money, usually somewhere in the area of $4,000 to $5,000 to help facilitate all the travel that takes place and plus…these kids want to have money when they get there. And they need to make sure someone is purchasing the tickets…they need a driver and a facilitator to get them to the airport.… So there is, I don't like to use the word "team," but there is an organization that makes this happen. But usually there is one principal person that…I call "The Guide" that can take this person in this [radicalized] ideological state and guide them to Syria or wherever it might be.… and of course, there are people in the Middle East…that are constantly feeding and supporting this decision.[13]

Somalis first began arriving in the United States in the early 1990s, thanks to a taxpayer-funded refugee resettlement program run by the State

Department. In my 2011 book, *The Terrorist Next Door,* I described how tens of thousands of Somali Muslims, with the U.S. government's help, have left the chaos of their homeland over the past few decades and settled in places such as Nashville, Boston, San Diego, Columbus, Ohio, Portland, Maine, and especially the Twin Cities.

The exodus is not hard to explain. Somalia has had no functioning central government since 1991 and is among the most dangerous countries in the world (as the 1993 Black Hawk Down incident, in which nineteen U.S. servicemen were killed in a raging gun battle against warlords and jihadists in the capital city of Mogadishu, showed so vividly). It's also a hotbed for Islamic terrorism, with the al Qaeda–linked al-Shabaab perpetrating acts of horrific carnage not only inside Somalia but in neighboring Kenya—where al-Shabaab terrorists laid siege to an upscale Nairobi shopping mall for four days in September 2013, murdering sixty-seven people, including several Western tourists.

Many Somali-Americans are undoubtedly grateful to have escaped the chaos of their homeland and started a new life in the United States. But in reporting extensively since 2008 on the growth of Islamic radicalism in Somali-American communities throughout the U.S., I have found time and again that failure to assimilate—and in some cases, a lack of any desire to do so—is a major issue for a significant chunk of Somali immigrants.

For an unemployed, isolated nineteen-year-old Somali with little education who doesn't feel quite at home in the United States, the lure of being a gun-toting jihadi rock star in the Islamic State—and a supposed champion and defender of Muslims around the world—can be quite appealing.

But ISIS doesn't attract just high school dropouts and pot-smoking knuckleheads. Omar Jamal, a longtime Somali community activist based in the Twin Cities, told me that while the Islamic State does indeed target the "confused, lost-identity kids" and high school dropout types, he had come to realize that "Even an 'A' student in universities and colleges is...vulnerable to [ISIS's] powerful propaganda machine.... It has been very successful—kids are responding to it.... The attraction is a very strict, ideological-driven message and indoctrination process. Kids are led to believe they are part of a bigger mission, something much bigger than them. They feel grandiose."[14]

Department of Homeland Security chief Jeh Johnson paid a visit to Little Mogadishu in November 2014, meeting with local and state law enforcement and community leaders to devise strategies to combat "violent extremism" among Twin Cities residents.[15] Unfortunately, branding the problem of Islamic terrorism with the vague, evasive label of "violent extremism," is getting off on the wrong foot. To be crystal clear: the root cause of the virtual terror pipeline from Minnesota to the Islamic State is a powerful, well-defined Islamic jihadist ideology that, as we'll see throughout this book, resonates among a significant number of Muslims of all races, nationalities, education levels, and socio-economic backgrounds.

ISIS's influence in the United States can be felt not only among the Somali communities of the Twin Cities, or in the "lone wolf" terrorist attacks it has inspired in places such as Oklahoma and New York City, but among radicalized young Muslims across the country, all interconnected by a manic ISIS social media campaign for which the group and its supporters blast out some ninety tweets per minute.[16]

Twitter is only one means by which ISIS reaches an English-speaking American audience with its message. The crown jewels of its multimedia onslaught are its propaganda videos, which feature ultra-slick production values reminiscent of a Hollywood action flick.

One ISIS video released in November 2014—featuring the gruesome beheadings of American aid worker Peter Kassig and twenty-two captured Syrian soldiers—had an estimated equipment cost of $200,000, used multiple takes, and took between four and six hours to film.[17] Needless to say, the days of Osama bin Laden staring into a single camera and droning on in Arabic for hours are long gone. ISIS has singlehandedly revolutionized jihadi multimedia in an ambitious effort to appeal to Western Muslims—the same American and European recruits that reportedly crave Snickers, Pringles, and Red Bulls upon their arrival to the rugged Islamic State.[18]

Take, for instance, ISIS's magnum opus, a graphic, fifty-five-minute documentary entitled *Flames of War* that debuted on jihadi websites in September 2014. The film features an ISIS fighter speaking in American-accented English. In one scene, he presides over captured Syrian soldiers as they dig their own graves. As Ryan Mauro of the Clarion Project describes,

> The film utilizes romantic imagery carefully crafted to appeal to dissatisfied and alienated young men, replete with explosions, tanks and self-described *mujahedeen* winning battles. Anti-American rhetoric provides the voice-over to stop motion and slow motion action sequences. The use of special effects such as bullet-time is interspersed with newsreel footage.
>
> This up-to-date, sophisticated cinematography combined with the bloodthirsty message makes the film *Flames of War* reminiscent of Hitler propagandist Leni Riefenstahl's 1935 film *Triumph of the Will*.[19]

The decision to make an American the face of a high-profile project such as *Flames of War* was a stroke of strategic brilliance by ISIS that surely did not go unnoticed in the jihadi underground of the United States. The message of the film is unmistakable: *Our movement knows no racial, ethnic, or national boundaries. It does not matter where you are from or what language you speak. Unlike America, the Islamic State does not discriminate. My American brothers, you, too, can rise in the ranks, slaughter the unbelievers and pagans, avenge Islam, and be among the founding fathers of a new caliphate that will one day rule the world. You will become legend. Join us.*

ISIS really does know no boundaries. One of the most influential "spiritual authorities" inspiring ISIS fighters is based not in Raqqa or Fallujah but in the midwestern United States. According to a study by the London-based International Centre for the Study of Radicalisation and Political Violence, some 60 percent of foreign fighters in Syria follow a Dearborn, Michigan–based imam named Sheikh Ahmad Musa Jibril on Twitter.[20] The report found that Jibril is playing a very subtle game. He "does not openly incite his followers to violence nor does he explicitly encourage them to join the Syrian jihad. Instead, he adopts the role of a cheerleader: supporting the principles of armed opposition to [Syrian dictator Bashar al-] Assad, often in highly emotive terms, while employing extremely charged religious or sectarian idioms."

At the time of this writing, Jibril, who is in his early forties, had upwards of 245,000 likes on Facebook and over 26,000 followers on Twitter. He has "spent six years in federal prison for crimes including money laundering, tax evasion and trying to bribe a juror" and was reportedly banned from one Michigan mosque for "urging his followers to kill non-Muslims."[21] Upon his release from prison in 2012, Jibril quickly became a favorite among young Western jihadis and has even interacted directly with foreign fighters in Syria via Twitter.[22]

U.S. intelligence agencies are undoubtedly aware of Jibril's influence. He's subject to restrictive bail conditions that limit his movements, but he remains a free man, reportedly living in his father's Dearborn bungalow, in the shadow of Detroit.[23] Jibril's output on social media has dipped with increased scrutiny of his activities, but other American citizens are eager to spread the ISIS message.

Consider the case of a twenty-nine-year-old single mother named Heather Coffman. Coffman, who lived with her parents and seven-year-old son in rural Henrico County, Virginia, was arrested by federal agents in November 2014 and charged with making false statements to the FBI about her connections to ISIS. According to an FBI affidavit, she posted pro-ISIS material on Facebook under various accounts and tried to help an undercover FBI agent facilitate a fictional Islamist sympathizer's travel to the Islamic State.[24]

If you're surprised that a single mom living with her parents in rural Virginia would convert to Islam and enter the dark world of ISIS, don't be. As we'll see in chapter four, the ideology and triumphs of the fledgling Islamic State have resonated with a host of troubled men and women throughout America who are not repelled by, but drawn to, its gleeful sadism and massive success. ISIS is not just a movement—it is an event.

In just a few years of existence, ISIS has upended the geography of the Middle East, drawn America back into the region, and quite possibly changed the course of world history in the process. It is a growing global phenomenon that profoundly threatens America from within and without.

And it is just getting started.

CHAPTER ONE

THE CALIPHATE RETURNS

"WE'RE TALKING ABOUT EGYPT TODAY BUT IN A FEW MONTHS, everybody will be talking about Iraq. Trust me."

It was mid-August 2013, and as we chatted in the green room of Fox News Channel's Washington, D.C., bureau, a friend who is a decorated U.S. military veteran and had spent significant time in Iraq throughout that year was providing an ominous glimpse of things to come.

"Iraq is out of control right now and no one is even paying attention," he lamented. "We left, but the jihadists didn't."

At the time of our conversation, the major story in the Middle East was the second Egyptian revolution and the demise of Mohammed Morsi's Muslim Brotherhood regime. Iraq had largely disappeared from the headlines despite a horrific wave of violence that commenced practically from the moment U.S. forces withdrew in December 2011. Most of the bloodshed was carried out by an ultra-violent terror group called the Islamic State of Iraq and al-Sham (Syria), otherwise known as ISIS, that would soon—through an unprecedented campaign of conquest and carnage—make Iraq the biggest story in the world once again, just as my friend was predicting.

ISIS, or the Islamic State, is more than just a terrorist organization. It is a fully fledged terrorist army boasting some thirty-five thousand battle-hardened jihadists[1] and controlling roughly thirty-five thousand square miles of territory across vast swaths of Syria and Iraq, smack dab in the middle of the Middle East.[2] To put it in perspective, that's an area that's been described as roughly the size of Jordan (or the state of Indiana). It is home to some 8 million unfortunate souls living under ISIS's sadistic rule.[3]

ISIS and its followers are adherents of Jihadist-Salafism, the most extreme and violent interpretation of Islam—and the ideology of choice for Sunni Islamic terrorists. Salafi jihadists despise the West, modeling themselves after Islam's prophet Mohammed and his earliest followers in the seventh-century Arabian desert. In the modern era, this worldview has translated into the merciless application of Islamic sharia law in all areas under ISIS control. As we'll examine in chapter two, public beheadings, amputations, crucifixions, sexual slavery, and slave-trading are all normal features of life in the Islamic State caliphate. Religious minorities and women have particularly precarious positions in ISIS's sharia society; they're subjected to mass persecution and second-class-citizen status in places such as Raqqa, Syria—the de facto capital of the Islamic State.

To say that ISIS's emergence has captured the attention of Islamists worldwide would be an understatement. The prospect of a reborn Islamic superpower dominating the world stage has loomed large in the imaginations of Muslim radicals for almost a century; ever since the last caliphate came to an end in 1924 after the collapse of the Turkish-led Ottoman Empire, Islamists great and small have pined for its return.

So, needless to say, when ISIS announced the reestablishment of the caliphate, or Islamic State, on June 29, 2014, the news sent shockwaves throughout the Muslim world. Abu Bakr al-Baghdadi was declared the *caliph*, or political and spiritual leader of all Muslims worldwide, and demanded their allegiance—a move that was met with disapproval in many Islamic corners (in many cases not out of opposition to a caliphate, but to ISIS's presuming to declare and claiming to lead it) but embraced in others.

Al-Baghdadi had the audacity—and with ISIS's military prowess and territorial gains, the means—to do what al Qaeda, the Muslim Brotherhood, Hizb ut-Tahrir, the Iranian regime, and virtually every prominent radical Islamic entity has dreamed of doing for the past ninety years. Regardless of their tactical and even theological differences (Shia Iran, for instance, seeks more of an "Imamate," with an Iranian ayatollah at the helm), all radical Islamist organizations share the ultimate goal of re-establishing a caliphate, or pan-Islamic super state, that will confront Israel and the West and return Islam to its former glory days. This grand, borderless coalition of Islamic nations governed by sharia law would ideally be united politically, economically, and militarily; control a large share of the world's oil supply, and boast nuclear capability. A formidable foe, without question—and one with big shoes to fill, historically:

- Under the Umayyad Caliphate, the second of the four major caliphates after Mohammed's death in 632 AD, the Muslim world empire reached its zenith. Between 661 and 750 AD, the Umayyads, whose capital was Damascus, ruled over 5 million square miles of contiguous land, including Spain and Portugal—rebranded "Al Andalus" by their Muslim conquerors—and drove into central France before being repelled by the armies of Frankish warrior Charles Martel. Despite the setback in France, the caliphate continued its advance elsewhere. The island of Sicily eventually came under Islamic control, and Muslim armies launched frequent raids into southern Italy, even plundering suburban Rome in 846 AD. These were only the beginnings of a long struggle between Europe and Islam that only intensified under the Ottomans and still goes on today, albeit in a different form, as we'll see in chapters six and seven.

- The Ottoman Caliphate was established in 1571 and at its height encompassed most of the Middle East, North Africa, and the Caucasus, not to mention a large chunk of southeastern Europe, including Greece, Romania, Bulgaria, Albania, the former Yugoslavia, and parts of modern-day Hungary. The Ottoman Turks even reached the gates of Vienna twice before being turned back. Yet by the dawn of the twentieth century, the Ottoman Empire had declined to the point that it was known as "the sick man of Europe." Its caliphate gradually shrank in size and influence and was ultimately abolished by the secular Turkish ruler Mustafa Kemal Ataturk in 1924.

- The Muslim Brotherhood was founded in Egypt four years later as a direct response to the dissolution of the caliphate, an event the Brothers and their founder, Hassan al-Banna, considered a catastrophe.

- But the Brotherhood's slow-and-steady incremental strategy for reviving the caliphate was insufficient for al Qaeda and other more impetuous Brotherhood offshoots that broke away from the "Brother-ship" with the goal of establishing a sprawling Islamic state—stretching from the Himalayas in the east to the Atlantic Ocean in the west—through violent jihad.

- Finally ISIS took the al Qaeda formula, added tens of thousands of foot soldiers and heavy weaponry, and ran with it, succeeding where AQ and the Brotherhood had failed and violently imposing an Islamic State across a large area of Iraq and Syria—the heartland of the caliphates of old.

Compared to the Umayyad and the Ottoman, the self-declared ISIS caliphate is tiny. But those previous caliphates weren't built in a day, either. The ultimate long-term goal of ISIS, as of its predecessors, is to expand its current mini-empire to the four corners of the earth, imposing Islamic sharia law on all mankind and either slaughtering those who do not comply or forcing them to live a humiliating second-class existence as *dhimmis*. Of course, given ISIS's track record of wholesale massacres in the areas that it has conquered thus far, there would likely be few people left to dhimmify.

Another important aspect of the Islamist vision is that all areas—including Israel and European nations such as Spain—that were ever part of the caliphate at some point in history are still considered Muslim land and must be brought back into the fold, through violent jihad if necessary. On that, there can be no compromise.

While global domination is the endgame, in the short term ISIS will settle for expanding the current borders of the Islamic State into the countries in its immediate backyard: Jordan, Lebanon, Saudi Arabia, and the remaining areas of Iraq and Syria that it has not yet conquered, including the big prizes of Baghdad and Damascus. In ISIS's vision, assaults on Israel and the hated Shia stronghold of Iran would also come at some point, followed by forays into North Africa and South Asia. Does that sound like an unlikely scenario? It may seem that way. But it's not impossible in today's wildly unstable Middle East.

As recently as November 2010, just before the first stirrings of the Arab Spring in Tunisia, few foresaw the toppling of secular Arab strongmen whose iron-fisted regimes had ruled for decades (much easier to predict, unfortunately, were the radical Islamic regimes that would follow them). Who would have predicted that two massive revolutions would engulf Egypt, the most populous and influential Arab Muslim nation, in the span of just two years? And what about ISIS's lightning seizure of Mosul, Iraq's second-largest city, in June 2014, a geopolitical earthquake that apparently took the Obama administration, and much of the world, completely by surprise? The point is that events are unfolding so rapidly and unpredictably in today's Middle East—and the West's response is so weak, disjointed, and muddled—that nothing is beyond the realm of possibility in the region, including an ISIS caliphate stretching well beyond its current borders.

And as the Twin Cities terror pipeline shows, ISIS's influence is felt far beyond the Middle East. While the bulk of ISIS's soldiers hail from Syria and Iraq, at least a third of its ranks consist of foreign fighters who have flocked to the Islamic State caliphate from eighty countries around the world,[4] including thousands from Europe and approximately 130 from the United States.[5] Boasting fanatical adherents on six continents and flush with tons of cash, territory, and heavy weaponry, ISIS may very well go down as the most powerful and influential terrorist movement in history. It is already the richest, with an estimated overall worth of $2 billion.[6]

It is also the most brutal—"a group of marauders unparalleled in Mesopotamia since the time of the Mongols"[7]—crucifying, raping, pillaging, and beheading their way across Iraq and Syria and gleefully posting videos and pictures of the slaughter on YouTube, Facebook, Twitter, and Instagram for their devoted followers worldwide to revel in. Old and young, male and female, Christians and Kurds, Yazidis and Shiites: none are immune to ISIS's savagery.

Thanks to its sweeping gains in Iraq and Syria and its recruitment of some fifteen thousand foreign fighters from every corner of the globe, ISIS has overtaken al Qaeda—the group from which it was spawned—as the top jihadist organization on the planet. Think about it. Al Qaeda has branches around the world and remains an extremely dangerous beast, but it controls no territory and cannot field a standing army. The genocidal terror group Hamas has run the tiny Gaza Strip into the ground, creating a miserable mini–Islamic emirate with little influence beyond its immediate neighborhood, outside of fundraising. The Taliban ruled the war-ravaged wasteland of Afghanistan for just five years, but only took the country even deeper into the Stone Age.

While al Qaeda, Hamas, and the Taliban are all formidable in their own ways (particularly Hamas, with its large rocket arsenal that can now reach every corner of Israel), none of them can match ISIS's lethal combination of funding, foot soldiers, territory, global reach, multimedia influence, and advanced weaponry. Further, all three of the above-named organizations have been around for years and absorbed heavy blows to their leadership and infrastructures. They have likely already hit their ceilings, whereas ISIS, in its current incarnation, only exploded (no pun intended) onto the world scene in 2013 yet has already risen to the top of the jihadi heap.

The only entity comparable to ISIS is Hezbollah. The two terror heavyweights have battled each other in Syria and Iraq over the past few years as part of the ongoing Sunni-Shia strife sweeping the region (more on that in chapter eight), with Hezbollah's top leader Sheikh Hassan Nasrallah warning, "The capabilities, numbers and capacities available to ISIS are vast and large. This is what is worrying everyone and everyone should be worried.... This [ISIS] monster is growing and getting bigger."[8]

Unlike the Islamic State, Hezbollah's home base of southern Lebanon does not constitute a vast territory. But Hezbollah, essentially operating as a state within a state, does exert tremendous sway over the Lebanese government and also wields a global terror network that is active on six continents. Most important, Hezbollah is sponsored by the state of Iran, which has supplied it with tens of thousands of rockets and advanced missiles. Hezbollah also boasts a well-trained paramilitary force that has battled both the Israeli military and Syrian rebels in ground engagements.

Although (as we'll see in later chapters) funds from Turkey, Qatar, and the Persian Gulf states have almost certainly fallen into its hands, ISIS, unlike Hezbollah, has no clear state sponsor behind it—but ISIS *is* a state sponsor of terrorism. The territory controlled by the Islamic State encompasses large chunks of northern and western Iraq and eastern and northern Syria, from the outskirts of the Iraqi capital Baghdad to the periphery of Aleppo, Syria's largest city. Clearly, ISIS possesses the geographical expanse of a "state." And it is beginning to build up other trappings of statehood as well, developing a sophisticated bureaucracy, issuing annual progress reports, minting its own currency, and even reportedly issuing its own Islamic State passports.[9]

It's also a good bet that, if left unchecked, the ISIS caliphate—like other state sponsors of terrorism—will export terror beyond its borders very soon, quite possibly to a neighborhood near you. In fact it has already exported terror, if only indirectly, in the form of Western sympathizers who have been inspired by ISIS to carry out solo "lone wolf" jihadi attacks in Canada, New York City, Australia, and Oklahoma.

As for rockets and missiles, ISIS could begin to close a wide gap with Hezbollah by, for starters, seizing some of the Syrian regime's missiles and launching pads—a scenario that is certainly not outside the realm of possibility. ISIS actually showcased a captured Scud missile during a military parade in Raqqa in June 2014. It's unclear whether the Scud was of Syrian or Iraqi origin, and experts believe it was inoperable.[10]

Nevertheless, ISIS more than makes up for its deficiencies in surface-to-surface missiles with the other spoils it has seized in its victories over the Syrian and Iraqi militaries. The vast ISIS arsenal reportedly includes:

- Dozens of Soviet-made tanks.
- American-made armored Humvees.
- Howitzers and other field artillery.
- Chinese-made field guns.
- Anti-aircraft guns.

- Shoulder-fired RPGs (rocket-propelled grenades).
- Anti-tank missiles.
- Untold bundles of machine guns and AK-47s.[11]
- ISIS may also have older-model Soviet MiG fighter jets in its possession—no match, obviously, for U.S. fighter jets, but enough to give ISIS the beginnings, at least, of an air force.[12]
- Perhaps most alarming for U.S. officials is ISIS's reported use of advanced surface-to-air missiles, or MANPADS (Man Portable Air Defense System), which can be used to shoot down not only American fighter jets currently flying over Syria and Iraq but also civilian airliners. ISIS has even issued its foot soldiers a "how-to" guide on shooting down U.S. Apache helicopters using MANPADS.[13]

The bitter irony is that a sizable chunk of ISIS's arsenal was made in the United States. According to an extensive study by the London-based group Conflict Armament Research, "Islamic State forces have captured significant quantities of US-manufactured small arms and have employed them on the battlefield."[14] Much of that haul was acquired when ISIS forces rolled into Mosul in June 2014.

ISIS's conquest of Mosul—Iraq's second-largest city, rich in history and culture and home to nearly two million inhabitants—was an unprecedented event in the modern era of Islamic terrorism. Not only did ISIS jihadists seize Mosul's central bank and close to $500 million, but also, according to the *Los Angeles Times*,

[Iraqi] Government forces retreated en masse from the [ISIS] onslaught, leaving behind a military hardware bonanza, including the U.S.-made armored Humvees as well as trucks, rockets, artillery pieces, rifles, ammunition, even a helicopter. Some of the seized materiel was old or otherwise non-functioning; but a lot was promptly put to use on the battlefield.

Pictures of grinning Islamist warriors cruising in U.S. Humvees bedecked with white-on-black militant flags flooded the Internet and became the signature image of the ISIS rampage.[15]

So much for the years of training and equipment and $25 billion in aid that the U.S. has invested in the Iraqi military, whose brave warriors ran for the hills at the first sight of a jihadi-filled pickup truck, all but gift-wrapping loads of U.S. military hardware for ISIS. The effects of this shameful retreat were profound and quickly reverberated elsewhere in Iraq. One senior Kurdish official lamented that ISIS, "took the weapons stores of the 2nd and 3rd [Iraqi army] divisions in Mosul, the 4th division in Salah al Din, the 12th division in the areas near Kirkuk, and another division in Diyala.... We're talking about armaments for 200,000 soldiers, all from the Americans."[16]

ISIS's seizure of a Saddam Hussein–era chemical weapons depot outside Baghdad in June 2014 may have given it access to rockets filled with sarin gas,[17] Obama administration officials downplayed the incident and said that any chemical materials still stored at the facility were likely unusable.[18] But then reports began flooding in about ISIS using chemical weapons—in the form of chlorine gas—against Iraqi security forces.[19] Similarly, news that ISIS stole eighty-eight pounds of uranium from Mosul University, also in June, was essentially dismissed by the UN's nuclear agency, which branded the materials "low-grade" and not "high risk"[20]...until an alleged ISIS weapons maker referring to himself as Muslim al-Britani began boasting on Twitter that "A Radioactive Device has entered somewhere in Europe" and that ISIS was in possession of a dirty bomb thanks to uranium taken from—you guessed it—Mosul University in June 2014.[21] The same uranium the UN dismissed as low risk.

Perhaps al-Britani was lying. And perhaps the uranium does indeed pose no threat. Whatever the case, the fact that ISIS—an organization that regularly engages in mass executions and has already attempted genocide against Iraqi Christians and Yazidis—is actively working to procure weapons of mass destruction is anything but a low risk scenario.

Exhibit A: Syria. Although the Assad regime, under pressure from the United States, has supposedly destroyed all of its "declared" chemical arsenal, Western intelligence officials are concerned that Assad still has a secret stash of "undeclared" chemical weapons, not to mention a biological weapons program.[22] The ISIS jihadists who are continuing their advance in Syria would no doubt love to get their hands on these chemical and biological agents and do horrible things with them.

In the meantime, ISIS has reportedly developed its own makeshift biological weapon in the form of "scorpion bombs." According to the *Daily Mail*, "Militants fighting for the Islamic State in Iraq have unveiled…bombs containing hundreds of live scorpions designed to spread fear among their enemies. Canisters packed with poisonous varieties of scorpion are being blasted into towns and villages, which explode on impact—scattering the scorpions and causing panic among the innocent local population."[23]

Whether through beheadings, torture, mass rape, or scorpions, ISIS seems prepared to make infidels' worst nightmares come true—and to relish every minute of it.

■   ■   ■

So how did we get here? After all, a global movement that controls thirty-five thousand square miles of prime Middle Eastern real estate, rakes in up to $3 million per day in revenue (much of it in the illicit oil trade), draws thousands of Westerners to its ranks, beheads American citizens, and pulls the United States back into the world's most tumultuous region couldn't have just appeared overnight—although, if you were listening to the Obama administration from 2012 through the first half of 2014, you'd be forgiven for thinking so.

Throughout the 2012 presidential campaign, President Obama continually trumpeted the death of Osama bin Laden while proclaiming that al Qaeda was "on the run," and "on the path to defeat"—"decimated," as the president asserted on the campaign trail, and "on its heels."[24] Even after al Qaeda–linked terrorists attacked the U.S. consulate in Benghazi, Libya, on September 11, 2012, killing four Americans, including Ambassador J. Christopher Stevens, Obama doggedly stuck to his narrative that al Qaeda was in its death throes.

While the president was busy scoring political points and willfully misleading the American people about the nature of the Islamic terror threat, al Qaeda was not contracting but expanding—to the point where AQ and its affiliates and allies cover more geographical ground today than they did on 9/11: from the tribal regions of Pakistan to Somalia, Yemen, Syria, Iraq, Nigeria, Libya, Sinai, Europe, India, and the Sahara desert region covering northern Mali and southern Algeria. Yes, jihadist organizations like al Qaeda are "on the run" indeed—*overrunning* large areas of the Muslim world.

None more so than ISIS. When ISIS roared into the city of Fallujah, in western Iraq, in January 2014 and declared it part of an Islamic State, you'd think that would have been a massive wake-up call for the Obama administration. Not only does Fallujah lie just forty-five miles from the Iraqi capital of Baghdad. In 2004 U.S. forces had reclaimed the city, which had become the nerve center of an al Qaeda–led insurgency, after two hellacious battles that were the bloodiest—and costliest—of the entire Iraq War. Over one hundred American troops were killed and hundreds more wounded in brutal building-to-building fighting against Sunni terrorists. One can only imagine the agony that veterans of the Fallujah campaigns must have felt as they watched ISIS raise its black banner above a city they had fought so valiantly to liberate just a few years earlier. Talk about a bitter pill to swallow. President Obama, however, seemed completely unfazed.

In an interview with the *New Yorker* magazine just a few days after ISIS had seized Fallujah in a jihadist takeover rife with strategic and symbolic significance, the president dismissed the growing strength of al Qaeda affiliates and offshoots such as, well, ISIS:

> "The analogy we use around here sometimes, and I think is accurate, is if a jayvee team puts on Lakers uniforms that doesn't make them Kobe Bryant," Obama said, resorting to an uncharacteristically flip analogy. "I think there is a distinction between the capacity and reach of a bin Laden and a network that is actively planning major terrorist plots against the homeland versus jihadists who are engaged in various local power struggles and disputes, often sectarian.
>
> "Let's just keep in mind, Falluja is a profoundly conservative Sunni city in a country that, independent of anything we do, is deeply divided along sectarian lines. And how we think about terrorism has to be defined and specific enough that it doesn't lead us to think that any horrible actions that take place around the world that are motivated in part by an extremist Islamic ideology are a direct threat to us or something that we have to wade into."[25]

Obamaspeak translation: *The only jihadists that matter are al Qaeda's core leaders in the tribal regions of Pakistan. Our war is against them and them only and we're literally droning them to death. ISIS and its ilk are small-time, provincial hacks—JV!—and tough break and all, but Fallujah was an Islamist hotbed that was bound to go over to the dark side anyway. Above all, none of this poses any threat to the United States. As I have told you all again and again, Osama bin Laden is dead and al Qaeda is on the path to defeat. Period. You guys can trust me. Now let's go play some golf.*

The president had a vested interest in downplaying ISIS's gains in Iraq. Throughout the 2008 campaign and during his first term in office, he had promised to end the unpopular war in Iraq and bring the troops home. It was a cornerstone of his foreign policy—indeed, during his 2012 reelection campaign, he trumpeted the fact that he had "ended" American involvement in Iraq (except, as we'll see, al Qaeda apparently didn't get the memo).

Against the advice of his top commander on the ground, General Lloyd J. Austin III (who recommended keeping twenty-four thousand U.S. troops in Iraq), and other top military officials, President Obama had authorized the complete withdrawal of American troops from the country.[26] In December 2011, as the last U.S. troops were departing Iraq, America's commander in chief gave a speech at Fort Bragg declaring, "We're leaving behind a sovereign, stable and self-reliant Iraq, with a representative government that was elected by its people. We're building a new partnership between our nations. And we are ending a war not with a final battle, but with a final march toward home."[27]

Got that? Bush's unnecessary war in Iraq was *over*. El fin. Case closed. Not because the jihadists had conceded defeat in their quest to turn Iraq into an Islamic State, or had abandoned terrorism against U.S. and Iraqi interests. Far from it. No, the war in Iraq was ended because President Obama said so. Same with al Qaeda being "on the path to defeat"—we had the president's word for it. In the president's Middle East and national security playbook, if you repeat a mantra often enough and wish hard enough for it to become true, it does. Or not.

By the time ISIS was rampaging through Mosul in June 2014—five months after the president's "JV" quip—it was clear that someone in the White House had some serious explaining to do. Although the president later laid the blame at the feet of the U.S. intelligence community—saying it had "underestimated what had been taking place in Syria" with ISIS prior to its foray into Mosul—ABC News reported that, in fact, "for nearly a year, senior officials in the U.S. government had been warning about the

alarming rise of ISIS...and the inability of the Iraqi government to confront the threat." More than once:

- In testimony before a House Foreign Affairs subcommittee
  in November 2013, Brett McGurk, deputy assistant secretary of state for Iraq and Iran, had stated bluntly, "There is
  no question that [ISIS] is growing roots in Syria and in
  Iraq." McGurk "cited the group's alarming campaign of
  suicide bombings, its growing financial resources and its
  expanding safe haven in Syria."[28]
- Then in January 2014 the U.S. ambassador to Iraq, Robert
  Beecroft, had called the situation in Iraq "very precarious"
  following ISIS's seizure of Fallujah and part of the city of
  Ramadi, warning that, "a misstep anywhere could set off a
  larger conflict in the country."[29]
- Perhaps most damning to the Obama administration's
  strategy of feigning shock and then throwing the intel community under the bus in the wake of the Mosul debacle was
  testimony from the Pentagon's top intelligence official,
  Lieutenant General Michael Flynn, in February 2014.
  Flynn, quite presciently, told the Senate Armed Services
  Committee that "[ISIS] probably will attempt to take territory in Iraq and Syria to exhibit its strength in 2014, as
  demonstrated recently in Ramadi and Fallujah, and the
  group's ability to concurrently maintain multiple safe
  havens in Syria."[30]
- Interestingly enough, President Obama's own handpicked
  CIA director, John Brennan, had made a similar assessment
  earlier that same month, testifying before the House Permanent Select Committee on Intelligence that al Qaeda
  camps in Syria and Iraq posed a threat to the United States.[31]
  Not bad for a JV team.

The Obama White House was surely aware of Brennan's assessments, Flynn's testimony, and similar dire warnings by Beecroft, McGurk, and other top experts about the rise of ISIS in the months prior to the fall of Mosul. According to James Jeffrey, the U.S. ambassador to Iraq from 2010 to 2012, the Obama administration, "not only was warned by everybody back in January [following ISIS's invasion of Fallujah], it actually announced it was going to intensify its support against ISIS with the Iraqi armed forces. And it did almost nothing."[32]

Jeffrey has said that he believed keeping U.S. troops in Iraq beyond 2011 was "critical."[33] He, like other U.S. diplomatic and military officials who had spent significant time in Iraq and knew the dynamics of the country, realized that a complete U.S. withdrawal would leave a vacuum that would be filled by very bad actors. That much was clear as far back as 2003, after the American ouster of Saddam Hussein, as the organization that would one day become known as ISIS first began making its presence felt in Iraq—and the region—in a major way.

ISIS: THE GENESIS

With apologies to the Obama administration, ISIS did not appear out of thin air one balmy day in Mosul in June 2014. By then, the roots of the Islamic State already stretched back more than a decade. They were laid down by a former street thug and ex-con who has been described as "barely literate."[34] Abu Musab al-Zarqawi followed a long, twisted, and bloody road from petty criminal to founding father of the world's most successful jihadist terror organization. By the time he was killed by a U.S. airstrike in Iraq in 2006, al-Zarqawi had become one of the world's most wanted men and the face of the Sunni jihadist insurgency against Coalition forces. Unfortunately, his dark vision for the Middle East would outlive him and eventually change the face of the entire region. Al-Zarqawi is revered by ISIS's leadership and in its official publications today. ISIS youth groups are nicknamed "al-Zarqawi's [lion] cubs," and an Islamic State training base in Raqqa is also named after the terror kingpin.[35]

In 1989, al-Zarqawi abandoned a shiftless life of petty crime, leaving his hometown of Zarqa, Jordan, and joining the jihad in Afghanistan. He returned to Jordan in 1993 as a battle-tested jihadist zealot and ended up serving six years in prison for plotting terror attacks on Jordanian soil. After being released from prison, al-Zarqawi eventually made his way back to Afghanistan, where Osama bin Laden provided him with seed money to set up a terrorist training camp in the city of Herat, near the Iranian border. Despite this early financial assistance, bin Laden and al-Zarqawi reportedly had a contentious relationship, with al-Zarqawi refusing several times to give *bayat*, or a vow of allegiance, to the al Qaeda mastermind.[36]

Following the 9/11 attacks, al-Zarqawi made his way into Iran and bounced between there and the Kurdish regions of Iraq, building up his terror network, before setting up shop in Iraq for good in 2003, a few months after the U.S. invasion, and quickly becoming a key figure in the burgeoning insurgency against Coalition forces.

In 2004, al-Zarqawi finally pledged bayat to bin Laden and founded al Qaeda in Iraq (also known as al Qaeda in the Land of Two Rivers)—the organization that would eventually become known as ISIS. Al-Zarqawi's group went on to spearhead a wave of terror and extreme brutality throughout Iraq that included the same kind of tactics that are ISIS staples today: beheadings, suicide bombings, torture, executions, and the rabid targeting of Shiites, whom al-Zarqawi considered apostates and hated with a passion. In the process of inflicting unspeakable cruelty upon Iraqis of all backgrounds, al-Zarqawi angered al Qaeda's core leadership (much as ISIS has done today, as we'll see shortly) who realized that his frequent attacks against Shia Muslims and their mosques were turning Muslim opinion against al Qaeda.[37]

After al-Zarqawi's death, al Qaeda in Iraq became part of an umbrella organization of Sunni terrorist groups called the Islamic State of Iraq (ISI).

They continued al-Zarqawi's wave of terror, particularly in western Iraq's Anbar province (an ISIS stronghold once again today), until the American military, working with local Sunni tribes, smashed ISI in a campaign that became known as "The Surge." ISI was further weakened in 2010 when Iraqi security forces, aided by U.S. forces, killed two of its top leaders, Abu Hamza al-Muhajir and Abu Omar al-Baghdadi. Ironically enough, their deaths elevated the man who would go on to become the caliph of the Islamic State.

THE RISE OF ABU BAKR AL-BAGHDADI

Bookish. Quiet. Bespectacled. Pious. A fine soccer player. A family man.

Judging by the accounts of those who knew him before the U.S. invasion of Iraq in 2003, the bloodthirsty fanatic who would one day declare himself leader of the world's Muslims, become the most wanted jihadist on the planet, and direct the most powerful, vicious terrorist organization in memory was, in a word, unimpressive. Little is known of the background of ISIS leader—and self-declared caliph—Abu Bakr al-Baghdadi (a.k.a. "Abu Du'a") but the scant information that is available about his early days does not suggest a budding terrorist mastermind.

Reportedly born in 1971 and raised just north of Baghdad in the town of Samarra in Iraq's Sunni heartland, al-Baghdadi (real name: Awwad Ibrahim Ali al-Badri al-Samarra) was an introverted loner as a child. Described as "studious, pious and calm," he was focused on Islam and soccer, where he excelled playing for a team sponsored by his local mosque.[38] At the age of eighteen, al-Baghdadi moved to the Iraqi capital to study Islam, eventually earning a Ph.D. in sharia law from Baghdad's Islamic University. For a decade, he lived among both Sunnis and Shias in the run-down neighborhood of Tobchi on the western edge of the city. He married, had children, and apparently showed no overt signs of rabid extremism, magnetic charisma, or bold leadership.[39]

Perhaps al-Baghdadi was, as one former acquaintance mused, "a quiet planner" who was merely waiting for the right moment to burst onto the world stage and implement a carefully crafted ideology that would enslave millions. He helped organize a jihadist group called "Jeish Ahl al-Sunnah al-Jamaah" following the U.S. invasion of Iraq, an act that led to his detainment by American forces and imprisonment at Camp Bucca in southern Iraq.[40] Some believe he was "radicalised by jihadists" from al Qaeda while at Camp Bucca, although he seems already to have been well on his way down the jihadist path at the time of his arrest.[41]

Accounts of al-Baghdadi's time at the U.S.-run prison—which was home to some twenty-four thousand inmates and has been likened to "a summer camp for ambitious terrorists"—vary. It's not clear even which years he was imprisoned there.[42] Some say he arrived at Camp Bucca in 2004, others say 2005. Was he released in late 2004? 2006? 2009? Like everything surrounding al-Baghdadi, it seems no one can say for certain. One associate, a man calling himself Abu Ahmed who met al-Baghdadi at Camp Bucca and later joined him in ISIS, has described the future caliph as "someone important" who had "a charisma," but added that, "there were others who were more important. I honestly did not think [al-Baghdadi] would get this far." Still, Abu Ahmed says, he "got a feeling from [al-Baghdadi] that he was hiding something inside, a darkness that he did not want to show other people. He was the opposite of other princes who were far easier to deal with. He was remote, far from us all."[43]

Al-Baghdadi may have provided a chilling glimpse of his future plans when, deemed no longer a threat, he was released from Camp Bucca. Upon his departure, he told a group of U.S. troops, "I'll see you in New York":

> "He knew we were from New York, and he knew he was going to get out," said Col. Kenneth King, who oversaw the former detention facility near the Kuwaiti border.

King told Fox News Channel that he escorted al-Baghdadi on a flight to Baghdad, where the handover took place. Al-Baghdadi was ultimately released by Iraqi government officials.

"Their decision to let him go was personally disappointing," King said. "But I have to respect the decisions of a sovereign government."

In another interview with *The Daily Beast*, King said he took al-Baghdadi's words as something of a joke—"like, 'This is no big thing. I'll see you on the block.'"

But al-Baghdadi didn't seem like the type who'd end up leading an insurgency that threatens to topple Iraq's government.

"I'm not surprised that it was someone who spent time in Bucca, but I'm a little surprised it was him," King said. "He was a bad dude, but he wasn't the worst of the worst."[44]

Al-Baghdadi, true to form, appears to have been intentionally inconspicuous during his time at Camp Bucca. Today, although he is arguably the world's most infamous terrorist, he continues to shroud himself in mystery like a jihadi Keyser Söze. Before he emerged in a Mosul mosque on July 5, 2014, clad in black turban and black robes, and declared himself caliph, there were only two grainy photographs of him known to exist. Dubbed "the invisible sheikh," he almost never appears on video. During meetings with ISIS commanders, he reportedly wears a mask.[45] One Raqqa man who was present at a mosque where al-Baghdadi made a rare public appearance described the scene:

> "The minute he entered, the mobile coverage disappeared," says a 29-year-old resident of Raqqa in Syria—who asked to be identified only as Abu Ali—recalling the flawless security on one occasion when al-Baghdadi entered a mosque. "Armed guards closed the area. The women were sent upstairs to the women's

section to pray. Everyone was warned not to take photos or videos. It was the most nerve-racking atmosphere.

"What made it [more nerve-racking] is that when Baghdadi finally showed up, wearing black, head to toe, the guards started shouting, 'Allah akbar! Allah akbar!' [God is great.] This made us even more scared," says Ali. "The guards then forced us to swear allegiance to him. Even after Baghdadi left, none of us were allowed to leave the mosque for another 30 minutes."[46]

The U.S. State Department has placed a $10 million bounty on al-Baghdadi's head. Not surprisingly, he moves around often—likely between Raqqa and Mosul.[47] In early November 2014, Iraqi officials claimed that al-Baghdadi had been injured in an airstrike in Iraq, but a few days later, he released an audiotape mocking the United States, calling for attacks on Saudi Arabia, and encouraging ISIS's supporters to "Erupt volcanoes of jihad everywhere" and "Light the Earth with fire."[48] It appeared the caliph was very much alive and kicking, to the delight of his followers worldwide. It is unclear whether ISIS has a suitably charismatic successor in the wings capable of galvanizing support should al-Baghdadi be killed. Adding to al-Baghdadi's mystique is his claim to be a direct descendant of Islam's prophet Mohammed (a claim made, no doubt, to bolster his credentials as caliph).

Al-Baghdadi's meteoric rise began in 2010, after his stint at Camp Bucca, when he assumed leadership of the Islamic State of Iraq and proceeded to revive an organization—the former al Qaeda in Iraq—that had been pulverized by the U.S. military. Al-Baghdadi's moment had finally arrived, and he would soon give new meaning to the term "silent but deadly." When the last U.S. troops departed Iraq in December 2011, the path was cleared—as the Obama administration had been warned it would be—for al-Baghdadi to "rebuild [ISI] and gather strength to renew its terrorist campaign against the Shi'ite population and the central Iraqi government."[49] In an ominous sign of things to come, some 434 people, mostly Shiites, were killed in terror attacks across Iraq in the first month after U.S. forces withdrew.[50] Things would only get worse:

- Under al-Baghdadi's direction, ISI embarked on a wave of suicide bombings throughout Iraq in 2012 and 2013. The effects were immediately apparent: three thousand people were killed in suicide bombings between September and December of 2013 alone; altogether there were ninety-eight suicide bombings that year.[51]

- In the meantime, ISI initiated a year-long campaign called "Breaking the Walls" that saw it carry out a number of jailbreaks, freeing countless hardened al Qaeda operatives who would replenish ISI's ranks—including five hundred inmates from Abu Ghraib prison in July 2013.[52]

- The prison breaks coincided with yet another coordinated campaign engineered by al-Baghdadi, dubbed "Soldiers' Harvest," in which ISI targeted members of the Iraqi security forces for assassination. According to the Combating Terrorism Center at West Point, "In addition to demolitions of soldiers' homes, the first six months of 'Soldiers Harvest' witnessed a sharp 150% increase in the number of sophisticated close quarters assassinations of troops manning checkpoints and effective under-vehicle improvised explosive device (IED) attacks on key leaders."[53]

The stunning resurgence of the Islamic State of Iraq, meticulously mapped out by al-Baghdadi (who has gained a reputation as a skilled military tactician) and the ISI brain trust (which included former high-ranking members of Saddam Hussein's Baathist regime intimately familiar with every corner of Iraq), was in full swing. At the same time, al-Baghdadi's rapidly growing organization was also becoming much better acquainted with Iraq's next-door neighbor. Soon, ISI's foray into Syria would not only dramatically expand ISI; it would also transform the organization into a transnational movement with a new name that would become synonymous with terrorist mayhem: the Islamic State of Iraq and al-Sham (Syria), better known as ISIS.

THE CALIPHATE COMETH

Even by the gruesome standards of the Middle East, the numbers are staggering.

As of January 2015, the Syrian Civil War had already claimed the lives of over two hundred thousand people in under four years. The dead included some sixty-three thousand civilians, including more than ten thousand children, according to the UK-based Syrian Observatory for Human Rights.[54] At the same time, millions of Syrian refugees have fled the fighting, flooding into Turkey, Jordan, Lebanon, and Iraq and creating a massive humanitarian crisis. In short, the Syrian conflict is a hellish, unmitigated disaster on every level, with no end in sight. And ISIS could not be happier.

When the uprising against the regime of Syrian dictator Bashar al-Assad erupted in March 2011, Abu Bakr al-Baghdadi, continuing his reboot of the Islamic State of Iraq, saw an opportunity. Late that year, he sent a contingent of his soldiers across the border into Syria to join the fight against Assad's forces. Led by Abu Mohammed al-Golani, these ISI jihadis established a group called the "al-Nusra Front" that quickly gained battlefield success and followers "from both inside and outside" Syria.[55]

As the Syrian Civil War became the go-to destination for battle-hungry jihadists worldwide, the al-Nusra Front became increasingly independent and drifted from its parent organization, ISI, prompting al-Baghdadi to declare "the unification of the two organizations under his leadership" in April 2013.[56]

Al-Baghdadi, seeking to reassert absolute control, christened the merger of the two organizations, The Islamic State of Iraq and al-Sham, or ISIS. Yet things did not go according to plan and an "As the Jihad Turns"–like sequence of events followed:

- Al-Golani rejected the merger and instead pledged his allegiance to al Qaeda's top overall leader, Ayman al-Zawahiri.
- Al-Zawahiri supported al-Golani and weighed in against the merger. He ordered al-Baghdadi (at the time still technically his subordinate) to limit his operations to Iraq and cede Syria to al-Golani's al-Nusra Front.
- Al-Baghdadi refused.
- Al-Zawahiri formally disowned ISIS and kicked it out of the al Qaeda network in February 2014. The al-Nusra Front was now the sole representative of al Qaeda in Syria.

Much as his predecessor, Abu Musab al-Zarqawi, had done nearly a decade before, al-Baghdadi had alienated (and threatened) al Qaeda's core leadership through a combination of hubris, ruthless ambition, and wanton violence that targeted "apostate" Muslims every bit as much as non-Muslims.

Booted from al Qaeda, ISIS was now officially an independent actor, and al-Baghdadi wasted no time outmaneuvering the rival al-Nusra Front in pursuit of his boundless vision: "Abu Bakr [al-Baghdadi] . . . set about establishing himself in Syria, drawing away a great many of al Nusra's foreign members. ISIS quickly became a dominant force in Syria and as well as attracting recruits from al Nusra and other rebel groups, it also received donations and support from outside the area, both as a successful salafist/takfiri group, and as an opponent to the regime of Bashar al Assad."[57]

Although the al-Nusra Front continues to be a formidable fighting force today, crushing competing rebel groups and controlling large areas of northwestern and western Syria (including along the border with Israel, near the Golan Heights) with possible designs on declaring an emirate of its own, ISIS has clearly eclipsed it in virtually every way. The two organizations' bitter rivalry has, at times, spilled over into open battle in Syria, but recently there have been signs of a thaw.

Jihadists from ISIS and the al-Nusra Front crossed from Syria into Lebanon in August 2014, attacking the Lebanese town of Arsal. The combined jihadi force killed and wounded dozens of Lebanese soldiers and kidnapped twenty-nine others, beheading some of them. At the time of this writing, reports persist that the Arsal incursion was a "dry run," and that the two jihadi organizations were preparing to open a new front in Lebanon.[58] Such a move would certainly fit with ISIS's vision of an expanded caliphate.

In November 2014, improbable as it would have seemed not so long ago, leaders of ISIS and the al-Nusra Front reportedly met outside Aleppo to discuss a merger—the same kind of arrangement al-Nusra leader Abu Mohammed al-Golani had rejected just a year and a half before. It's funny how the establishment of a caliphate in the heart of the Middle East can change the equation.

Serious differences between the two organizations remain, but as ISIS continues to steamroll its way across the region, gaining fresh recruits and (as we'll see in chapter two) new affiliates, the al-Nusra Front and other jihadi groups may soon be forced to come to a realization.

If you can't beat 'em, join 'em.

■   ■   ■

In 2005, a Lebanese journalist named Fouad Hussein published details of an al Qaeda "twenty-year plan" that had been leaked to him by AQ members. The plan had seven phases, culminating in "Definitive Victory" in the year 2020.

Interestingly enough, the fifth phase of the plan, which al Qaeda projected would unfold between 2013 and 2016, was "to establish an Islamic state, or caliphate." In 2014, ISIS—an al Qaeda offshoot—did exactly that. "The Plan," it seems, is right on course. We now appear to be moving toward the sixth—and next to last—phase: "Total Confrontation," in which "al-Qaida anticipated an all-out war with the unbelievers" between the years 2016 and 2020.[59]

In 2014, that war began to take shape, not only in the Middle East—where ISIS is actively pursuing genocide against any group that does not share its bleak vision—but also in the West, where homegrown ISIS supporters are laying the groundwork for a virtual guerrilla war in American and European cities. How the war will end depends largely on Western leaders, who, at the moment, seem absolutely flummoxed as to how to confront the Islamist threat, both at home and abroad. As we'll see throughout this book, the results of their impotence and ignorance have already been disastrous.

The caliphate has returned—and in its short, ugly existence, has already heaped untold misery upon millions of people.

And there's much worse in store.

CHAPTER TWO

HELL AWAITS: WELCOME TO THE ISLAMIC STATE

"WHAT REALLY TOOK A TOLL ON ME WAS HEARING WHAT THEY DID after they kidnapped Yazidi and Christian women. It was too much."

As ISIS raped and pillaged its way through Iraq's Nineveh province in the summer of 2014, Steven Nabil spent hours wide awake through the night, on the phone and on social media, listening as anguished Yazidi and Christian women told him the horrors inflicted upon their sisters and daughters by the invading jihadist hordes. Nabil, a twenty-six-year-old Iraqi-American activist with a network of contacts throughout Iraq, including in government and military circles, was even able to communicate with some of the prisoners directly to get firsthand accounts of the atrocities.

"I have never really dealt with that kind of emotional pain," he told me as we talked by phone in September 2014. "A captured Yazidi girl told me how ISIS had just brought two more busloads of Yazidi women to the place where she was being held captive. She said she could hear them scream throughout the night as they were being raped. They had two choices. The ones who converted to Islam were married off to ISIS terrorists or given as gifts to [Iraqi] tribal leaders who had sworn allegiance to [ISIS]. The ones who didn't convert were just raped."[1]

Nabil described another occasion, when he received a phone call from a local Yazidi friend living in Phoenix. "It was a man, older than me," Nabil said. "He was weeping. He said, 'ISIS is moving toward Yazidi villages, people are fleeing to the mountains—Steven, you are the only one who can help me.'"

"That's how my nights are," Nabil sighed. "It all got me so down that I didn't even go out for about two months."

Despite the often gut-wrenching nature of his work, Nabil did not shy away. Instead, he became a go-to source for breaking information out of Iraq, receiving regular updates from his contacts in Mosul and elsewhere and posting them on Facebook and other social media sites in real time. As ISIS closed in on Mosul in early June 2014, Nabil, a native Arabic speaker, warned on social media about the impending invasion. And as ISIS began to inflict atrocities upon Iraqi civilians, Nabil received harrowing on-the-ground accounts and photos that he shared with his many followers online. In the meantime, he was still holding down a 9-to-5 day job.

"Iraqi intelligence started watching my postings to get updates," he told me. "Even the Iraqi air force started to benefit from some of the information I was sharing."

But his work isn't limited to social media. On June 13, 2014, just three days after the fall of Mosul, Nabil, along with other Iraqi-Americans, helped organize what he calls the world's first Iraqi-led protest against ISIS, in downtown Phoenix. Such activities have not gone unnoticed by the Islamic State.

"ISIS has threatened me on social media," Nabil shared. "They've tried to hack into my Facebook page numerous amounts of times. They publicly attacked my page three times and they were finally able to disable it for a while."

"I've paid out of my pocket, out of my time, out of my time off from work, to do this," he continued. "I'm not benefiting financially. I'm just doing it to fight ISIS."

I first met Nabil in 2011 when, despite his youth, he was already becoming a leading advocate for the persecuted Christians of the Middle East, holding several demonstrations in downtown Phoenix calling attention to their plight. For Nabil, it was personal: he was born and raised as an Assyrian Christian in northern Iraq before coming to the U.S. as a foreign exchange student.

After attending high school in Virginia, he graduated from Arizona State University and, in July 2013, started a daily online video journal that he used to communicate with young Iraqis. He quickly gained a large following of Iraqis from all religious backgrounds, and by the time ISIS roared into Mosul in June 2014 Nabil had built up an extensive network of friends and contacts eager to share their stories.

Their accounts of life under ISIS are frequently horrifying. For instance, Nabil has spoken to nurses in Mosul hospitals who have treated girls for internal bleeding caused by rape at the hands of ISIS terrorists.

"For Shias, Yazidis, or Christians inside the caliphate, there is death unless you convert," Nabil told me. "There are beheadings every day and mass shootings. Crucifixions are very common—in Syria, there are lots of them. Also, if you're caught with beer or cigarettes, you're sentenced to eighty lashes."

By summer 2014, the kind of brutality Nabil's contacts were describing, combined with ISIS's boundless ambition—both in the Middle East and among its fanatical Western supporters—had spurred calls for the Obama administration to take action against the Islamic State. Remember, the president had essentially shrugged off ISIS's seizure of Fallujah and parts of Ramadi in January 2014 as an isolated outburst by a group of al Qaeda castoffs—a mere blip on the national security radar screen, perpetrated by a terrorist "JV" team that posed no threat to the United States.

That position became considerably more difficult to sustain a few months later when ISIS conquered Mosul—a city of nearly two million people and Iraq's second-largest—embarrassing the U.S.-trained Iraqi Army and preparing to advance on Baghdad. Then came Abu Bakr al-Baghdadi's declaration of a caliphate and the revelation that thousands of Western passport holders—including several Americans—were fighting for the fledgling Islamic State, raising the strong possibility that they would one day return home and continue their jihad on U.S. or European soil. The clear and present danger ISIS posed to the region and to the United States had now become undeniable.

Yet all the while President Obama insisted that he would "not be sending US troops back into combat in Iraq."[2] After all, he said, it was "ultimately... up to the Iraqis, as a sovereign nation, to solve their problems."[3] That certainly is the goal, at some point. But Iraq's army had just folded like a cheap suit as soon as the first ISIS flag showed up in Mosul. And the Iran-friendly, Shia-dominated government of Iraqi Prime Minister Nouri al-Maliki, who had alienated Iraq's Sunni minority (undoubtedly driving many into the arms of ISIS), had proven completely unequipped to confront Iraq's many problems, let alone its biggest one: ISIS. Although al-Maliki would step down from his post as prime minister under heavy pressure in August 2014, the same daunting challenges remain.

Indeed, what was true as U.S. troops withdrew prematurely in December 2011 remained true as ISIS knocked on Baghdad's doorstep in the summer of 2014: Iraq, although technically a sovereign nation—as President Obama pointed out continually while deflecting suggestions of U.S. military force against ISIS—was nowhere near the point of being able to provide for its own stability and security. The unpleasant reality of Iraq's repeated defeats at the hands of a terrorist caliphate bent on attacking the United States meant that Mesopotamia's problems were—once again—America's problems.

- ISIS's takeover of the Mosul Dam in August 2014 was a prime example. The dam, described by the U.S. Army Corps of Engineers as the most dangerous in the world, thanks mainly to its unstable foundation, is Iraq's largest, "holding back 11 billion cubic meters of water and producing over 1,000 megawatts of electricity." Seizing it gave ISIS control of "the water flowing into Baghdad and to the agrarian areas south of Baghdad," putting the jihadists "in a position to impose a famine on the rest of Iraq" or to simply destroy the dam and flood areas as far south as Baghdad with a "60-ft. wave" that would leave hundreds of thousands of dead Iraqis in its wake and have far-reaching economic impacts (including skyrocketing oil and gas prices).[4]

Thankfully, Kurdish forces, backed by U.S. airstrikes, retook the dam later in August. But ISIS's control of it, however brief, demonstrated the catastrophic potential of the Islamic State.

- So did ISIS's lightning advance into areas of northern Iraq that same month. ISIS conquered the town of Sinjar and surrounding villages, killing or capturing (and selling into slavery, as we'll see shortly) thousands of members of Iraq's Yazidi minority—an ancient sect that ISIS labels "devil worshippers."[5] At the same time, tens of thousands of survivors fled onto nearby Mount Sinjar, many with nothing but the clothes on their backs. ISIS surrounded the mountain with the intention of slaughtering the trapped Yazidis, who were stranded on the mountaintop in the sweltering summer heat with no food, water, or medical supplies. As dozens of elderly people and small children succumbed to exposure to the elements and died, the Yazidis were left with no options other than remain on the mountain and watch their family members die of thirst, or leave and meet a merciless fate at the hands of ISIS below.[6]

- Meanwhile, ISIS routed outgunned Kurdish Peshmerga forces that had been defending Sinjar and moved closer to the city of Erbil, capital of the autonomous Kurdistan region in northern Iraq. The potential fall of Erbil—a prosperous hub of pro-American sentiment and home to a consulate where dozens of U.S. personnel are stationed—combined with the very real prospect of a wholesale ethnic cleansing of Yazidis on Mount Sinjar, finally compelled President Obama to act. He ordered limited U.S. airstrikes against ISIS forces around Sinjar and Erbil and authorized humanitarian airdrops for Yazidis stranded on Mount Sinjar. The airstrikes had an effect, as up to twenty thousand Yazidis were able to flee the mountain and make their way to Kurdistan.[7]

Although President Obama declared the ISIS siege of Mount Sinjar broken following those initial airstrikes, at least seven thousand Yazidis remained trapped on the mountain for over four more months, until they were finally freed thanks to an offensive by Kurdish forces in December 2014.[8]

■ On August 19, 2014, shortly after the Sinjar siege unfolded, ISIS released a graphic propaganda video featuring a black-clad, masked butcher dubbed "Jihadi John" hacking off the head of captured American photojournalist James Foley. Two weeks later, ISIS released a similar video showing Jihadi John beheading another captured American journalist, Steven Sotloff. ISIS blamed its executions of the two men on U.S. airstrikes against Islamic State positions in Iraq.[9] As of this writing, ISIS has also released videos of Jihadi John decapitating American aid worker Peter Kassig and two British citizens, David Haines and Alan Henning.

President Obama has had a typically confounding response to ISIS's onslaught of beheadings, rapes, and torture. He—along with Secretary of State John Kerry and British Prime Minister David Cameron—has declared that ISIS is "not Islamic."[10] In other words, the self-described "Islamic State"—whose leaders quote copiously from Islamic texts and frequently cite Islamic history to justify their actions—is just a gang of miscreants who have completely twisted Islamic teachings.

Take beheadings, for instance. Following the release of an ISIS video showcasing the severed head of Peter Kassig in November 2014, President Obama declared that ISIS's rampant beheadings, "represent no faith, least of all the Muslim faith."[11] So Hindus, Jews, Buddhists, and Christians would all be more likely to behead someone than Muslims, who, in the president's view, apparently, are the "least" likely of all religions to engage in that sort of violence. *That's right, you bigoted Islamophobes. Koran-and-hadith-compliant Muslims would never harm a hair on anyone's head—because there is absolutely, positively nothing in Islamic texts that extols violence. Islam is an inherently peaceful religion that teaches only love and coexistence. Imam Obama hath spoken.*

And it wasn't his first fatwa. During his infamous Cairo speech in 2009, the president intoned that he considers it part of his "responsibility as President of the United States to fight against negative stereotypes of Islam wherever they appear."[12] The Founding Fathers must have forgotten to write that one into the job description. They certainly would have never envisioned an American president saying, as President Obama did before the UN General Assembly in 2012, that "the future must not belong to those who slander the prophet of Islam."[13]

In the future, our Theologian in Chief may want to brush up on his Islamic history before playing armchair sheikh. As we learned in chapter one, previous Islamic caliphates were not established by jovial Muslim missionaries handing out tracts on street corners. Rather, Islam spread mainly by the sword, and its prophet, Mohammed, was not just a spiritual leader but also a military-political leader, conqueror, and warrior. This is all part of the historical record to which Muslims—moderate and extreme alike—will readily attest. Further, the Koran refers to the characteristically Islamic concept of jihad no less than 164 times (mostly in a violent context).[14]

Does every Muslim in the world subscribe to these unsavory teachings, and take them literally? Of course not. Most Muslims want no part of jihad or sharia and just want to get on with their daily lives. At the same time, it's estimated that up to 15 percent of the world's 1.6 billion Muslims (or roughly 240 million) are indeed radicalized—and presumably take Koranic admonitions such as "slay the idolaters wherever you find them" quite literally.[15] Further, they believe that any Muslim who disagrees with their viewpoint is really not a Muslim at all and should be killed—and that they have a compelling Koranic argument for their actions.

In ISIS's literalist view, beheading is not only accepted in Islam—it is mandated. For instance, Surah 8, verses 9-13 of the Koran command Muslims to "smite [slice]...unbelievers...above their necks." Additionally, Surah 47 of the Koran states: "When you encounter the unbelievers on the battlefield, *strike off their heads* until you have crushed them completely; then bind the prisoners tightly [emphasis added]."

In ISIS's view, there isn't much wiggle room there—particularly above the collar. As we'll explore further in chapter four, throughout history Islamic conquerors have put the above-mentioned beheading verses into action, using head-chopping as a means of terrorizing their enemies. It is an unpleasant fact that may make inside-the-Beltway strategists and network news honchos squeamish—but it is a fact nonetheless (with apologies to Imam Obama).

Thankfully, the American people are catching on to the danger ISIS represents. A November 2014 CNN/ORC poll found that most Americans believe ISIS poses a serious threat to the United States.[16] And according to an October 2014 NBC News/*Wall Street Journal* poll, 41 percent of Americans believe that U.S. ground troops, and not just airstrikes, are needed to defeat the Islamic State.[17] It's likely that for some of those polled, the beheadings of James Foley and Steven Sotloff were their introduction to ISIS—and the sight of two U.S. citizens clad in prison-style jumpsuits crudely murdered in the middle of the desert by a trash-talking jihadist didn't go over well.

The Foley and Sotloff murders shifted the national conversation from striking ISIS in Iraq to extending the U.S. bombing campaign to ISIS safe havens in Syria—such as the city of Raqqa, the unofficial capital of the Islamic State caliphate. If President Obama really wanted to defeat ISIS, as he had vowed to do,[18] then northern and eastern Syria, which make up a large chunk of the caliphate, were an ideal place to start. Yet when pressed by reporters about possibly striking ISIS in Syria following the Foley beheading, the commander in chief admitted that his administration had not quite gotten that far—in fact, it had gotten nowhere:

> "We don't have a strategy yet," Mr. Obama said of his plans for defeating the Islamic State in Syria. "We need to make sure that we've got clear plans. As our strategy develops, we will consult with Congress."
>
> … the president said he has ordered his military advisers to give him "a range of options."
>
> But Mr. Obama tried to tamp down the suggestion that his decision was imminent, saying "folks are getting a little further ahead of where we're at than we currently are."
>
> "We need to make sure that we've got clear plans, that we're developing them," Mr. Obama said at a White House news conference. "There's no point in me asking for action on the part of Congress before I know exactly what it is that is going to be required for us to get the job done."[19]

By this time, it had been eight months since ISIS roared into Fallujah. In the ensuing months ISIS, using a bevy of Western recruits, had overrun large parts of Syria and Iraq, declared a caliphate, lopped off the head of an American citizen, and vowed to strike the United States. Yet, incredibly, President Obama still had not devised a strategy to counter the rapidly growing Islamic State. In his words, he had no "clear plans" and no idea of what was "required…to get the job done." This was dereliction of duty, plain and simple. But it was not surprising.

Not only does President Obama have a stunning and potentially fatal misunderstanding of the Middle East (as we'll see in chapter eight), he also has a profound lack of interest in national security issues, period. A damning report released by the Government Accountability Institute in September 2014 showed that the president had missed over half of his daily intelligence briefings during his second term in office.[20] Indeed, an Obama staffer admitted that the president hadn't received regular in-person intel briefings since early 2009, preferring to get them in writing instead—an arrangement that, presumably, prevents him from picking the brains of his national security team and asking pointed questions as he would be able to do during an in-person meeting.[21] One wonders if written briefings would be the norm if the topic of our national security were as near and dear to the president's heart as, say, Obamacare.

President Obama may blow off his intel briefings, but he makes sure never to miss a date on the golf links, no matter how dire the circumstances. On August 20, 2014, just minutes after giving a somber speech vowing that justice would be done in the wake of ISIS's beheading of James Foley, the president, along with an entourage that included former NBA star Alonzo Mourning, headed right to the golf course, where he spent the next few hours "laughing, fist-bumping his friends and driving a golf cart with Mourning in the passenger seat."[22]

The president was roundly criticized afterward for his insensitivity— needless to say, yukking it up on the links immediately after addressing the brutal murder of an American citizen did not make for good optics, particularly in a mid-term election year. Despite the public relations disaster the golf outing created for the White House, at least we finally had a name for the president's ISIS strategy.

Golf and Awe.

■   ■   ■

President Obama has vowed repeatedly that any U.S. military operations against ISIS "will not involve American combat troops fighting on foreign soil."[23] As of this writing, however, the president had authorized the return of up to three thousand U.S. soldiers to Iraq, albeit in noncombat roles. For now, they are supposed to be "limited to advising local commanders and retraining elements of Iraq's army" while "confined to military headquarters or training bases at four sites" around the country.[24] How long that arrangement can last is uncertain. First, military experts across the board (and even former British Prime Minister Tony Blair)[25] have argued that ISIS cannot be defeated through airstrikes alone. Second, ISIS may eventually drag some of those three thousand U.S. advisors into, at the very least, limited ground engagements whether the Obama administration likes it or not.

In December 2014, for instance, a contingent of over three hundred U.S. troops stationed at a base in Anbar province came under fire from Islamic State jihadists, who "repeatedly hit the base with artillery and rocket fire."[26] Thankfully, there were no American casualties in the attacks. But as more U.S. troops arrive in Iraq and are based in ISIS strongholds such as Anbar, they'll become highly desirable targets. Imagine the propaganda value for the Islamic State if it were able to kill some American soldiers, or perhaps kidnap one to feature in a beheading video. All of a sudden, the Obama administration's strict "no ground operations" policy would be nearly impossible to sustain.

For now, though, the strategy for Operation Inherent Resolve—as the U.S.-led military campaign against ISIS is known—remains limited to airstrikes against Islamic State positions in Iraq and Syria (yes, after much golfing, the president ultimately decided to extend the bombing campaign to the other half of the caliphate). The strikes, which have also targeted the "Khorasan Group," a contingent of senior al Qaeda members inside Syria, are being conducted by a coalition that includes the U.S., France, Great Britain, Australia, and Canada, as well as a handful of Muslim nations that are petrified of the new caliphate next door.

While it's nice that Jordan, Saudi Arabia, Qatar, UAE, and Bahrain have offered some assistance—ISIS is conquering territory in their backyard, after all—America, predictably, is doing the heavy lifting and carrying out the overwhelming majority of the airstrikes.[27] But as we'll see in chapter eight, the Obama administration is eagerly seeking to enlist the help of none other than the terrorist regime in Iran to take some of the pressure off—and American military hardware is falling into the hands of Iraqi Shia militias loyal to Tehran.[28]

Although boots on the ground are needed to truly cripple ISIS, even limited Coalition airstrikes have unquestionably had an effect. As of December 2014, some 1,100 ISIS jihadists had reportedly been killed in Syria.[29] In Iraq, U.S. air cover had enabled Kurdish Peshmerga forces (who have begged for more American weaponry)[30] to mount a counter-offensive and retake some northern towns from ISIS.[31] In addition, a months-long ISIS siege of the Syrian town of Kobane, strategically located along the Turkish border, had stalled thanks to a combination of fierce Kurdish resistance and Coalition airstrikes.[32]

ISIS's earlier successes in Mosul, Sinjar, and elsewhere can be attributed largely to its ability to surprise its opponents with lightning onslaughts and then continue to push forward relentlessly, pausing only briefly to con-solidate its gains. If ISIS's momentum is stunted in Iraq, look for it to potentially drive westward in an attempt to open up new fronts and keep some semblance of momentum going:

- As we saw in chapter one, Lebanon is clearly in the Islamic State's crosshairs. In January 2014, the head of Lebanon's main security apparatus said that "more than 1,000" ISIS fighters had already holed up inside the country near its border with Syria.[33]
- Meanwhile, in December 2014, ISIS destroyed at least six Jordanian border control stations along that country's boundary with Iraq.[34]
- The following month, a group of ISIS jihadists (including one who detonated a suicide vest) killed three Saudi guards at Iraq's border with Saudi Arabia.[35] The Saudis are now building a six-hundred-foot wall along their northern bor-der with Iraq to keep ISIS out. The wall will feature "a ditch

and a triple-layered steel fence, with 40 watchtowers spread
out along it."[36]
- As we'll see in chapter eight, ISIS is also beginning to inch
closer to Syria's border with Israel, thanks in part to Syrian
rebel groups in the region that have pledged allegiance to
the Islamic State.

American-led airstrikes may have helped slow ISIS's momentum
on the battlefield in certain areas of Iraq and Syria, but they have not
been able to dampen enthusiasm for the Islamic State among radicalized
Muslims around the world. According to one study, over six thousand
new fighters have joined ISIS *since* the first American airstrikes began
in August 2014.[37] As of late October 2014, some one thousand foreign
fighters were reportedly flowing into Syria to join the group each month,
the same rate as before the airstrikes.[38]

As ISIS continues to draw fanatical young jihadists from six continents
to its ranks, it has also gained the support of several regional jihadist organizations, stretching from South Asia to North Africa. These groups, some
more significant than others, have pledged allegiance to the Islamic State
and its caliph, providing ISIS with satellites (or *wilayats*) beyond the borders of the Islamic State. Among the most prominent:

- **Ansar Beit al-Maqdis (ABM)**: Based in Egypt's Sinai Peninsula,
ABM gives ISIS a strategic perch from which it can conduct attacks against
both Israel and Egypt and coordinate with ISIS sympathizers in the nearby
Gaza Strip. ABM is estimated to have anywhere between several hundred
and a few thousand fighters that "have killed hundreds of members of
Egypt's security forces in a series of suicide bombings, drive-by shootings
and assassinations" since July 2013 alone.[39] They've also carried out attacks
in Cairo and against targets in southern Israel and—in true ISIS fashion—
have shown a fondness for beheading their hostages.[40]

▪ **ISIS in Derna, Libya**: As Libya continues to spiral into terrorist chaos and civil war in the wake of the 2011 ouster of longtime dictator Muammar Gaddafi by NATO forces (an event hailed by the Obama administration as a great foreign policy victory), Derna has been overrun by jihadists who've pledged allegiance to ISIS and transformed this port city of eighty thousand people into "a colony of terror":

> [Derna] is the first Islamic State enclave in North Africa. The conditions in Libya are perfect for the radical Islamists: a disintegrating state, a location that is strategically well situated and home to the largest oil reserves on the continent. Should Islamic State (IS) manage to establish control over a significant portion of Libya, it could trigger the destabilization of the entire Arab world.[41]

Incidentally, Libya's next-door neighbor Tunisia has supplied more foreign fighters to ISIS (possibly as many as three thousand) than any other country.[42]

▪ **Soldiers of the Caliphate**: This small Algeria-based outfit made a gory splash in September 2014 when it pledged allegiance to ISIS and promptly kidnapped and beheaded a French tourist. Algerian Special Forces say they killed the group's leader in December 2014. It's unclear whether the "Soldiers" have staying power, but Algeria has long been a hotbed for Islamic militancy.[43]

▪ **Pakistani Taliban (TTP) jihadists**: In October 2014, the spokesman for the influential Pakistani Taliban, along with five of TTP's commanders, gave their allegiance to the Islamic State. They were subsequently banished from the Pakistani Taliban for disloyalty.[44] The leader of Jamaat-ud-Dawa, another major South Asian terrorist organization that boasts approximately 150,000 members, has also reportedly expressed support for ISIS, albeit without offering any sort of official pledge of allegiance.[45]

In supporting the Islamic State caliphate, these organizations and individuals have not only chosen to get behind a "strong horse." They have given their seal of approval to one of the most depraved, violent, and barbaric societies in memory.

■   ■   ■

He played dead, and so he lived.

He was the only one.

When ISIS tore through the Iraqi city of Tikrit (Saddam Hussein's hometown), about 150 miles south of Mosul, in June 2014, twenty-three-year-old Ali Hussein Kadhim was one of hundreds of Iraqi military recruits who were rounded up by the jihadists to be executed en masse.

Kadhim, a father of two small children, had joined the Iraqi military on June 1 in hopes of making a salary that could support his young family. Instead, not long after enlisting, he ended up staring into a freshly dug trench alongside hundreds of his fellow Shia Muslims, sentenced to death for apostasy by ISIS's Sunni jihadists. Yet miraculously, Kadhim survived. He recounted his harrowing ordeal for the *New York Times*:

> As the firing squad shot the first man, blood spurted onto Mr. Kadhim's face. He remembered seeing a video camera in the hands of another militant.
>
> "I saw my daughter in my mind, saying, 'Father, father,'" he said.
>
> He felt a bullet pass by his head, and fell forward into the freshly dug trench.
>
> "I just pretended to be shot," he said.
>
> A few moments later, Mr. Kadhim said, one of the killers walked among the bodies and saw that one man who had been shot was still breathing.

"Just let him suffer," another militant said. "He's an infidel Shia. Let him suffer. Let him bleed."[46]

Kadhim lay in the trench, playing dead, for "about four hours…until it was dark and there was only silence." He spent the next three weeks traveling through "insurgent badlands," making his way to safety in Kurdistan before finally returning home to his family in southern Iraq. ISIS claimed that it killed 1,700 people in the mass execution (Human Rights Watch put the number between 560 and 770 deaths).[47] Kadhim is the only known survivor. As you can see in his video interview with the *Times*, he could scarcely believe his good fortune. It's not hard to see why: since first capturing territory in Syria in 2013, ISIS has proven to be a well-oiled, ruthless, killing machine with zero regard for the populations it has conquered—particularly if the vanquished are not Sunni Muslims. The Islamic State caliphate was founded upon the corpses of thousands of Shias, Yazidis, Christians, and any Sunni Muslims who dared to dissent from its barbarous vision.

A former ISIS fighter captured by Kurdish forces has explained, "Whenever ISIS goes into an area…the people there who don't adhere to their Islamic law are apostates.… Everything has to follow ISIS' way. Even women who don't cover their faces…women would get their heads chopped off." Another captured ISIS fighter told CNN, "…there are different kinds of death—they would torture you for sure, they might decapitate you, or cut off your hands. They will not simply shoot a bullet in your head."[48]

ISIS blazed an appalling trail of murder and mayhem across Iraq throughout 2014 in Mosul, Sinjar, Tikrit, and Anbar province. And according to the Syrian Observatory for Human Rights, ISIS jihadists killed nearly two thousand people, mostly civilians, in Syria between June and December of that same year. ISIS also reportedly executed 120 of its own members, "most of them foreign fighters trying to return home."[49] In the Hotel

Killafornia that is the Islamic State, you can check out anytime you like, but you can never leave.

ISIS doesn't just conquer towns—it utterly ravages them, slaughtering men and women, children and the elderly. Survivors of the months-long ISIS siege of Kobane, a town in northern Syria located near the Turkish border, described for the *Daily Mail* a stomach-churning orgy of bloodletting reminiscent of the Mongols' devastation of the Middle East eight centuries earlier:

> According to those who escaped [Kobane], the jihadis' savagery is more hideous than anyone feared.
>
> Headless corpses litter the streets of the besieged Syrian border town, they say, and some of the mainly Kurdish townsfolk have had their eyes gouged out.
>
> Refugees who made it to Suruc, just across the border in Turkey, tell of witnessing appalling horrors in hushed tones, as if they can barely believe it themselves.
>
> Father-of-four Amin Fajar, 38, said: "I have seen tens, maybe hundreds, of bodies with their heads cut off. Others with just their hands or legs missing. I have seen faces with their eyes or tongues cut out—I can never forget it for as long as I live. They put the heads on display to scare us all."
>
> It worked. Mr Fajar, a floor fitter from Kobane, and his wife and children aged three to 12, ran for their lives.
>
> "The children saw the headless people. They saw them," he said quietly, sitting cross-legged on a rug in his tent in a squalid refugee camp in Suruc.[50]

As of this writing, ISIS was on its heels in Kobane, beaten back by Kurdish ground forces supported by Coalition airstrikes. Many other towns in Syria and Iraq, however, have been successfully absorbed into the

ISIS caliphate—and once they're cleansed of non-Sunni Muslims (who are either killed or sold into slavery), their inhabitants are forced to live under sharia law. The disciplined ISIS bureaucracy, including several important councils that help the caliph, Abu Bakr al-Baghdadi, govern his territory and make decisions, dispatches religious police, called the "al-Hesbah" force, around the caliphate to ensure that sharia norms are followed—and to deal out harsh punishments if they find otherwise.

Interestingly enough, two former members of Saddam Hussein's Baath Party, Abu Muslim al-Turkmani and Abu Ali al-Anbari, are al-Baghdadi's top deputies, overseeing Iraq and Syria, respectively. According to a comprehensive report by the Soufan Group, a respected security and intelligence firm:

> Abu Bakr [al-Baghdadi] and his two senior advisors set the overall strategic objectives of the group, which are then passed down through the hierarchy with each lower rung having a degree of autonomy in their fulfillment. This is especially true in military operations where a local commander will know what he has to achieve, and even where to attack, but the exact timing and method may be left to his discretion. This system of devolved authority has enabled The Islamic State to operate on many fronts at more or less the same time, both administratively and militarily....
>
> The Councils are responsible for the military and administrative organization of The Islamic State, providing advice to [al-Baghdadi] and overseeing strategic planning, military operations, and civilian administration. The Shura Council is the highest advisory body and theoretically must approve [al-Baghdadi's] appointments and even the choice of who should succeed him as Caliph, which is decided by the Sharia Council. Theoretically, it also has the power to dismiss the

Caliph if he fails to carry out his duties in accordance with the guiding (sharia) principles of the organization.[51]

The report notes that ISIS also maintains a Security and Intelligence Council "responsible for eliminating rivals to Abu Bakr [al-Baghdadi] and rooting out any incipient plots against him," as well as Military, Finance, and Media Councils and a Provincial Council that "oversees the civilian administration of the State through its 18 provinces."[52] In addition, the red-bearded Abu Omar al-Shishani (real name: Tarkhan Batirashvili), an ethnic Chechen—one of many in ISIS's ranks—who served as a sergeant in the Georgian army, has been described as ISIS's top military commander, reportedly helping to engineer some of its most important conquests, including the takeover of Mosul.[53]

At the end of 2014, ISIS bragged of a $250 million surplus, with plans to use the extra money left over from its $2 billion budget "to help fund [the Islamic State's] war against the West and western allies."[54] The Islamic State is financially independent and, while it does receive donations from wealthy donors based in Persian Gulf countries like Kuwait, Saudi Arabia, and Qatar (longtime hotbeds of terrorism financing), is not beholden to any nation. ISIS controls several oil fields in western Iraq and eastern Syria and is driven, in large part, by oil money. ISIS was making as much as $3 million per day by selling oil in the Levant region's black market (which thrives in Syria, Turkey, Iraq, and Jordan)[55] until U.S. airstrikes reportedly put a dent in its revenue.[56]

Nevertheless, the Islamic State continues to rake in the dough via a mixture of private donations, oil sales, smuggling, blackmail, ransoms (European nations have paid tens of millions of dollars to free citizens held by ISIS)[57] and taxation and extortion in the areas it has conquered.[58] ISIS pays its fighters about $400 per month, certainly not a princely sum but reportedly more than members of the various Syrian rebel groups and the Iraqi military earn.[59]

For ISIS foot soldiers, the glory of jihad and the spoils of war more than make up for what they lack in salary. They are not driven by money but by a fanatical ideological commitment to expanding the caliphate and enforcing their totalitarian vision upon the Middle East and the world—beginning, of course, with Syria and Iraq.

THE CROSS IN THE CROSSHAIRS

Assyrian Christians in Iraq's Nineveh province had a proud history stretching back two thousand years.

That history is now over.

After ISIS swept into Mosul, the capital of Nineveh province, the city was literally emptied of its Christian population. In July 2014, ISIS handed out leaflets to Christian leaders in Mosul informing them that they had three options if they decided to stay: convert to Islam, pay the *jizya* (an exorbitant tax levied against non-Muslims under sharia law), or die. And they only had a few days to decide. Most of Mosul's estimated three thousand Christians left the city by the deadline, quickly gathering their belongings and beginning new lives as refugees, joining some five hundred thousand others who had fled Mosul after ISIS's arrival.[60] Laying low and staying in Mosul was not a viable option: Islamic State jihadists had spray-painted the Arabic letter for "N" in red to mark homes and businesses that were owned by Christians. The N stood for "Nazarene," indicating followers of Jesus of Nazareth.[61] Reportedly, ISIS has even turned churches into torture chambers in Iraq and Syria—after looting them of invaluable artifacts and relics to sell on the black market—and in July 2014, used sledgehammers to destroy the tomb of the biblical prophet Jonah in Mosul.[62]

ISIS's blitzkrieg across the Christian areas of northern Iraq was the climax of a decade-plus wave of persecution that began after the U.S. invasion of Iraq in 2003, when jihadists, led by ISIS's predecessor, al Qaeda in

Iraq, embarked on a campaign of church bombings and murders that have resulted in over a million Christians leaving Iraq. As of the summer of 2014, three hundred thousand still remain but if ISIS continues its rampage, they won't be there for long.[63]

Canon Andrew White, the Vicar of St. George's Church in Baghdad, the city's last remaining Anglican church, visited CBN's Jerusalem bureau in November 2014 and shared eyewitness accounts of the horrors ISIS is inflicting upon Iraqi Christians. White is a native of England whose ministry, the Foundation for Relief and Reconciliation in the Middle East, offers humanitarian and spiritual aid to Christians in Iraq and Syria who've seen their worlds turned upside down thanks to ISIS. In an interview with my CBN News colleague Chris Mitchell, he described the unfathomably hellish situation:

> In Iraq at the moment, it is impossible to describe how it really is. It is so awful. Most of our people originate from Nineveh, which is Mosul, and they come from there because that is really where our faith started.... Things were bad in Baghdad and there were bombs and shootings and our people were being killed, so so many of our people fled from Baghdad back to Nineveh—their traditional homes. It was safer. And then one day, ISIS...came in...and hounded all of them out. Not some, all of them. And they killed huge numbers. They chopped the children in half, they chopped their heads off. And they moved north.... they said to one man, an adult, they said "Either you say the words of converting to Islam or we kill all your children." He was desperate. He said the words. And then he phoned me, "Abounah, Abounah [Father], I said the words. Does that mean Yeshua [Jesus] doesn't love me anymore? I've always loved Yeshua, but I said those words because I couldn't see my children being killed." I said, "Elias, no, Jesus still loves you. He will

always love you." A few days later…ISIS turned up and they said to the children, "You say the words, that you will follow Moham-med." And the children, all under fifteen, all of them, they said, "No, we love Yeshua, we have always loved Yeshua, we have always followed Yeshua. Yeshua has always been with us." [ISIS] said, "Say the words." They said, "No we can't." They chopped all their heads off…. That is what we are going through. Most of my staff are still in the north of Iraq trying to look after all the displaced people. [ISIS was] threatening to kill me, they were after me. They wanted that Abounah from England….[64]

When children are being beheaded and cut in half, crucifixion is a logical next step in the savagery department. Sure enough, ISIS has taken to hanging bodies on crosses in Syria—and not just of Christians. The victims include one seventeen-year-old Muslim boy who allegedly took pictures of ISIS's military headquarters in Raqqa. His body was hung on a cross for three days in the city's central square, where he met an agonizing death. ISIS uses crucifixions and beheadings as a way to intimidate the local population—in Raqqa, severed heads hanging from street posts are a familiar sight.[65] Perhaps the Islamic State will include those details in its travel brochure.

MODERN-DAY SLAVERY

Even her father pelted her with stones.

At point blank range.

ISIS had accused the unnamed Syrian woman of committing adultery. The sentence for her alleged crime was stoning. And in accordance with sharia law, ISIS carried out "justice" in grisly fashion, stoning the woman (whose face was covered) to death and then posting a video of the deed online. Her father refused to forgive her despite her pleas and chose instead to participate in the execution, hurling stone after stone at his own daughter's head as ISIS jihadists encouraged him.[66]

That's just a small sampling of what life is like for women in the Islamic State. But while Muslim women are subjected to stonings, repression, and second-class status, non-Muslim women are treated worse than animals. Simply put, captured Christian and Yazidi women are being subjected to mass rape by Islamic State jihadists, who have created a thriving sex slavery trade. Thousands of Yazidi women, in particular, have been rounded up "like cattle" by ISIS, which places price tags on them at markets in cities like Mosul and Raqqa.[67] In many cases, their family members have already been executed by ISIS. The women are all alone, destined to live a life of inhuman servitude in the power of "sex jihadists." According to an op-ed by two former CIA analysts in *Foreign Policy*: "The Islamic State's (IS) fighters are committing horrific sexual violence on a seemingly industrial scale: For example, the United Nations…estimated that IS has forced some 1,500 women, teenage girls, and boys into sexual slavery. Amnesty International released a blistering document noting that IS abducts whole families in northern Iraq for sexual assault and worse. Even in the first few days following the fall of Mosul…women's rights activists reported multiple incidents of IS fighters going door to door, kidnapping and raping Mosul's women."[68]

In September 2014, the *Telegraph* recounted how an Italian newspaper was able to get in touch with a seventeen-year-old-Yazidi girl, who, along with some forty other Yazidi women, was being kept as a sex slave by ISIS "in a building with barred windows and guarded by men with weapons":

> The woman said her captors had initially confiscated her mobile and those of all the other women, but had then "changed strategy", returning the phones so that the women and girls could recount to the outside world the full horror of what was happening to them.

"To hurt us even more, they told us to describe in detail to our parents what they are doing. They laugh at us because they think they are invincible. They consider themselves are [sic] supermen. But they are people without a heart.

"Our torturers do not even spare the women who have small children with them. Nor do they spare the girls—some of our group are not even 13 years old. Some of them will no longer say a word." The woman, given the false name Mayat by *La Repubblica*, said the women were raped on the top floor of the building, in three rooms. The girls and women were abused up to three times a day by different groups of men.

"They treat us as if we are their slaves. The men hit us and threaten us when we try to resist. Often I wish that they would beat me so severely that I would die.

...If one day this torture ever ends, my life will always be marked by what I have suffered in these weeks. Even if I survive, I don't know how I'm going to cancel from my mind this horror.

"We've asked our jailers to shoot us dead, to kill us, but we are too valuable for them. They keep telling us that we are unbelievers because we are non-Muslims and that we are their property, like war booty. They say we are like goats bought at a market."[69]

If you think this type of medieval barbarism is due solely to a backwards Middle Eastern culture, think again. ISIS jihadists of French and British origin have openly bragged on social media of using Yazidi women as sex slaves.[70] And as we'll see in chapter six, British women who have migrated to the Islamic State actually run brothels where they provide sex slaves for ISIS fighters.

An ISIS handbook released in December 2014 entitled "Questions and Answers on Taking Captives and Slaves" justifies these atrocities, stating, "It is permissible to have sexual intercourse with the female captive. Allah the almighty said: '[Successful are the believers] who guard their chastity, except from their wives or [the captives and slaves] that their right hands possess, for then they are free from blame' [Koran 23:5-6]."

The handbook also goes on to condone sexual intercourse "with the female slave who hasn't reached puberty if she is fit for intercourse; however if she is not fit for intercourse, then it is enough to enjoy her without intercourse."[71]

Inside the Islamic State, such directives are taken quite literally. According to some reports, girls as young as nine years old have been raped by ISIS fighters.[72] Indeed, the exploitation of children is a way of life inside the caliphate and is not limited to the horrors of sexual molestation:

- In Raqqa, children under fifteen are "forcibly" conscripted and placed in ISIS training camps where they're taught to behead infidels, using dolls with blonde hair and blue eyes for practice.[73]
- They're also taught how to handle automatic weapons and shown videos of beheadings, stonings, and crucifixions.[74]
- Supplementing the daily brainwashing at the training camps, ISIS provides a handbook for mothers that encourages them to train their children in all forms of physical fitness (including martial arts) "from the time they are babies" in order to prepare them to one day assume the mantle of jihad for the Islamic State.[75]

◾   ◾   ◾

To the average Westerner, all of it is unthinkable: the mass rapes, the slave markets, the crucifixions, beheadings, stonings, and child soldiers. Yet growing numbers of American and European citizens not only agree with these Islamic State "values"—they wish to see them enforced on Western soil.

From Paris to Ottawa to New York City, they've proven ready and willing to maim, murder, and menace their fellow citizens.

If they can't live inside the caliphate, they'll do the next best thing.

Bring the caliphate home.

CHAPTER THREE

TARGET AMERICA: WHY YOU SHOULD CARE ABOUT ISIS

"WOW, THAT GUY LOOKS REALLY ANGRY."

"At what?"

"At us."

My cameraman, Ian, directed my attention to a café a few feet from where we were standing. An elderly Somali man inside was wildly gesticulating at us through the window with a look of fury in his eyes. His long beard was dyed bright orange with henna in emulation of Islam's prophet Mohammed, who is said to have worn his beard in a similar fashion.

Since we were separated by glass, I couldn't make out what the colorfully bearded old man was shouting at us. But I could guess that it wasn't "Peace be upon you."

"I think he's mad that we're filming," Ian said.

"We've overstayed our welcome," I agreed.

We had been shooting footage at the Karmel Square mall and Suuqq (or "souk": Arabic for mall or bazaar) in southwest Minneapolis for a series of reports I was producing about ISIS recruitment in the Twin Cities—particularly among the area's large Somali Muslim community. Known to locals as the "Somali Mall," the Karmel facility hosts some 150 Somali-owned businesses, plus an Islamic prayer center that was under construction when we visited in September 2014. Area sources had told me the sprawling complex was an exclusively Somali enclave that was indicative of that community's troubling lack of assimilation.

The existence of such an enclave came as no surprise. In my 2011 book, *The Terrorist Next Door*, and in several on-the-ground reports for CBN News, I've documented the troubling insularity of Somali communities in the United States in places such as rural Shelbyville, Tennessee. These communities have a predisposition to self-segregate and circle the wagons. Their members face massive cultural barriers to engagement with the larger American culture, and they tend to gravitate to what is familiar, particularly Islam. Combine Islamic radicalism with alienation and a resistance to assimilation, and you have a combustible mix. Witness the dozens of young Somalis from the Twin Cities who have traveled abroad to join ISIS.

I've been to outdoor souks in the Middle East. The Karmel mall had the same noisy Third World feel, only moved indoors. Its maze-like halls were packed with stalls and small shops selling an abundance of hijabs, niqabs, and Islamic clothing as well as jewelry, carpets, cell phones, and other assorted knick-knacks. There were also cafés where groups of men sat and chatted. Other than Ian and me, there was nary a non-Somali in sight, and we received quizzical looks from shop owners and patrons who didn't know quite what to make of the two tall white men wielding a video camera. We engaged in some small talk with an older Somali man who told us he loved the mall because it felt like home. "It is like Mogadishu came to Minnesota," he said with a laugh.

Yet the longer we lingered, filming, the more intense the stares grew. We were outsiders who had stepped into a world that was very remote from Minneapolis and St. Paul. And we had a video camera, the sight of which made the Somali women, who were dressed in conservative Islamic garb, visibly uncomfortable. It was obviously time to go—a fact that was only underlined by the enthusiastic send-off from our orange-bearded friend.

As we left, I couldn't help but recall my conversation the previous day in nearby St. Paul with Omar Jamal, a local Somali activist who has long warned of jihadist infiltration in the Twin Cities' Somali communities. Jamal told me that, "even an 'A' student" in a university can be vulnerable to the ISIS propaganda machine and that jihadi recruitment in the Twin Cities doesn't only happen in mosques. "It can happen anywhere," he said. "A coffee house, a basement, university, colleges, in meeting rooms."

Perhaps even in an isolated Somali mall.

■   ■   ■

While the Twin Cities' Somali communities have arguably become America's number one terrorist breeding ground, the lure of jihad extends far beyond the upper Midwest. According to reliable estimates, as of August 2014 at least a hundred American citizens were fighting alongside jihadist groups in Syria, including ISIS.[1] Some have placed the number as high as three hundred.[2] Of course, neither of those estimates includes the untold number of ISIS sympathizers already living inside the United States and gleefully re-tweeting Islamic State beheading videos.

When American jihadists are through learning the finer points of bomb-making and hostage-taking from their ISIS brethren in Syria—not to mention gaining invaluable battlefield experience and ideological training—at least some of them will return to the United States. What happens then is anyone's guess. The Islamic State isn't exactly turning out the type of upstanding young gents who can be expected to transition back into a quiet, jihad-free existence upon returning from the caliphate. A guy who just last week was dismembering Yazidi sex slaves or screaming "Allahu Akbar" as he charged Syrian Army positions isn't likely to get a 9-to-5 job or go back to school and get his bachelor's degree. Rather, these U.S. passport holders, assuming they clear customs, are prime candidates to follow the example of Mehdi Nemmouche.

Nemmouche, a French citizen, gunned down four people at a Jewish museum in Brussels after returning to his native Europe following a stint with ISIS in Syria. It was tragic, horrific—and, sadly, predictable. A former ISIS hostage described how Nemmouche relished torturing prisoners and boasted of raping and murdering a woman before beheading her baby.[3] All in a day's work for the guardians of the Islamic State.

Nemmouche is no outlier. The ranks of ISIS are filled with sadists and murderous sociopaths of his ilk. And it's not alarmism or exaggeration to say that some of them could be coming soon to a neighborhood near you. Welcome to Unpleasantville.

The Anti-Defamation League (ADL) studied twenty U.S. citizens who fought alongside terrorist groups abroad, or attempted to do so, in 2013 and 2014. Some of the report's key findings, in the ADL's words:

- They range in age from 18 to 44, but the majority are in their 20s....
- 13 of the 20, or 65%, are reportedly converts to Islam.
- They come from across the country: Six came from California, two each from Minnesota, Michigan, North Carolina, Florida and New York. Other states represented include Texas, Pennsylvania, Illinois, Massachusetts and Arizona.
- Only two of the 20 were women. (ADL has documented 13 female citizens and permanent residents of the U.S. arrested on terrorism charges since 2002.)[4]

FBI Director James Comey told *60 Minutes* in an October 2014 interview that he was "aware of" only "about 'a dozen or so' Americans who have joined ISIS,"[5] versus the one hundred or more that Obama administration officials had maintained for months were with the jihadists.[6] Comey said the FBI knew who the twelve Americans were and that the Bureau was keeping an eye on them. He added that if these same U.S.-born jihadists wished to return to America, they are "entitled to come back," unless their passport is revoked. The fact that they have committed treason by joining a terrorist group committed to our destruction apparently does not change that equation. Welcome to Obama's America, where even ISIS recruits are "entitled."

But never fear: according to Comey, "Someone who has fought with ISIL, with an American passport, [that] wants to come back, we will track them very carefully."[7] Forgive me if I don't feel reassured.

If Comey and the Bureau have things under control, how do they explain Moner Mohammad Abusalha? A twenty-two-year-old U.S. citizen who was born and raised in Florida, Abusalha fought with the al Qaeda–affiliated al-Nusra Front terror group in Syria, eventually blowing himself up in a suicide bombing against Syrian troops. He recorded the now-obligatory "martyrdom" video prior to carrying out his suicide mission, warning, "You think you are safe where you are in America. You are not safe."

Abusalha had actually made two separate trips to Syria. After the first trip in early 2013, he returned to the United States—and moved around the country, free and unmonitored, for months. According to the *Washington Post*, "There were no U.S. air marshals watching the newly clean-shaven passenger on the transatlantic flight, no FBI agents waiting for him as he landed in Newark in May 2013 after returning from Syria's civil war." He was selected for "additional screening," but the TSA did little but search his luggage and call his mother to verify that he had been "visiting relatives in the Middle East," as he claimed. Then he "was waved through without any further scrutiny or perceived need to notify the FBI that he was back in the United States.... His movements went unmonitored despite a major push by U.S. security and intelligence agencies over the past two years to track the flow of foreign fighters into and out of Syria."[8]

FBI field agents have done some fantastic work since the 9/11 attacks, and the Bureau's performance overall in breaking up terror plots and arresting aspiring terrorists—including some who had planned to join ISIS—should be commended. But as the case of Moner Mohammad Abusalha shows, the FBI is not infallible. Further, it's unclear whether the Bureau is being completely forthcoming about the extent of the domestic ISIS problem. For example, New York Congressman Tim Bishop, a Democrat and Obama supporter, has said that some forty of the hundred U.S. citizens who have traveled to Syria to join ISIS have already returned home and "are under FBI attention and surveillance. So they are known and being tracked by the FBI."[9] That's a far cry from the supposed twelve American ISIS fighters Comey alluded to in his *60 Minutes* interview.

Former longtime CIA clandestine services officer Brian Fairchild gave me a chilling assessment of the threat posed by these American jihadists once they return home from the Islamic State:

> ISIS's American recruits pose an extremely dangerous threat to the American homeland. Many of them have direct combat experience during which they have honed their military skills. They've killed during combat, and they've executed captives, raped and enslaved women, and beheaded their enemies. They are religious zealots who believe that they are fighting a holy war against the United States, which they consider to be the premier enemy of their religion. Worse, they believe that Allah directly commands them to kill us. Armed with this sanction they have no moral red line, and will not hesitate to commit the same heinous crimes here.[10]

Perhaps some of these ISIS returnees will form a cell and attempt a Mumbai-style attack—a very plausible scenario that Western intelligence officials have long been concerned about. In a 2008 jihad attack in Mumbai,

India, ten well-trained young Pakistani terrorists—each armed with assault rifles and bombs—spread out across the streets of the world's second-largest city and slaughtered 164 people while wounding over three hundred more. Jihadists everywhere took note. In October 2013, four Muslim men were arrested in London on charges that they were plotting to carry out a Mumbai-like attack in Britain. In *The Terrorist Next Door* I described the effects such an assault on American soil could have:

> The Mumbai operation presented an appealing package to the jihadist world. It garnered massive media coverage and dominated the international news cycle for nearly a week. It was cheap, low-tech, and didn't take much manpower to pull off, yet it still caused immense carnage and crippled the world's second-largest city for days. It also created the kind of psychological terror and economic damage that Islamic terrorist groups yearn for, and showed how a major city could be completely unprepared for a coordinated onslaught by jihadi foot soldiers.... How many lives would be lost, how much devastation would ensue, before a ten-man team of well-armed, well-trained jihadists could be subdued in a city like Columbus, Ohio? Local police would take them on at first. The FBI, SWAT, and potentially even the National Guard would later rush to the scene. Eventually the situation would be brought under control—but not before many people were killed and countless more wounded.[11]

The Mumbai blueprint was utilized to devastating effect by Somali terrorists in Kenya on September 21, 2013, but with a despicable new twist. A small band of heavily armed jihadists from the al Qaeda–linked terror group al-Shabaab fanned out, not across a city neighborhood, but throughout Nairobi's upscale Westgate shopping mall, a destination frequented by Western tourists. They slaughtered at least sixty-seven people, including several Westerners, and wounded hundreds more during a gruesome four-day siege that left the mall in ruins (it has never reopened). The terrorists intentionally targeted non-Muslims for death during the siege, asking hostages to name the Islamic prophet Mohammed's relatives or recite the *shahada*, the Muslim profession of faith. If hostages answered incorrectly, exposing themselves as non-Muslims, they were immediately killed. Al-Shabaab later said it carried out "a meticulous vetting process," to ensure that Muslims would not be killed and only "kuffar" would be targeted.[12]

It is no stretch to say that America is completely unprepared for a Westgate-style attack on a crowded suburban mall by a team of ISIS terrorists during the height of the Christmas shopping season. In fact, a Mumbai- or Westgate-type cell is not necessary to create bedlam in an American city or town. Think of the carnage wrought at Fort Hood by a lone Islamic terrorist, Nidal Hasan, who massacred thirteen of his fellow soldiers while yelling, "Allahu Akbar." And the Boston bombings were carried out by a pair of brothers who managed to kill four people, wound some 264 more, and shut down the city of Boston for the better part of a week, grabbing international media coverage.

Fort Hood and Boston represented what I call "chip away" attacks: smaller-scale, low-tech acts of terrorism that can nevertheless chip away at America's psyche and security if carried out on a regular basis. Al Qaeda has advocated this "death by a thousand cuts" strategy for years now, urging Western Muslims to act alone if necessary to become a one-man (or -woman) jihad, à la Nidal Hasan, against soft targets in the United States such as buses, trains, outdoor cafés, and shopping malls. ISIS is making a similar call to Muslims in the West—and with much greater effect than al Qaeda ever dreamed.

Consider the chaos that unfolded at a chocolate café in Sydney, Australia, over a sixteen-hour span in December 2014, when fifty-year-old Man Haron Monis—an Iranian-born ISIS sympathizer and jihadist rabble-rouser who had long been on Australian authorities' radar screen—held seventeen hostages at gunpoint. During the siege Monis forced the hostages to hold up the black flag of jihad in the café's window. Australian police eventually stormed the café and killed Monis, but not before the terrorist was able to murder two of his hostages.[13]

As we'll explore further in chapter five, the Islamic State's ubiquitous in-your-face social media presence, horror movie violence, and stunning battlefield successes—culminating in the declaration of the long-awaited caliphate—have galvanized radicalized Muslims across North America, Europe, and beyond, as we saw in Sydney.

If potential "lone wolves" needed any extra motivation, they received it in a September 2014 audio release. ISIS spokesman Abu Mohammad al-Adnani urged Muslims in the West, "If you can kill a disbelieving American or European—especially the spiteful and filthy French—or an Australian, or a Canadian, or any other disbeliever from the disbelievers waging war, including the citizens of the countries that entered into a coalition against the Islamic State…kill him in any manner or way however it may be."[14]

ISIS jihadists have also encouraged their followers in the United States to track down American soldiers online and from their personal information on social media, then go to their homes and slaughter them.[15] The threats only promise to increase as the United States increases its military involvement against the Islamic State caliphate.

The ultimate aim here for ISIS is a jihadist guerilla war—carried out mainly by homegrown "lone wolves"—that will turn America into a battlefield. Bear in mind that there have already been over sixty Islamic terror plots against America since 9/11 and that the overwhelming majority of them have been homegrown.[16]

As we saw in the days and weeks immediately following the release of al-Adnani's audiotape on September 21, 2014, there is no shortage of budding Western *mujahideen* willing and eager to answer ISIS's call and take up the mantle of domestic holy war:

■ On September 25, 2014, at a food-processing plant in Oklahoma, an American grandmother was beheaded by a Muslim radical. That vicious jihadist attack, which we'll discuss in more detail in chapter four, was carried out by an ISIS sympathizer and generated national outrage. What you may not have heard is that in the very same week when the beheading took place and in the very same town—Moore, Oklahoma—an Arab man walked into a local high school and started asking some very peculiar questions. According to the Daily Caller,

> A fortysomething Middle Eastern man described as having a thick Arabic accent waltzed into Moore High School in Moore, Okla. without authorization last week and asked a number of "suspicious" questions, according to police.... The man, who entered the school without permission through an unlocked door and then made his way into the cafeteria, queried two students and a teacher.
>
> …the man wanted to know the number of police officers who work at the school on a regular basis and the location of the closest police department. The odd question-asking incident lasted only a couple minutes. Then, apparently, the man disappeared.

According to Jeremy Lewis, a spokesman for the Moore police department, it was "very concerning that he was able to enter the school unannounced, unconfronted, that's concerning. That's something that has to be fixed."[17]

Yes, I would say the security situation at Moore High School needs some fixin'. And fast: "*The incident, which was caught on surveillance video, was not reported to police for two days, according to Fox affiliate KOKH* [emphasis added]."

Although police would not identify the Middle Eastern man and said he faced no criminal charges, the FBI was notified about the incident and it was reportedly under investigation.[18]

Police added that the man was not a threat and that his incursion onto school property had no connection to the nearby jihadist beheading that week—which the same Moore Police Department described, memorably, as an act of "workplace violence." Move along, nothing to see here.

Why should we be concerned? Well, consider the horrific three-day siege at Beslan, North Ossetia, in 2004. Terrorists, mainly from Chechnya and surrounding Muslim areas in Russia's Caucasus region, seized an elementary school in the town of Beslan in southern Russia. The ensuing hostage standoff ended in a nightmarish bloodbath that shocked and revolted the world. Three hundred and thirty-four people, including 186 children and many parents, were killed after being subjected to days of hellish abuse by their terrorist captors.

The possibility of a Beslan-style school siege has caused some restless nights for U.S. intelligence types and terrorism analysts as well as members of Congress who are regularly briefed on the terror threat. I'm based inside the Beltway and speak with such folks on a regular basis. In the decade-plus since Beslan, the school siege scenario has frequently come up in conversations as a serious concern. It's not hard to see why.

■ On September 23, 2014, just two days after ISIS spokesman Abu Mohammad al-Adnani released his call for lone wolf terror attacks, specifically mentioning Australia, an eighteen-year-old Afghan native brutally knifed two Australian counterterrorism police. Abdul Numan Haider was summoned to meet with counterterrorism agents at a Melbourne police station because of his suspected ties to terrorism. When the ISIS sympathizer was greeted outside the station by two agents, he promptly attacked them with a knife, seriously wounding one of them with slashes to the neck, head, and stomach. The other agent shot and killed Haider before the teenage jihadist could carry out his full plan "to stab the cops, behead them, wrap their bodies in the Islamic State flag and post photos of the killings online." Authorities found another, larger knife and an ISIS flag on Haider's body.[19]

Less than one week before Haider's one-man jihadi outburst, Australian authorities arrested fifteen people in connection with a plot to carry
out so-called "demonstration killings" in Sydney. ISIS sympathizers allegedly planned to kidnap a random person off the street, cover that person
in an Islamic State flag, and behead him or her for the camera in a sickening "demonstration" of the subterranean depths of ISIS's evil—and its
ability to carry out attacks in Western countries.[20] If successful, the plot
would have sent shockwaves throughout the world and left citizens from
Paris to Toronto to New York looking over their shoulders on their morning commutes.

ISIS-style beheading has already come to the West. Besides the September 2014 beheading of the Oklahoma grandmother by an ISIS supporter, in May of 2013 we saw a British soldier nearly decapitated in broad
daylight on a London street by a pair of jihadists. The Sydney beheading
plot was simply another sign of the times and a harbinger of things to come
in ISIS's budding guerilla war against the West.

■ The week of October 20, 2014, marked the official arrival of Islamic
terrorism to the Great White North. Canadian authorities had arrested
several terror suspects in the years following 9/11. The "Toronto 18," for
example, was a massive, eighteen-person cell in Ontario that planned to
behead Canadian Prime Minister Stephen Harper. But no Islamic terrorist had ever struck successfully on Canadian soil until a white convert to
Islam named Martin Rouleau-Couture—who went by the monikers
"Ahmad Rouleau" and "Abu Ibrahim Al-Canadi" in pro-ISIS rants
online—mowed down two uniformed Canadian soldiers with his car as
they walked across the parking lot of a Quebec strip mall, killing one of
them and wounding the other. Rouleau, who was well known to Canadian
authorities prior to the attack, then led police on a high-speed chase that
ended when his car flipped over into a ditch. He emerged from the car,
knife in hand, and charged police, who shot and killed him.[21] During the
car chase he had phoned a 911 dispatcher and said he carried out the attack,
"in the name of Allah."[22]

Just two days later, another radicalized convert and ISIS sympathizer, Michael Zehaf-Bibeau, shot and killed a Canadian soldier who was standing guard at the National War Memorial in Ottawa. Zehaf-Bibeau then stormed the nearby Canadian parliament building, filled with senior government officials, and opened fire before being shot and killed by the parliament's sergeant-at-arms.[23]

The sum of Rouleau and Zehaf-Bibeau's respective "chip away" attacks was two dead Canadian soldiers—both murdered on Canadian soil in the span of three days—plus wall-to-wall international media coverage. The case of Zehaf-Bibeau also exposed the glaring security vulnerabilities of Canadian government facilities and managed to cripple Canada's capital city for several hours as police hunted for any possible accomplices.[24]

A disturbingly impressive accomplishment for a mere "lone wolf" armed with nothing more than a hunting rifle.

■ On October 11, 2014, the FBI issued a bulletin warning that U.S. law enforcement personnel could be targeted by ISIS supporters.[25] Twelve days later, yet another Muslim convert, a thirty-two-year-old man named Zale Thompson, attacked four rookie New York City police officers with a hatchet in broad daylight on a Queens street. Thompson, whose Facebook page featured the obligatory radical Islamic imagery, critically wounded one of the officers with a hatchet blow to the head before being shot and killed. NYPD brass determined that Thompson's explosion of violence was indeed an act of terrorism, and that Thompson was "self-radicalized."[26]

So why are so many recent Muslim converts, like Thompson, drifting into terrorism? Bernard Squarcini, former head of France's domestic security service, has described the stunning speed and ease with which an individual can become radicalized: "An ideological transformation can be done in three months on the web," he said. "An individual can at night auto-radicalize himself via the [Internet] and get in touch with leaders of terrorist organizations."[27]

It's unclear what path a New Jersey native named Ali Muhammad Brown took to become a one-man walking jihad. Brown was not a recent convert; he had been a Muslim for some time. Also, his killing spree occurred in the months before ISIS declared a caliphate and called for attacks against Western civilians. Nevertheless, Brown, who gunned down three people in Washington state and one in New Jersey between April and June 2014, was clearly motivated by Islamist ideology. He told a police investigator, "My mission is vengeance. For the lives, millions of lives are lost every day… [in] Iraq, Syria, Afghanistan, all these places where innocent lives are being taken every single day…. So, a life for a life."[28] This is classic jihadist grievance rhetoric, the kind that all too often resonates with Western Islamists who wish to help their beleaguered brothers overseas. Sometimes they wire money to fund jihad. Other times, as in the case of Brown, they turn to violence.

Former CIA and State Department official Fred Fleitz, now with the Center for Security Policy in Washington, D.C., observed, "While Brown was not radicalized by ISIS, I believe recent ISIS propaganda and publicity pushed Brown over the edge to conduct terrorist killings."[29] Fleitz also noted the glaring lack of interest in Brown's case by the Obama administration and the mainstream media. I guess it would be tough to brand a cross-country murder spree as "workplace violence."

The lone wolf attacks described above—all of which, besides Ali Muhammad Brown's multi-state jihadist frenzy, occurred over a span of just four weeks—represent the new normal for the West in the age of ISIS. The flurry of violence by ISIS sympathizers was no coincidence. Each time the Islamic State issues a call for attacks on Western soil, as Abu Mohammed al-Adnani did in September 2014, you can bet that at least some of its fanatical supporters in Europe, the United States, Canada, and Australia will respond with rudimentary yet deadly effective lone wolf attacks—or perhaps something much worse.

Take the massacre in Paris of twelve people, including two police officers, at the offices of the French satirical magazine *Charlie Hebdo*. Al Qaeda had long called for attacks against the magazine for its irreverent cartoons featuring Islam's prophet Mohammed. On January 7, 2015, Said Kouachi, thirty-four, and his brother, Cherif, thirty-two—both French citizens—responded and stormed the offices of *Charlie Hebdo*, gunning down eleven people, including the magazine's editor, and then executing a French policeman (who was Muslim) on the street outside of the building. The assault was carried out in a highly professional manner—not surprising, since it was later revealed that the brothers had trained with al Qaeda in Yemen (which claimed responsibility for the attack).[30] The pair, who were on both U.S. and UK terror watch lists, fled the scene of the attack and were on the run for two days before being killed by French police in a hostage standoff near Charles De Gaulle Airport.

On January 8, one day after the massacre at *Charlie Hebdo*, another French Muslim, thirty-two-year-old Amedy Coulibaly, an acquaintance of the Kouachi brothers (and, like them, on a U.S. terror watch list),[31] shot and killed a French municipal police officer in Paris. The next day, Coulibaly turned up at a Kosher Jewish supermarket in Paris, murdering four people and taking several more hostage before being shot and killed by French security forces.[32] In a video published online by the Islamic State after his death, Coulibaly pledged allegiance to ISIS.[33] Just two months before his rampage, ISIS had called for attacks against France.[34]

These sorts of attacks, which were once sporadic, promise to only increase in frequency thanks to ISIS's continued success in expanding its caliphate and inciting its followers through social media. Shortly after the attacks by Coulibaly and the Kouachi brothers in France, Belgian authorities broke up a terror cell that was reportedly directed by the Islamic State. Members of the cell "had traveled to Syria and met with ISIS" to plan attacks in Europe.[35]

The ultimate goal, again, is to instill terror in the hearts of Western citizens and turn cities into virtual battlefields, as in Mumbai, Paris, Boston, and Ottawa. ISIS wishes to create an environment in which Western cities are besieged—not just sporadically, but on a sustained basis by self-starter jihadists hitting a variety of civilian, military, and law enforcement targets. If you're an American ISIS supporter seeking to wage jihad, the calculation is simple: Why travel to the battlefields of Syria and Iraq when you can create one in your own backyard, striking not against Iraqi, Syrian, or Kurdish troops but against Islam's greatest enemy, the United States? Die in a firefight with Iraqi security forces in Anbar province, and you fade into the dustbin of history. Die killing a few police in an attempt to storm the U.S. Capitol, and you become famous, your bushy-bearded mug plastered on media worldwide as jihadists far and near extol your praises.

All of this means we've entered a frightening—and personal—new phase in radical Islam's war on the United States. Will Americans glance up from their smartphones and put down their video game consoles in time to notice? And what about our government? Terrorism expert and investigative journalist Patrick Poole has found that American lone wolves may be better described as "known wolves"—virtually all of them were already on law enforcement and counterterrorism authorities' radar *before* engaging in, or attempting to engage in, terrorist activity on U.S. soil.[36] But no need to worry: James Comey and the Obama national security team have things completely under control.

■   ■   ■

The trauma and anger that a wholesale massacre of American schoolchildren or mall shoppers at the hands of Islamic terrorists would unleash cannot be overstated. If that massacre was committed by terrorists who had crossed America's southern border—which has gone from shamefully porous under President Bush to a virtual sieve under President Obama—the federal government would bear the full brunt of the American people's righteous anger.

Between April and July 2014 alone, some two hundred ninety thousand illegal immigrants from Central America—including fifty thousand unaccompanied minors—entered the United States through its southern border and were detained by federal authorities, only to be relocated to cities and towns throughout the country.[37] Mind you, those were only the migrants who were caught. Who else is here?

According to a U.S. Customs and Border Protection document obtained by Breitbart, some 474 illegal aliens from terrorism-linked countries—known as Special Interest Aliens, or SIAs—were apprehended trying to enter America's borders in the first seven months of 2014 alone. They hailed from majority-Muslim nations such as Afghanistan, Pakistan, Iraq, Iran, Somalia, Yemen, Lebanon, Egypt, and Syria, all of which have a sizable jihadist presence. Again, these were only the ones we caught.

As Breitbart reported, the same leaked U.S. government document showed, "Human smuggling routes from Syria into the U.S. go through South America, Central America, and the Caribbean before reaching Mexico.… Syrian human smugglers reportedly use the U.S.-Mexico border to enter America."[38]

Last time I checked, ISIS ruled a large swath of Syria, while the al Qaeda–linked al-Nusra Front and its allies also controlled a piece of the pie. In other words, the new, borderless America, targeted by "Syrian human smugglers" and God knows who else, is an Islamic terror attack waiting to happen:

- In October 2014, Congressman Duncan Hunter—a California Republican not prone to wild exaggeration—maintained that Border Patrol sources told him that ten ISIS operatives had been detained while attempting to enter the U.S. through its southern border. The Department of Homeland Security immediately denied Hunter's claim.[39]

- A month earlier, another well-respected Republican House member, Utah's Jason Chaffetz, alleged during a House hearing that sources had told him four men with Middle Eastern terrorist ties had crossed the U.S.-Mexico border. Homeland Security Secretary Jeh Johnson later dismissed Chaffetz's claim, arguing that the four men were indeed apprehended after crossing the border illegally—but that they had no terror ties and claimed merely to be members of the Kurdish Workers' Party (also known as the PKK), a group "that is actually fighting against ISIL and defended Kurdish territory in Iraq." He promised that the quartet would be deported.

Chaffetz noted that the PKK has been designated a foreign terrorist organization by the U.S. government. "I don't think that should be dismissed as insignificant...." Chaffetz told CBS News. "These are terrorists nonetheless and they had no trouble crossing our southern border." Chaffetz wondered why the men had not been prosecuted. "There's no doubt in my mind that they're tied with terrorists," he said. "To try to say that they were good terrorists is a bit concerning coming from the Homeland Security Secretary. We were lucky that they're not tied with ISIS. They could have been."

Chaffetz described how the four men had "fl[own] into Mexico City, hired a coyote to help them reach and cross the Rio Grande, and then make their way to a safe house. They intended to make their way to New York City."[40]

How many ISIS operatives intend to take a similar path? And how many from the Islamic State, the PKK, and other terror groups have already slipped through the cracks and taken advantage of the deluge of illegal immigrants swarming America's wide-open southern border?

■ Two other Republican House members, Texas's Ted Poe and Tom Cotton of Arkansas, have warned that ISIS could work with Mexican drug cartels. Poe, a member of the House Judiciary Committee's Subcommittee on Crime, Terrorism, and Homeland Security, said in August 2014 that ISIS and the cartels seem to be "talking to each other." He continued, "The drug cartels use the same operational plan as terrorist groups do... They kill their opponents, they behead their opponents, they brag about it and they have operational control of many portions of the southern border of the United States. They're vicious as some of these other terrorist organizations."[41]

I'd add that they also have no allegiance to anyone or anything other than the almighty dollar and have no love lost for the United States.

▪ Meanwhile, then–Texas Governor Rick Perry warned in an August 2014 speech that there was a "very real possibility" that ISIS may have already used the southern border to enter the United States, while acknowledging that there was no evidence that such an incursion had occurred.[42]

▪ Even General Martin Dempsey, chairman of the Joint Chiefs of Staff, has sounded the alarm, warning of "the number of Europeans and other nationalities" that have gone to the Middle East to link up with ISIS and other terror groups. "And those folks can go home at some point," Dempsey said at a Pentagon press briefing. "It's why I have conversations with my European colleagues about their southern flank of NATO, which I think is actually more threatened in the near term than we are. Nevertheless, because of open borders and immigration issues, it's an immediate threat. That is to say, the fighters who may leave the current fight and migrate home."[43]

To recap: America's top general, four congressmen, and the popular governor of a border state all warn that ISIS operatives have infiltrated, or may be planning to infiltrate, the U.S.-Mexico border. And why wouldn't they? Report after report has documented how murderers, gang members, drug smugglers, rapists, and every other criminal element have already done so, along with members of various terrorist groups, including the likes of Hezbollah.[44]

Another not-so-fun fact: close to 167,000 illegal immigrants have been convicted of crimes and are scheduled to be deported, yet they remain at large inside the United States.[45] Most of them undoubtedly entered the U.S. through its southern border. Yet that same border continues to be virtually ignored by the Obama administration, recklessly and brazenly putting American lives at risk.

How dangerous is the "borderless" game the Obama team is playing? When I asked Brian Fairchild, a former career CIA case officer who ran clandestine operations in seven CIA stations around the world, which kinds of possible attacks on the U.S. homeland concerned him most, he laid out the following scenario:

What I'm concerned about is that whatever spectacular approach [ISIS leader Abu Bakr] al Baghdadi decides on might include Weapons of Mass Destruction. It is a fact that he controls munitions from Iraq's Muthanna chemical weapons complex that contain Sarin, VX, and mustard gas, and, in addition to that, we know that his fighters seized approximately 90 pounds of uranium compounds from a university in Mosul that can be used to construct a dirty bomb. And, of course, there is always the possibility that biological weapons could be employed against us, so I'm afraid that whatever spectacular attack he imagines might well include the use of these WMDs.

This is where the vulnerabilities of our southern border come into play. While many foreign fighters can enter the U.S. via American airports with U.S. or Western European passports and then find weapons or the materials to construct bombs after their arrival, it is highly unlikely that they would be able to smuggle chemical weapons or radioactive elements in this way.

The U.S. border with Mexico, however, is a huge sieve through which people and drugs are smuggled into the country on a daily basis, so it is likely that a dedicated team of terrorists could smuggle WMDs, RPGs, MANPADs, or other weapons into the country.[46] [emphasis added]

Fairchild's clandestine work for the CIA saw him operate under both official and non-official cover—including a stint as chief of base in a hostile "denied area"—that is, territory under enemy control. He's a serious, razor-sharp guy with loads of experience working in the shadows in some of the most dangerous places on earth. When he tells me America's southern border is a disaster waiting to happen, I take his word for it. As for ISIS and chemical arms, the Islamic State reportedly has already used such weapons against Kurds in Syria.[47] In addition, an August 2014 *Foreign Policy* piece detailed the alarming contents of a laptop captured from a Tunisian jihadist named "Muhammed S." who had studied chemistry and physics before joining ISIS in Syria. On his laptop was a nineteen-page Arabic document detailing "how to develop biological weapons and how to weaponize the bubonic plague from infected animals":

> "The advantage of biological weapons is that they do not cost a lot of money, while the human casualties can be huge," the document states.
>
> The document includes instructions for how to test the weaponized disease safely, before it is used in a terrorist attack. "When the microbe is injected in small mice, the symptoms of the disease should start to appear within 24 hours," the document says.

Also on the same laptop was a twenty-six-page fatwa from Nasir al-Fahd, an Islamic cleric currently imprisoned in Saudi Arabia, justifying the use of WMDs: "'If Muslims cannot defeat the kafir [unbelievers] in a different way, it is permissible to use weapons of mass destruction.... Even if it kills all of them and wipes them and their descendants off the face of the Earth.'"

As *Foreign Policy* noted, "The fear now is that men like Muhammed [S.] could be quietly working behind the front lines—for instance, in the Islamic State–controlled University of Mosul or in some laboratory in the Syrian city of Raqqa, the group's de facto capital—to develop chemical or biological weapons." The possibilities are chilling: "'Use small grenades with the virus, and throw them in closed areas like metros, soccer stadiums, or entertainment centers,' the 19-page document on biological weapons advises. 'Best to do it next to the air-conditioning. It also can be used during suicide operations.'"[48]

As Fairchild pointed out, why try to smuggle these kinds of weapons into the United States on an airplane when you can waltz across the Rio Grande undetected?

Although America's southern border is surely enticing, it isn't the only means by which ISIS jihadists and their sympathizers can penetrate the United States and carry out attacks. As we've seen, from beheading grandmothers to attacking police officers with hatchets in broad daylight, Islamic State barbarians are not just at the gates. They're already inside them.

CHAPTER FOUR

HEARTLAND HORROR: THE AMERICAN RECRUITS

FROM THE MOMENT I STEPPED INSIDE FAITH BIBLE CHAPEL IN
Arvada, Colorado, it felt like a homecoming.

I was in town to speak at the church's thirty-sixth annual Israel Awareness Day, a vibrant interfaith event designed to show unwavering support for Israel and the Jewish people in the face of world hostility.

For this four thousand five hundred–member congregation located just outside Denver, Israel Awareness Day, which is capped by a "Night to Honor Israel" celebration featuring high-profile speakers, music, and worship, presents an opportunity to show both Christian and non-Christian alike what they are all about.

Pastor George Morrison and his team are kind and welcoming. They love Jesus. They love Israel. They preach the Gospel boldly and without apology.

And Shannon Conley hated them for it.

At the time of my visit in October 2014, it had been nearly one year since Conley, a nineteen-year-old ISIS sympathizer and aspiring jihadist, had stalked the Faith Bible campus on Sundays carrying a large backpack and dressed in Islamic garb. I spoke to a member of the church's security team who described how Conley took notes as she wandered around various areas of the church, testing doors, recording sanctuary activities, and documenting the location of security cameras. She was also seen pacing near Sunday School areas filled with children. When security and church staff asked to review her notes, Conley refused to let them.

In the church parking lot, a member of the Faith Bible security team observed a camouflage U.S. Army jacket draped over the passenger seat of Conley's car—bearing a patch showing the Saudi flag (which features the Islamic *shahada*, or creed, along with a sword). When a staffer asked Conley if she was coming to church because she was interested in converting to Christianity, she answered in the negative, saying she was devoted to Islam.

Naturally, this kind of alarming behavior by a devoutly Muslim woman at an evangelical Christian church raised eyebrows. Particularly at Faith Bible, where a 2007 shooting spree by a deranged man at a missionary training center had left two people dead (the shooter went on to kill two more people at a church in Colorado Springs that same day).

Given that tragic history and Conley's erratic displays and lack of cooperation with security, church leaders eventually had no choice but to ask her to leave Faith Bible Chapel. They alerted the Arvada Police Department about Conley's behavior, and the investigation was then turned over to the Colorado branch of the FBI. In April 2014, a few months after the church stalkings, federal agents arrested Conley at Denver International Airport. She was on her way to Syria, via Turkey, to marry an ISIS fighter she had met online. Conley, a certified nurse's aide, told agents she hoped to be "a housewife and the camp nurse" and help treat wounded ISIS fighters. She was also willing to engage in armed jihad if called upon.[1]

As for Faith Bible Chapel, Conley told the FBI that she detested the church's pro-Israel stand, stating, flatly, "I hate those people." She added,

"If they think I'm a terrorist, I'll give them something to think I am." Mission accomplished. Shannon Conley—raised in a comfortable, middle-class suburb of Denver—had become a committed, and unlikely, Islamic radical. According to a *Los Angeles Times* profile,

> Conley had been "among the brightest kids" at Arvada West High School, said principal Rob Bishop, adding that she was the daughter of a professor at a Catholic university, was enrolled in honors courses and presented no discipline problems.
>
> Sometime during her junior year, Bishop said, Conley had begun to wear traditional Muslim dress. Several girls complained that she was kneeling on the bathroom floor three times a day for her prayers.[2]

Conley eventually took the Arabic name Halima, describing herself on her Facebook page as a "slave to Allah." Her rapid conversion surprised her family and neighbors. One neighbor recalled sometimes seeing her, "sitting alone in a neighborhood park, drifting silently on the playground swing" and looking "kind of lost."[3] It's likely that Conley discovered fundamentalist Islam where so many radicalized converts do, on the Web. She began corresponding online with a Tunisian ISIS jihadist and agreed to relocate to Syria and marry him.

Following her arrest, Conley was generally portrayed in the mainstream media as a bungling sad sack who was a threat to no one but herself. Yet in preparation for her new life abroad as a jihadi bride, Conley managed to receive military training at a Texas camp run by the U.S. Army Explorers.[4] During a search of her Arvada home, agents found jihadist videos, including sermons by notorious al Qaeda cleric Anwar al-Awlaki (who was killed in a U.S. drone strike in 2011). They also discovered shooting targets marked with the distance and number of rounds that had been fired.

If Conley had made it to Syria and taken up arms, she wouldn't have been the first woman to participate in violent jihad. According to one estimate, as of August 2013, at least "46 women [had] turned themselves into suicide bombs in Russia, committing 26 terrorist attacks (some attacks involved multiple women). Most of the bombers were from Chechnya and Dagestan."[5] These Chechen and Dagestani "Black Widows" typically have lost husbands or sons in the ongoing Islamic insurgency against Russian forces in the Caucasus region. The Widows conduct suicide bombings against Russian civilians in a sick form of revenge for their deceased loved ones.

Conley had no such personal motivation for joining with ISIS, but she was fanatically committed to its cause nonetheless. FBI agents met with her, face to face, eight times between November 2013 and April 2014 and met six times with her parents during that same span. The agents tried repeatedly to dissuade Conley from traveling to Syria and warned that what she was planning was illegal, but to no avail.[6] "Halima" was hell-bent on traveling to Syria, marrying a jihadist, and helping ISIS. While the mainstream media was busy dismissing Conley as a harmless wannabe, they ignored the obvious question: Had she not chosen to wage jihad in Syria, what's to say that this increasingly fervent ISIS sympathizer wouldn't have turned her sights on local targets like Faith Bible Chapel instead?

In September 2014, Conley pleaded guilty in a Denver District Court to "providing material support to al-Qaeda and affiliates, including ISIS." In January 2015, she was sentenced to four years in federal prison for her attempts to travel overseas and join ISIS.[7] According to the *Denver Post*, "As part of a plea agreement, prosecutors agreed not to file additional charges, and [Conley] promised to divulge information about co-conspirators and possibly testify in court."[8]

Perhaps one day Conley will share insights into why so many young Western women like her from middle class backgrounds are gravitating toward the most misogynistic, undemocratic, and depraved society on the planet. The growing list of female Islamic State recruits includes three teenage girls who lived not far from Conley in Aurora, Colorado, outside Denver.

The trio—two sisters of Somali descent aged seventeen and fifteen and their friend, a sixteen-year-old girl of Sudanese descent—were taken into custody at Germany's Frankfurt Airport in October 2014 as they prepared to board a flight to Turkey with plans to travel to Syria and join ISIS. They were encouraged in their mission by an "online predator," or recruiter, who enticed them into traveling to the Islamic State.[9] The two sisters stole passports and $2,000 from their parents' home before heading out with their friend on a quest, not just to be jihadi brides, but "to join the fight" alongside ISIS.[10] And they are not alone in that quest.

As of November 2014, at least four Somali-American women had reportedly left Minneapolis and St. Paul and made their way to the Islamic State.[11] The Twin Cities' Somali community has been a virtual conveyor belt for foreign terrorist organizations over the past several years. Bob Fletcher, who served as sheriff of Ramsey County, which includes St. Paul, for sixteen years, told me that young Somali women in the Twin Cities are being recruited online. "They are constantly getting messages," he said. "Especially from the women [of ISIS]. These young women [in the Islamic State] . . . are feeding these other women propaganda, if you will, to come."[12]

Much of the online propaganda is coming from ISIS's plentiful crop of British female recruits inside Syria. The *Guardian* reported that, "Some British women and girls have posted pictures of themselves carrying AK-47s, grenades and in one case a severed head, as they pledge allegiance to ISIS. But they are also tweeting pictures of food, restaurants and sunsets to present a positive picture of the life awaiting young women in an attempt to lure more from the UK."[13]

Their strategy is working. An estimated fifty British girls and women have reportedly joined ISIS, with many of them now based in the city of Raqqa, the Islamic State's de facto capital.[14] As we'll see in chapter six, British jihadists—both male and female—are taking on important roles in the Islamic State. Reports have emerged of British women leading an all-female sharia police unit called the "al-Khansaa Brigade" that brutally enforces

Islamic law and dress codes among female civilians inside Raqqa.[15] This terror squad composed of British citizens is even reportedly running brothels that force captured Iraqi women into sex slavery in the service of ISIS fighters.[16]

If needed, the al-Khansaa Brigade will find no shortage of willing Western accomplices to assist in their dark work. At least forty German women have relocated to Syria and Iraq to join the Islamic State, while over sixty French women have joined ISIS and other terrorist groups in the region, with many more reportedly eager to take the jihadi plunge.[17]

Fletcher, who left the St. Paul police force in 2013 and now works closely with local Somali leaders to battle Islamic radicalism within their community, knows the jihadi recruiting process well, having seen dozens of Somalis from the Twin Cities join terror groups overseas in recent years. ISIS's targeting of women comes as no surprise to the former sheriff. "Their handlers and their recruiters in Syria, they want them to help build a society," he told me. "While they are recruiting men, they also promised them wives when they get there. They need women in their society to keep their fighters content. It's a scary thing, but the women are really being used in a variety of ways once they get there."

Yes, you need women to build a caliphate—after all, someone has to make babies and raise them up to be good *mujahideen* while Daddy is off plundering. And ISIS likes 'em young. The average age for ISIS's female recruits is between sixteen and twenty-four—and some are even younger.[18] Once they arrive in Syria, they don't stay single for long. The Islamic State has its own jihadi Mingle-style dating service: a "marriage bureau" near Raqqa that seeks to match new arrivals with male ISIS fighters.[19]

ISIS has also established a special institute for these female recruits, called "al-Zawra," intended to "prepare sisters for the battlefields for jihad." According to Vocativ: "To prepare women for their roles as mujahedeen, al-Zawra offers classes in five areas, including domestic work such as sewing and cooking, medical first aid, Islam and Sharia law, weaponry, and in a surprisingly progressive twist, training in social media and computer programs for editing and design."[20]

Al-Zawra instructs aspiring female jihadists to get in shape, learn first aid, and learn to sew and cook. And of course, to watch YouTube and learn weapons training, because ISIS wants gals who are, "interested in explosive belt and suicide bombing more than a white dress or a castle or clothing or furniture."[21] *Frozen* is apparently not very popular in the Islamic State.

A pair of Austrian teenagers found out the hard way about a girl's life in the caliphate. Austrian authorities believe Samra Kesinovic, seventeen, and Sabina Selimovic, fifteen, two pretty friends from Vienna, were radicalized online and at a local mosque.[22] In April 2014 the pair left a note for their parents that read, "Don't look for us. We will serve Allah, and we will die for him." They then departed for Syria to join ISIS, ending up married—and reportedly pregnant—to two Islamic State fighters in Raqqa. Kesinovic and Selimovic soon became known as the "poster girls" of jihad, with images (reportedly doctored by ISIS) of them clad in burqas and brandishing AK-47s posted regularly to social media.[23]

When reports surfaced that the girls realized they'd made a horrible mistake and wished desperately to return to Austria, the seventeen-year-old Kesinovic gave an interview via text message to a French magazine saying the rumors were untrue and that she was happy in Syria. But Austrian security sources believe Kesinovic was being held at gunpoint by her doting hubby as she gave her answers.[24] Tragically, there have been reports that at least one of the girls has been killed during fighting in Syria.[25] The danger hasn't stopped other Austrian girls from wanting to trade in their tiaras for Islamic State burqas. In September 2014, Austrian police detained two girls, aged fourteen and fifteen, "with full suitcases…intending to go to Syria" and follow in the footsteps of Kesinovic and Selimovic.[26] Want to rebel and make Mom and Dad mad these days? Forget bringing home a guy with facial piercings and neck tattoos. Instead, run away to Syria and marry a bearded jihadi with a fondness for severed heads.

You'd think that young women and teenage girls brought up in the comfort, freedom, and security of the West would view ISIS with complete revulsion. As we saw in chapter two, the Islamic State engages in every form of sexual violence and degradation imaginable and imposes a dehumanizing, second-class existence upon women; it surpasses even the Taliban in sheer brutality. The eyewitness horror stories are readily available online—it's tough to romanticize gang rape, woman battering, sex slavery, and polygamy.

Yet ISIS continues to attract Western females: from the love-starved to the lost and naive, from anti-social loners to foolish young thrill-seekers looking for danger and a way to rebel against authority. Shannon Conley seems to have fallen into each of those categories to some varying degree. She seemed utterly convinced that she'd find a wonderful life in the new caliphate and help build an Islamic utopia where she would play a pivotal role.

And she is not alone.

■   ■   ■

What kind of person would leave a middle class suburb of Denver, London, Amsterdam, or Montreal to trek to a bloody war zone and into the embrace of the world's most sadistic terrorist organization? Former CIA case officer Patrick Skinner puts ISIS's fighters into three categories: the Psychopaths, the Pious, and the Sunni Pragmatists. He refers to the Pious as "True Believers" who are drawn to the caliph, Abu Bakr al-Baghdadi, and see the reestablishment of the caliphate as a religious duty. A good number of Western recruits undoubtedly fall into this category.

The Sunni Pragmatists, Skinner says, include Iraqi tribal sheikhs "whose allegiance to ISIS originates not in a cultish death wish but in a desire to win security and well-being, and who seem to be using the Psychopaths and the True Believers as convenient allies." This category does not apply to Western jihad seekers.

The Psychopaths, however, are a different story. Skinner describes them as having "more taste for grindhouse than Islamic jurisprudence…exemplars of the most lurid and photogenic of the three types of ISIS fighter." He says ISIS's foreign legion "tend to be hyperviolent," especially in comparison to more pragmatic indigenous fighters: "As men without significant military training—like most jihadis from Western or upper-class backgrounds—their main purpose is to create grotesque propaganda and, perhaps, to perform the low-skill role of blowing themselves up."[27]

The vulnerable, the impressionable, the lonely, the desperate, the troubled, the sinister, the violent, and the psychotic are leaving the comfort of Western societies behind to join the Islamic State. The Islamic State is like a valley of lost souls stretching across a vast swath of the Middle East; it has become a gathering place for the evil, the disturbed, and the depraved. In the Lord of the Rings trilogy, all of Middle Earth's malevolent forces flock to Mordor to serve the Dark Lord, Sauron, and destroy the forces of good. In Stephen King's post-apocalyptic novel *The Stand* a megalomaniacal dictator named Randall Flagg draws all of America's surviving psychopaths and criminal elements to Las Vegas, where he sets up a totalitarian society after a pandemic wipes out most of mankind. ISIS and its caliph are having a similar effect on an array of Western misfits and malcontents, men and women alike, who are drawn to the Islamic State's audacious violence, dark vision, and online bravado as to a magnet.

This is actually a phenomenon I had documented for years before ISIS's gory rise. In my 2011 book, *The Terrorist Next Door*, I included a chapter called "Freaks, Geeks, and Jihadis" that warned this Losers' Jihad would become, "increasingly familiar in the near future":

> In recent years, social outcasts have increasingly found appeal
> in Islamism. They might be lonely nerds, love-starved women,

ex-cons, or people who grew up in abusive families. Some are white converts to Islam, others are African-American or Hispanic. All have one thing in common: they find meaning and purpose in the jihadist cause that they previously lacked in life.... For the first time in what they themselves often view as their wretched lives, these misfits become part of something bigger, something that matters—a powerful, world-changing movement. Overnight, one can go from being a friendless sad sack or a directionless street thug to being a member of the ummah, or global Islamic community, simply by entering a jihadi chat room or sharing an Al Qaeda video on YouTube. For an ex-con or a lonely, tormented soul who blames his failures and unhappiness on a U.S. system and society that has done them wrong, aiding and abetting America's enemies in a jihad against that very power structure is a perfect way to gain revenge.[28]

For someone with a proclivity toward violent, anti-social behavior, the sight of ISIS raping, pillaging, and hacking off heads while calling for world domination is a major thrill. When a radical imam comes along online or at the mosque and tells that sort of person that there is a religious justification for his actions—that the wanton killing of innocent people will earn him a trip to heaven—these freaks and geeks can't sign up for jihad quickly enough. "In the old days," I wrote in *The Terrorist Next Door*, "they may have joined a cult, hooked up with a street gang, or listened to the darkest form of heavy metal music...the scary quiet kid with the distant stare, bad acne, and *Ozzfest* t-shirt that sat next to you in biology class is now a prime candidate to carry the banner of Islamic jihad. Ditto the thuggish troublemaker who was in and out of juvenile hall throughout high school."[29]

Today, if you're the troubled, rootless sort who is drawn to the darker side of life, it doesn't get any darker or more forbidden than ISIS and its army of serial killers.

What follows are the stories of a few American outcasts who have answered the Islamic State's call.

THE HEARTLAND BEHEADER

"SHARIA LAW IS COMING!!!"

Pronouncements like that on Alton Nolen's Facebook page left little doubt as to the ex-convict's religious and political beliefs. A Quaker he was not.

Nolen, who had taken to calling himself "Jah'Keem Yisrael" following his conversion to Islam in prison in 2011, frequently took to Facebook to post anti-American, anti-Israel, and pro-jihad screeds, as well as photos of Osama bin Laden, Taliban fighters, and the 9/11 attacks.[30] He also posted various photos of himself wearing Muslim garb at Oklahoma City–area mosques, including a snapshot of him with his index finger raised to the sky, which, as we'll see in chapter five, has become the unofficial hand gesture of ISIS fighters and sympathizers.

But one photo in particular, uploaded by Nolen on March 7, 2014—while he was still on probation, no less—would prove to be morbidly prophetic. It showed the gruesome image of a partially decapitated man along with the Koranic verse: "I will instill terror into the hearts of the unbelievers: smite ye above their necks and smite all their finger-tips off of them."[31] When this passage, from Surah 8, verses 9–13 of the Koran, talks about smiting unbelievers above their necks, it isn't talking about giving them a free facial—as Nolen would soon show he understood all too well.

On September 25, 2014, just six months after the Islamo-beheading propaganda appeared on his Facebook timeline, the thirty-year-old Muslim convert walked into the Vaughan Foods processing plant in Moore, Oklahoma, where he worked. Nolen, who had been fired by the plant earlier that same day for alleged racist rants against white people, was carrying a large knife. He encountered a co-worker, fifty-four-year-old grandmother Colleen Hufford, and attacked her from behind with the knife, decapitating her. He then slashed at another co-worker, forty-three-year-old Traci Johnson, wounding her seriously before the company's chief operating officer (a reserve deputy with the Oklahoma County Sheriff's Department) shot him with a rifle, ending the rampage. Nolen survived and is facing charges of first-degree murder at the time of this writing.

Before he was fired, Nolen had tried to convert others at the plant to Islam—and on the same day that he beheaded Colleen Hufford, he had allegedly engaged in an argument with co-workers in which he praised the Islamic practice of stoning female adulterers. He also reportedly shouted "Islamic phrases" as he severed Hufford's head.[32] Those facts, combined with his Facebook page glorifying jihad and beheading—not to mention his ISIS hand gesture and the very ISIS-esque nature of his crime—seem to leave little doubt that Alton Nolen's murderous outburst was motivated by Islamist ideology. That is, unless you're the Obama administration. The FBI is treating Nolen's case as an act of—brace yourself—"workplace violence."[33] That is the same description, of course, that the Pentagon infamously used to describe the actions of Fort Hood shooter Nidal Hasan—who yelled "Allahu Akbar" as he was gunning down thirteen American soldiers on November 5, 2009.[34] Hasan, who had communicated via e-mail with al Qaeda cleric Anwar al-Awlaki prior to carrying out the shootings and carried business cards that read "Soldier of Allah," has spent the past few years doing his best to refute the Pentagon's assessment. In August 2014, he wrote a letter to ISIS caliph Abu Bakr al-Baghdadi asking to become a citizen of the Islamic State caliphate.[35] Nevertheless, since the Obama administration's official line is that the Islamic State is "not Islamic," I suppose its "workplace violence" explanation for Nidal Hasan's actions still holds up just fine.

As for Alton Nolen's decapitation of Colleen Hufford, the Cleveland County prosecutor said, "There was some sort of infatuation with beheadings. It seemed to be related to his interest in killing someone that way."[36]

One wonders where Nolen would acquire such a sudden fascination with violently separating the head from the body. He had served two years of a six-year prison sentence after being convicted on drug charges and assaulting a police officer in 2011.[37] Serious crimes, to be sure, but not the type that would suggest that a beheading spree against middle-aged women would one day be in the works. It's no stretch to conclude that Nolen's macabre "infatuation" with beheading developed only after he converted to Islam and began watching ISIS slice and dice its way across the Middle East.

As the previously mentioned Koranic verse extolling Muslims to "smite" unbelievers "above their necks" shows, beheading infidels is not a novel concept in Islam. In 627 AD, after conquering the Jewish Banu Qurayza tribe in the city of Medina, Islam's prophet Mohammed ordered every man above the age of puberty to be decapitated. According to Muslim historical accounts, some seven hundred Jewish men of the Banu Qurayza tribe were promptly beheaded, and their wives and children were sold into slavery.[38]

Likewise, the brutal Muslim conqueror Tamerlane—who called himself "the Sword of Islam"—left a trail of headless bodies as he rampaged across Central Asia and the Middle East during the fourteenth and fifteenth centuries. One biographer said of Tamerlane, "The dreadful hallmark of his military campaigns, his battlefield signature...were the huge towers built from the severed heads of his slaughtered enemies and set alight as warnings to other cities not to oppose him."[39]

And the heads just keep rolling today. Tamerlane's strategy of intimidation-by-decapitation lives on in what ISIS is doing in Syria and Iraq. And Saudi Arabia, which the Obama administration has enlisted to aid in the fight against ISIS, is the only country to still regularly carry out execution by beheading, including for non-violent crimes such as "receiving drugs." In August 2014, the same month that ISIS began publicly sawing off the heads of American journalists, the Saudi government executed eight people by beheading.[40]

In the West, in addition to Alton Nolen's murderous frenzy and the 2013 killing of British soldier Lee Rigby on a London street by Islamic fanatics, there have been other, less publicized incidents in which Muslims have murdered by decapitation in recent years:

- In 2011, Muzzammil "Mo" Hassan was convicted of second-degree murder in upstate New York after savagely beating and then beheading his wife. Hassan was founder and CEO of Bridges TV, an Islamic TV network "aimed at countering Muslim stereotypes"—such as, presumably, wife beating and beheading.[41]
- In February 2013, an Egyptian Muslim from Jersey City, New Jersey, was arrested and charged with murdering two Egyptian Coptic Christians who lived nearby. Yusuf Ibrahim reportedly shot both men dead and then cut off their heads and hands, burying their remains.[42] Eyebrows were raised by the grisly nature of Ibrahim's alleged crime—which occurred during a period when supporters of Egypt's then-president, Muslim Brotherhood stalwart Mohammed Morsi, were intensifying attacks against Coptic Christians in a country already known for the frequent violent persecution of Copts by Muslims.
- On September 4, 2014, a deranged Muslim convert named Nicholas Salvadore attacked and beheaded an eighty-two-year-old woman in the back garden of her north London home. Salvadore—who, according to locals, had recently converted to Islam—hacked cats' heads off before encountering grandmother Palmira Silva and lopping her head off with a foot-long machete.[43]

The above incidents, in the context of ISIS's beheading fetish and the various foiled terror plots discussed in chapter three involving beheading, all point to a disturbing trend. Indeed, just a few days after Alton Nolen beheaded his co-worker at the Vaughan processing plant, another Muslim man was arrested for threatening to decapitate a female colleague at a nursing home in nearby Oklahoma City. Jacob Mugambi Muriithi, a Kenyan native, allegedly told the woman that he "represented ISIS and that ISIS kills Christians." According to the police detective's affidavit, Muriithi then told the woman he would behead her with a blade and post the images on Facebook. When the woman asked Muriithi why ISIS kills Christians, he reportedly replied, "This is just what we do."[44]

So we've noticed.

THE BODYBUILDING BRAWLER

For some, failure is a great motivator—it only makes them stronger. They learn from their failures along the way to achieving success.

For others, failure is deflating—even a temporary setback can leave a permanent scar. They become depressed. Discouraged. Angry. Bitter.

They may even do something criminal.

Donald Morgan, a country boy who grew up Catholic in North Carolina, suffered through a long string of personal disappointments and failures, after which he converted to Islam. Morgan told NBC News, "Islam presented this package that said: 'this is, this is it . . . this is the path and this is the way you're going to go. There is not going to be this way, that way.'"[45]

Morgan's "path" led him to the Middle East on a quest to enlist in the Islamic State's genocidal terrorist army. When NBC caught up with him in Beirut in the summer of 2014, "he was trying to figure out how to get into Syria and join ISIS." He had already attempted to enter Syria through Turkey but been stopped at the airport in Istanbul. "My reason for the support of ISIS is because they've proven time and time again to put Islamic law as the priority and the establishment of an Islamic state as the goal," Morgan explained.[46]

Morgan's upbringing in North Carolina would seem an unlikely beginning on the path to jihad. But throughout his life, he had gravitated toward jobs and activities that would enable him to channel his obvious aggression.

As a youngster, Morgan dreamed of joining the 82nd Airborne and U.S. Special Forces and serving "dutifully—duty, honor and country." He attended a military academy and then a boot camp that would have enabled him to deploy with the National Guard to Kuwait during Operation Desert Storm. Morgan, however, did not make it past the boot camp.

Failure number one.

His lifelong dreams of military heroism dashed, Morgan went on to become a sheriff's deputy for local law enforcement, a job that would still give him the opportunity to serve with honor and distinction. Yet he was fired after only a year and a half.

Failure number two.

After losing his job as a sheriff's deputy, Morgan went on a wild drinking and partying binge that led him into frequent brawls. During one fracas, he fired a gun into a crowded restaurant. He was arrested and served over two years in prison.

Failure number three.

Following his release from prison, Morgan seemed to get his life together, at least for a few years. He acquired a job in the auto business as a finance manager and became a devoted amateur bodybuilder. In 1999, he married a female bodybuilder and the couple had a son together. By 2007, they had divorced.

Failure number four.

A year after his divorce, Morgan converted to Islam, apparently drawn to its structured system of absolutes and, more than likely, the aggressive ideology of violent jihad. By 2012, he was on the road to radicalization thanks to "[p]ersonal disappointments and desires and exposure to increasingly radical social media."[47] Morgan began posting pro-jihad sentiments on Facebook and founded a small Islamic Center near downtown Salisbury, North Carolina.

First Morgan had thrown himself into his dream of becoming a military hero. He then went all out as a drinker and partyer, with no apparent concept of moderation. Later he became an obsessive bodybuilder. In short, Donald Morgan was a man of extremes. His embrace of Islam was no different.

In January 2014, Morgan made his way to Lebanon, with plans to ultimately enter Syria and wage jihad. By June of that year, Morgan had pledged allegiance to ISIS caliph Abu Bakr al-Baghdadi on Twitter, where he branded himself a *mujahid* or Islamic holy warrior and went by the handle, "Abu Omar al-Amreeki."

For some reason, possibly lack of funds, Morgan tried to reenter the United States in August 2014. Upon arrival, he was promptly arrested by U.S. officials at New York's JFK Airport on a weapons charge and held without bond.[48]

For Morgan, it was massive failure number five. For the United States, it was a dodged bullet. Who's to say whether, frustrated in his attempts to infiltrate Syria and join ISIS, the former military academy student and aspiring paratrooper, once home, wouldn't have targeted the United States—the same country he once dreamed of serving "dutifully"?

THE PIZZA MAN AND THE PUNKS

The affidavit said that Mufid Elfgeeh wanted infidel blood. And whether through recruiting jihadists for ISIS or striking American targets himself, he aimed to get it.

The thirty-year-old Elfgeeh, a food mart owner in upstate Rochester, New York, allegedly recruited three men with the intention of sending them to Syria to join ISIS. Two of the recruits were FBI informants.[49] Over the course of late 2013 and early 2014, Elfgeeh "helped them by doing things like paying one of their passport costs, coordinating travel arrangements and setting them up with contacts in the terror group under the guise of going 'to the university,' which was code for joining ISIS." Elfgeeh also allegedly sent $600 to another potential ISIS recruit. Referring to U.S. troops, he told informants, "We want…to start shooting those who were in the Army who went to Iraq." He fantasized about killing soldiers and civilians on U.S. soil himself: "five or ten already, 15, something like that."[50] His targets reportedly would have included Rochester-area Shiite Muslims—regarded as infidels by radical Sunnis like ISIS.[51]

At the same time that he was allegedly planning jihad, Elfgeeh owned and operated Halal Mojoe's, a Rochester pizza-and-chicken joint where, in December 2012, health inspectors found "insects [and] rodents present," along with several other health code violations.[52] One former employee would describe Elfgeeh, a native of Yemen, as "a crazy guy" who "should be in prison."[53] When Elfgeeh began posting inflammatory material to his Twitter account—including a declaration that ISIS "will one day rule the world with the will of Allah"—then purchased two handguns, silencers, and ammunition from an informant, federal authorities made their move. He was arrested in May 2014 on multiple charges related to his attempts to aid ISIS and kill U.S. citizens.[54] If the health inspection of Mojoe's was any indication, Elfgeeh may have also left a trail of damaged digestive systems in his wake.

Had Elfgeeh come across Mohammed Hamzah Khan prior to being arrested, the erstwhile pizza flipper would have thought he had struck the jihadi-recruiting jackpot. Khan, nineteen, was a committed, ISIS-worshiping fanatic and a U.S. citizen to boot. He lived in Bolingbrook, Illinois, a suburb of Chicago, but yearned to reside in the Islamic State. To Mohammed Khan, relocating to the caliphate was a religious obligation. During a search of his home, federal agents found a notebook containing pro-ISIS writings and drawings and also uncovered a letter Khan had written to his parents saying that Muslims must "migrate" to the caliphate. He invited his mother and father to join him there and warned them not to tell authorities about his travel plans.[55]

In the end, Khan never made it to the Islamic State. He was arrested at Chicago's O'Hare Airport on September 27, 2014, before boarding an Istanbul-bound flight. From Turkey he had planned to make his way to Syria to link up with ISIS. He later told authorities that he had met a terrorist recruiter online who paid for his $4,000 round-trip plane ticket to Turkey and gave him a phone number to call once he arrived in Istanbul.[56] Although the plane ticket covered a round-trip journey, Khan told authorities he did not intend to return to the United States.[57] It later emerged that Khan had been accompanied to the airport by his two younger siblings, aged sixteen and seventeen, who apparently planned to make the trip with him and wage jihad with ISIS.[58]

A few weeks before the Khan trio's arrest, another Windy City ISIS supporter ran into trouble with the law. On August 27, 2014, shortly after ISIS beheaded American journalist James Foley, a Muslim man waved an Islamic State flag outside his car window as he led police on a chase through the streets of southwest Chicago. Forty-nine-year-old Emad Karakrah was finally pulled over, but he reportedly threatened officers during his arrest, telling them he had a bomb in his car that he would detonate if they searched the vehicle. Thankfully, he was bluffing.[59] Federal authorities say a twenty-year-old Islamic convert from Ohio named Christopher Lee Cornell, however, meant business. In January 2015, he was arrested and charged with conspiring to attack the U.S. Capitol "with guns and pipe bombs in support of the Islamic State."[60]

Supporting ISIS doesn't always mean taking up arms. Pro-ISIS graffiti popped up around Washington, D.C., in the fall of 2014, prompting the FBI to take notice.[61] Around the same time, several leaflets bearing the Islamic State logo were found in Quantico, Virginia—site of a Marine Corps installation as well as the FBI training academy, two prime terror targets.[62]

Maybe the leaflets and the graffiti were just pranks carried out by a few knuckleheads. Or maybe they weren't. One Houston Muslim who operates online under the handles "Abdul-Rahman Baghdadi" and "Houston Baghdadi" certainly seems to mean business. He's become a one-man ISIS propaganda machine, plastering stickers with the group's logo around the city and tweeting out his support for the caliphate. He has also posted videos of himself clad in ISIS garb and stirring up trouble at Houston mosques. At one mosque, he pledges allegiance to ISIS caliph Abu Bakr al-Baghdadi in front of a police officer as he's being escorted off the premises.[63]

The mosque's rejection of the pro-ISIS rabble rousing of "Houston Baghdadi" is encouraging. However, opposition to jihad is the exception, not the norm, among the leadership of far too many Muslim houses of worship in the United States.

■   ■   ■

For a moment, I thought I was staring at Clint Eastwood.

When Abdullah walked into the hotel room where I was scheduled to interview him, he was clad in a poncho and wide-brimmed hat that recalled Eastwood's iconic Man with No Name character from the series of classic Westerns in the 1960s. But Abdullah's outfit wasn't meant as a Clint tribute. He had donned the elaborate get-up, which also included shades and a scarf, in order to disguise his appearance. Abdullah (a pseudonym) was about to share, on camera, facts about the activity of radical Islamists in the Boston area; and he feared for his safety. In addition to his disguise, he requested that we blur his face and alter his voice in post-production to add another layer of anonymity.

Abdullah's apprehension was understandable. A few weeks before our interview, a pair of brothers had killed three people and wounded 264 more when they set off bombs at the Boston Marathon in one of the deadliest Islamic terror attacks conducted on U.S. soil since 9/11. Tamerlan and Dzhokhar Tsarnaev later added to their body count by murdering an MIT security guard. Their trail of terror only ended when Tamerlan was killed in a shootout with authorities and his brother was seriously wounded and taken into custody.

I had traveled to Boston in the wake of the Marathon bombings to get a better handle on how two seemingly Westernized young brothers had become murderous jihadists. A Beantown contact had recommended that I speak to Abdullah, a moderate Muslim who had attended several Boston-area mosques and left horrified at what he witnessed. According to Abdullah, acolytes of the Muslim Brotherhood had gained an influential foothold in several of these mosques.

"They want to go after the young minds," he told me. "And the way they go after the young minds is, either they start scholarships in high school or they bring them to a certain level of obedience. It is called 'tarbiyya' [education and upbringing]. They have classes for them and so on."

Abdullah explained that tarbiyya sessions were often held in the wee hours of the morning in the mosques, with promising recruits drilled in the finer points of the Muslim Brotherhood's ideology.

"When some young man is ready to take the oath, he is given an oath so he will never leave the organization. They will do anything [for the Brotherhood]," he said.[64]

Were the Tsarnaev brothers at some point exposed to the Muslim Brotherhood's violent ethos of jihad and martyrdom? It would not be surprising. The Brotherhood—the world's oldest and most influential Islamic terrorist organization—has long served as a gateway to violent jihad. The Brotherhood's early ideologues such as Hassan al-Banna and Sayyid Qutb laid the foundation for the entire modern jihadist movement. The Brotherhood spawned al Qaeda (which in turn spawned ISIS) and Hamas, spreading genocidal anti-Semitism throughout the Muslim world. Although their tactics differ, the endgame for the Brotherhood and ISIS is exactly the same: the return of the caliphate and the global imposition of Islamic sharia law. Whereas ISIS knows only one way—violence—the Brothers often aim to accomplish these goals incrementally, through stealth and subversion. Smiling Western-educated MB spokesmen decked out in designer suits have hoodwinked clueless elites in Brussels and Washington, D.C., for years, deftly masking the Brotherhood's true, radical face.

Given the Brotherhood's nefarious agenda, I noted with great interest that the Tsarnaevs had attended the Islamic Society of Boston (ISB) mosque a few blocks from their home in Cambridge. Convicted terrorists have worshiped at that mosque—including "Lady al Qaeda," Aafia Siddiqui, who had plotted attacks against New York City, and for whom the Taliban reportedly wanted to trade U.S. Army Sergeant Bowe Bergdahl[65]—and it is known for its ties to the Muslim Brotherhood. Indeed, the ISB is operated by the Muslim American Society, an organization that federal prosecutors have called "the overt arm of the Muslim Brotherhood in America." Further, the Brotherhood's worldwide spiritual leader, Yusuf al-Qaradawi, is a former ISB trustee. The Muslim American Society also runs a sprawling mega-mosque in Boston's Roxbury neighborhood that serves as sister mosque to the one in Cambridge. Predictably, both mosques espouse the same Muslim Brotherhood worldview.[66]

Dr. Ahmed Mansour, an Egyptian native who now lives in the U.S., told me that he visited the Cambridge mosque with his wife in 2003 and found flyers and newsletters written in Arabic in its library that "…call[ed] for jihad against America and against the Jews and against the Christians…at that time, there was also a sheikh giving a sermon, and the sheikh was as fanatical as the written materials." Mansour, who taught at Egypt's famed al-Azhar University, was frequently threatened by the Brotherhood because of his moderate interpretation of the Koran. He eventually made his way to America and was shocked to find that the Brotherhood controlled many U.S. mosques. "I escape from them in Egypt and find them here," he lamented as we sat in his living room. "I say to myself, 'Where can I go? Can I go to the moon?'"[67]

We may never know what exactly the Tsarnaev brothers learned during their time at the Islamic Society of Boston mosque. But considering the mosque's radical track record and connections, the question certainly seems worth exploring—unless, of course, you're the Obama administration. As of this writing, the administration, never very enthusiastic in the investigation of radicalized mosques, reportedly has plans to prohibit federal agents from conducting undercover surveillance of American mosques unless they already have evidence that criminal activity is under way.[68] According to Steven Emerson, founder of the Investigative Project on Terrorism in Washington, D.C.,

> The FBI [has been constrained by] the Department of Justice [which] put out guidelines that restricted the FBI and other law enforcement agencies from using religious factors in identifying threats, national security threats to the United States in the homeland. That is so if someone was a religious extremist, though they didn't plot to carry out an attack, that [indicator] could not be factored into an investigation, into an intelligence investigation, into identifying them as a potential threat to the United States. Therefore, [law enforcement] would have to wait until they actually plotted to carry out an attack. Well, that's too late.[69]

It's no wonder the FBI has missed dozens of radicalized American Muslims who have traveled to Syria to join terror groups like ISIS. While federal agents will likely soon be handcuffed from monitoring mosques—81 percent of which, according to one comprehensive 2011 study, feature Islamic texts that promote violence[70]—jihadist recruiters are lining up to get inside. And they have a growing number of options. Between 2000 and 2011, the number of mosques in America increased by an astounding 74 percent—to 2,106 overall, and counting.[71] In dozens of cases where local jurisdictions have opposed the construction of new mosques, the Obama Justice Department has intervened, opening investigations that invariably weigh in favor of the mosques and against the will of the people.[72]

In its full-throated support of mosques, the administration isn't concerned with offending non-Muslim sensibilities. On October 4, 2014, nine
days after Alton Nolen beheaded Colleen Hufford, an administration
official traveled to the Oklahoma City mosque Nolen had attended and
read a personal letter of thanks from President Obama. "Your service is a
powerful example of the shared roots of the Abrahamic faiths and how our
communities can come together in shared peace with dignity and a sense
of justice," the letter to the Islamic Society of Greater Oklahoma City
reportedly read. The official's trip and the letter from the president were
"seemingly meant to counteract negative attention the mosque…received
following Nolen's gruesome murder of coworker Colleen Hufford."[73] No
word on whether the administration sent a letter of condolence or paid a
visit to Hufford's family.

Incidentally, following Nolen's slaughter of Hufford, one former
mosque-goer came forward and accused the Islamic Society of Greater
Oklahoma City of preaching jihad behind closed doors.[74] In light of the
Obama administration's jihad against mosque surveillance, we can only
hope that more courageous whistle-blowers step up to share what they
know and help stem the flow of recruits to the ISIS cause.

Because the recruits keep coming, thanks in large part to the Islamic
State's prolific social media machine, which is working non-stop—to the
tune of a reported ninety tweets per minute—to spread ISIS propaganda.[75]

All day. Every day.

CHAPTER FIVE

JIHADI COOL: HIP-HOPPIN' AND HEAD-CHOPPIN'

I NOTICED THE SHOES FIRST.

Old school Nikes. All-white leather. Some with a Velcro strap, others without. Very urban. Very hip-hop. The kind I had seen worn by literally thousands of teenagers and young men while growing up in working-class Philadelphia—and that I had sported myself in my younger years, before ultimately realizing that "Stak Diddy" was not my destiny.

For a moment, it was a whimsical trip down memory lane—until those same old school Nikes began violently stomping on an Israeli flag before my very eyes.

The unhappy feet belonged to members of the Islamic Thinkers Society—ITS for short—a Queens, New York–based Islamist group that, like ISIS, supports the establishment of a worldwide Islamic caliphate. On a day in February 2006, about twenty-five ITSers had gathered at the Danish Consulate in Manhattan to protest cartoons published in a Danish newspaper featuring Islam's prophet Mohammed—the same cartoons whose publication had sparked deadly riots across an endlessly riotous Muslim world (and set off a chain of events that, nearly nine years later, would result in the massacre of eleven people at the offices of the French magazine *Charlie Hebdo*). The ITS rally avoided any physical violence but did feature chants of "Death to Israel" to go along with the flag stomping, not to mention warnings of "Allah's wrath" and threats that Allah would "silence" disbelievers, or "scum," in the words of one ITS speaker.

As I observed in my 2011 book, *The Terrorist Next Door*:

> My first thought as I watched the ITS event unfold was that it was occurring just a few miles north of where the Twin Towers had fallen four and a half years earlier. My second thought was that I was quite possibly staring at a group of future Islamic terrorists. And sure enough, in the years since that February 2006 ITS rally, at least three men connected with the group have been arrested on terrorism-related charges. One NYPD intelligence analyst has said the group's "anti-Western, anti-democratic, anti-U.S., pro–al Qaeda message" makes the ITS "almost bug lights for aspiring jihadists."[1]

In fact, almost a third of those arrested and convicted of Islamic terrorism charges in the U.S. in recent years have reportedly been linked to two groups: ITS and Revolution Muslim (another NYC-based outfit, which disbanded in 2010).[2]

Which brings us back to the shoes. One of the reasons I was so concerned about ITS was that—other than a few stray skullcaps and a scattering of Islamic garb—these looked like the kind of young men found in any urban area of the United States or Western Europe. This was not a band of AK-47–waving mountain dwellers. It was a multi-ethnic mix that was clearly influenced by hip-hop culture. I could envision them selling their extremism to other urban young people in an appealing manner that, say, al Qaeda's grizzled, Arabic-speaking leadership in the tribal regions of Pakistan could not.

It came as no surprise to me then, that, perusing ITS's website in September 2014, I found the Thinkers strongly supported the caliphate, or "khilāfah," established by the reigning trendsetters of "jihadi cool," ISIS:

> [The caliphate] has returned, and is a reality, a nightmare for the forces against Islam and those who wish to see the light being extinguished. If the current Islamic State is attacked and blown up into smithereens, with "Caliph Ibrahim" being assassinated, there will arise another Muslim who will take his place.
>
> What has sparked off this new Islamic State cannot be stopped simply by carpet bombs and drones. It's an idea that is carried in the hearts of millions if not billions of people around the world. It's time for the elites such as the G-8 of this world to recognize that there is a new contender in the International Arena.
>
> Perhaps it is time for the G8 Nations to re-think their corrupt International Policies. Capitalist economic practices and the puppet and dictatorial regimes employed by capitalist nations are, perhaps, at the end of their days. The Khilafah, the Jewel of Islam, has returned.
>
> Only the spiritually and politically blind Muslims think that the Khilafah would come back and the status quo of the world would be unchanged. They are in error to think that the world would just simply accept an Islamic State while the tyrants still get to enjoy their throne. As if the world would shower the Khaleef with flowers and everyone would live happily ever after.[3]

Comforting sentiments, no doubt, for the NYPD's counterterrorism unit to hear.

ITS has been linked to Anjem Choudary, a notorious, ISIS-supporting cleric based in London whom we'll meet in chapter six. It has been alleged that some of Choudary's followers have traveled to Iraq and Syria to join the ISIS terror army.[4] I've interviewed Choudary in person at length and seen his followers up close: like ITS, they are multi-ethnic, predominantly young, and clad in urban street-wear. If not for their accompanying Islamic-tinged garb and beards, more than a few would pass unnoticed on the streets of any major city in the West.

One of Choudary's most infamous acolytes is former British light middleweight boxing champion Anthony Small. Small converted to Islam at age twenty-four, in the midst of a successful professional boxing career, and soon became radicalized. Now known as "Abdul Haqq," he released a series of YouTube videos in September 2014 defending ISIS's beheading of James Foley—which he justified as revenge for U.S. airstrikes against ISIS in Iraq—and referring to the slain American photojournalist as an "infidel." According to the boxer,

> We have to be objective and non-biased, that the beheading of James Foley, Mr. Beheaded infidel, not to be disrespectful to him or his family, I can't remember his name, Mr Infidel, it wasn't unprovoked.
>
> I say the exact same thing I said about Lee Rigby: people getting heads removed is an abnormal situation. It needs to be prevented. But we have to be objective.
>
> I don't want to say unprovoked because they could say I'm glorifying terrorism, but it was a retaliation, from the own words of those who conducted it, they said, not me said, they said it's a retaliation.[5]

Small blasted what he called the "United Snakes of America" and warned that the UK could be attacked by "sleeper cells" if it intervened militarily against ISIS. Lee Rigby, whom Small also referenced, was a British soldier killed, and nearly beheaded, by a pair of jihadists when they attacked him with a meat cleaver and knives in broad daylight on a London street in May 2013.

One of those jihadists, a Nigerian Brit named Michael Adebolajo, had been linked to—surprise—Anjem Choudary (who boasted after the horrific murder that he was "very proud" of Adebolajo and that Rigby would "burn in hellfire").[6] Like Anthony Small, both of Rigby's killers were raised Christian and later converted to Islam.

In the case of Small, one of the most striking aspects of his aforementioned YouTube rant was his appearance. His hair and beard closely cropped, Small—clad in a fashionably tight-fitting T-shirt—still looked every bit the strapping British sports figure that he had been during his boxing career, despite the Islamist bile coming out of his mouth.

Small's video diatribe was an ingenious bit of jihadi marketing. For starters, curiosity seekers were interested to hear what a former British boxing champ had to say on a hot button issue. And how many young British kids and aspiring boxers, particularly from immigrant communities, have looked up to Small over the years for his ring work and viewed him as a role model? How many of these same impressionable young minds watched the videos and took what Small had to say seriously? If even a handful of them adopt Small's beliefs, and their career paths lead not to the boxing ring but to ISIS's waiting arms, the results could be horrific.

Small, Choudary, ITS, and their extended networks are already on board with the Islamic State's vision. But ISIS is using social media and a highly sophisticated video and marketing campaign to broaden its appeal and reach young, untapped Muslims across the Western world—and old school Nikes fit right in.

■   ■   ■

"Chillin' with my homie or what's left of him."

As "humor" goes, it doesn't get much darker. Abdel-Majed Abdel Bary—the suspected beheader of American journalists James Foley and Steven Sotloff—had taken to Twitter to post a photo of himself proudly holding the severed head of a Syrian regime soldier (hence, the "what's left of him" quip).[7] In doing so, Abdel Bary—a former London rapper who performed, variously, under the names Lyricist Jinny, L-Jinny, and L-Jinn—managed to combine three qualities that have helped make ISIS so attractive to disaffected young Muslims raised in the West: 1) social media savvy, 2) glorification of brutal violence, and 3) hip-hop slang and cocky irreverence.

For an attention-craving, "selfie"-obsessed Millennial generation weaned on ultra-violent video games, gangsta rap lyrics, and gleefully sadistic horror films, ISIS is a cruel beast whose time has come. It's tough to shock this demographic—teens and twenty-somethings that have seen disturbingly realistic dismemberments and snuff film–like torture scenes flash across TV and movie screens for much of their young lives. Put a video game console in their hands and they can actually participate in the blood and gore, chopping, hacking, stabbing, and shooting into the wee hours of the night and then taunting their opponents online in 140 characters or less. It's a generation long on in-your-face swagger and short on attention span—and ISIS has a strategy to reach them, particularly if they are second- and third-generation Muslims in the West who (albeit profoundly influenced by American popular culture) feel disconnected from their host societies and are looking for meaning and a place to belong.

ISIS is engaged in a virtual hashtag jihad aimed largely at these perpetually wired, tech-obsessed Millennials—indeed, Twitter has become the de facto voice of the Islamic State:

> ISIS is online jihad 3.0. Dozens of Twitter accounts spread its message, and it has posted some major speeches in seven languages. Its videos borrow from Madison Avenue and Hollywood, from combat video games and cable television dramas, and its sensational dispatches are echoed and amplified on

social media. When its accounts are blocked, new ones appear immediately. It also uses services like JustPaste to publish battle summaries, SoundCloud to release audio reports, Instagram to share images and WhatsApp to spread graphics and videos.... British fighters have answered hundreds of questions about joining ISIS on Ask.fm, a website, including what type of shoes to bring and whether toothbrushes are available. When asked what to do upon arriving in Turkey or Syria, the fighters often casually reply, "Kik me," referring to the instant messenger for smartphones, and continue the discussion in private.[8]

In June 2014, as ISIS was in the process of seizing Iraq's second-largest city, Mosul, ISIS and its supporters worldwide posted nearly forty thousand tweets in one day alone. Want to get all the latest news on ISIS's various conquests? Yep, there's an app for that—it's called "The Dawn of Glad Tidings" and is available for Android phones.[9] Masters of propaganda and pop culture and keenly attuned to global political developments, ISIS's online legions of "E-hadis" are filled with snarky, English-speaking Westerners who can easily relate to frustrated kids in London, New York, or Toronto.

In August 2014, ISIS and its supporters tweeted regularly during racially charged protests over the shooting death of black teenager Michael Brown by a white policeman in Ferguson, Missouri. "So how is democracy treating you guys?" one ISIS tweet, clearly aimed at young African Americans, asked. Another mocked, "There are more blacks now than slaves before the Civil War. Are you truly free?" Black Americans were encouraged to rise up and embrace the caliphate, under hashtags such as #ISISinFerguson and #JihadinFerguson. To drive the point home, during one live CNN telecast from Ferguson a demonstrator was seen holding a large sign saying, "ISIS is Here."[10] Where this apparent supporter of the world's most barbaric terror group moved on to after Ferguson is anyone's guess.

The same month that Ferguson was dominating the headlines, ISIS minions used the trending hashtags #napaquake and #napaearthquake to post pro-ISIS taunts and pictures of dead U.S. soldiers in the aftermath of the costly 6.0 Bay Area earthquake. ISIS's hashtag hijacking meant that if you were a resident of northern California or had loved ones that were affected by the earthquake, there is a good chance your Twitter search for news updates resulted in a stream of ISIS propaganda.[11]

ISIS used a similar tactic during the 2014 World Cup, using the trending hashtag #WorldCup2014 while posting the latest news and photos from its brutal drive into Iraq. One tweet, showcasing ISIS's trademark depravity, featured a photo of an Iraqi officer's severed head with the caption: "This is our ball. It is made of skin. #WorldCup."[12] Likewise, in the days before an ISIS terrorist beheaded American journalist Steven Sotloff, ISIS used the hashtag #StevensHeadInObamasHands to spread taunts and threats against America on Twitter.[13]

One favorite tactic of ISIS supporters is to take pictures of themselves holding small ISIS flags or signs in front of Western landmarks. Their faces, shrewdly, are kept out of the shots. For example, a photo of an ISIS supporter in front of the Old Republic Building in Chicago created a stir when it was posted to Twitter in August 2014 (accompanied by the message "Soldiers of the Islamic State of Iraq and Syria will pass from here soon").[14]

Another pic of an Islamist, standing across the street from the White House, was posted that same month with the caption, "#AmessagefromUS toISIS we are here #America near our #target :) sooooooooooooooon."

The chilling photo—which emerged not long after an ISIS spokesman threatened to "raise the flag of Allah over the White House"[15]—was then re-tweeted by two other sympathizers who gloated, "we are everywhere #AmessagefromISIStoUS," and "#AmessagefromISIStoUS We are in your state We are in your cities We are in your streets You are our goals anywhere…"[16]

The grammar may be horrible, but it's the message and means of delivery that count. The tweets not only show that ISIS supporters are indeed in American cities and in close proximity to major terror targets;

they're delivered in a hip, "selfie" style with the kind of brash sarcasm that is so familiar in today's youth culture.

ISIS even has its own signature hand gesture that members flash incessantly for the cameras: a single index finger, raised in the air. Predictably, the raised index finger salute has caught on among ISIS sympathizers around the world—and as you might expect, it's more than just the jihadi version of a gang sign:

> When ISIS militants hold up a single index finger on their right hands, they are alluding to the tawhid, the belief in the oneness of God and a key component of the Muslim religion. The tawhid comprises the first half of the shahada, which is an affirmation of faith, one of the five pillars of Islam, and a component of daily prayers: "There is no god but Allah, Muhammad is the messenger of Allah." ... But for ISIS, the symbol is more sinister than a mere declaration of monotheistic beliefs. As Salafi jihadists, members of the group adhere to a fundamentalist interpretation of tawhid that rejects non-fundamentalist regimes as idolatrous. In other words, the concept of tawhid is central to ISIS' violent and uncompromising posture toward its opponents, both in the Middle East and in the West. When ISIS militants display the sign, to one another or to a photographer, they are actively reaffirming their dedication to that ideology, whose underlying principle demands the destruction of the West.... The gesture is equally important for what it means to Westerners, most of whom cannot read Arabic. By raising their index fingers, militants send an easy-to-understand message of the group's goals of theological supremacy and military hegemony. When potential ISIS recruits in London, New York, or Sydney see the symbol on Twitter, they can grasp the scale of ISIS' ambitions and its underlying aims. At

some visceral level, less-radicalized viewers understand that it means dominance.[17]

And if Western recruits would like to "flash their colors" by rocking a black ISIS hoodie or T-shirt, they can find plenty of them sold online, featuring various Islamic State logos and images.[18] For ISIS sympathizers, the options to latch on to jihadi cool are limitless. Ryan Mauro, a national security analyst with the Clarion Project who closely monitors ISIS's online activity, explains the group's appeal to young radicals weaned on Western culture:

> The personality profiles of ISIS supporters greatly differ from Al-Qaeda-types. You could never envision Bin Laden or Zawahiri dropping the f-bomb in a rap music video, making a crude joke, talking about videogames and complaining about not having enough Krispy Kremes. This is partially an outreach effort; ISIS wants to reach the young and show that you can enjoy parts of Western culture and still be a jihadist. But this isn't just an outreach effort. ISIS supporters genuinely enjoy American entertainment and have reconciled that with their anti-American ideology.[19]

The *New York Post* recounted how an ISIS supporter lamented the death of actor/comedian Robin Williams in August 2014:

> Even jihadist militants took a break from murder and mayhem to mourn Robin Williams.
> A 19-year-old self-proclaimed Islamic State supporter who goes by @mujahid4life on Twitter professed his sadness about Williams' death.
> "#RobinWilliams is dead? Weird. Grew up watching his movies," the poster, who calls himself Abdullah and is pictured on Twitter dressed in mujahideen garb, tweeted Monday.

"Shame. I liked Jumanji," responded @Ibn_Fulaan, a London-based Islamic State sympathizer. "I had it on video lol."

"Good movie. Loved it as a kid," Abdullah added. "'Jumanjihadi'? It's kinda catchy."

When other Twitter users started asking him about his love of Western films after the Williams tweet, Abdullah complained that people seems to think he grew up "in a mud hut." And

After numerous media outlets reached out to him, Abdullah became concerned that his love for Robin Williams would overpower his devotion to the Islamic State.

"Now I'm actually worried that people will start to follow me because they wanna hear about my favorite movies instead of reporting jihad."[20]

ISIS-loving jihadists engaging in pop culture patter—and gaining a curious, and even enthusiastic audience—are an unfortunate byproduct of a culture saturated with moral relativism and fascinated with the macabre. *Sure, ISIS does some things that are unadvisable and probably even wrong. But hey, who am I to tell them how to practice their religion? To each his own. Besides, other than all the jihad stuff, they seem like pretty normal dudes—watching Robin Williams flicks, listening to hip-hop … are we really so different? I'm actually kind of intrigued. What makes these guys tick?*

Doubt that ISIS is catching on? At least twenty-eight thousand pro-ISIS Twitter accounts were created in the two weeks following James Foley's beheading. In addition, some 10 percent of all tweets posted in the twenty-four hours after the beheading of Steven Sotloff characterized his murder positively.[21] Twitter's efforts to shut down these types of accounts—which frequently show horrific imagery of ISIS atrocities in Syria and Iraq—have been met with threats from supporters of the Islamic State, including one who called for the assassination of Twitter employees.[22]

The Islamic State's media savvy extends far beyond its veritable Twit-ter addiction and into the realm of video production. Jihadi videos, includ-ing those featuring beheadings, are certainly nothing new. In 2004, for instance, ISIS's predecessor, al Qaeda in Iraq, released videos showing its decapitations of American contractor Nicholas Berg and British contractor Ken Bigley. But while Foley and Sotloff met the same fate as Berg and Bigley and wore similar orange jumpsuits in their respective videos, the difference in production values and professionalism was striking:

> ... while Bigley and Berg's murder videos involved grainy and chaotic camcorder footage, Foley's differs from predecessors due to its comparatively high production values. The makers of ... [the] video used multiple cameras, and professional micro-phones.
>
> They worked competently with graphics and visual effects, and used editing tools to intersperse film of Foley with video of rolling news footage.
>
> While Bigley and Berg's videos were produced in Arabic, Foley's was in English, with subtitles. This should perhaps not come as a surprise: the Islamic State is now very well funded, due to its control of oil fields in Iraq and Syria (so it can afford expensive kit). It boasts an estimated 2,000 recruits from Europe, many of whom are well-educated, with backgrounds in IT or video production.[23]

ISIS's fifty-five-minute *Flames of War* propaganda video featured special effects, slow-motion explosions, and all the trappings of a Holly-wood action flick (including a teaser trailer posted online in the days before its release). In short, ISIS's ghoulish productions far surpass anything that has come before them in the jihadi video category, making them all the more appealing to a young Western audience weaned on 3-D, HD, and slickly made, graphic horror flicks:

In the evolution of modern jihadist propaganda, Bin Laden, addressing a single static camera with long-winded rhetoric in highly formal Arabic, represented the first generation. (His videos had to be smuggled to Al Jazeera or another television network to be aired.) The most prominent figure of the second generation was the YouTube star Anwar al-Awlaki, the American-born cleric killed in a drone strike in Yemen in 2011, who addressed Westerners in colloquial English, had a blog and Facebook page and helped produce a full-color, English-language magazine called *Inspire*.[24]

ISIS is the third generation—tech-savvy jihad on steroids—to the point that its video editors have even doctored footage of President Obama to make him appear older, washed out, and haggard. According to the *Telegraph*, in the Steven Sotloff beheading video, which featured a clip of the American president speaking at a podium, "Mr. Obama's blue jacket is made to appear a funereal black. His strands of grey hair are picked up and exaggerated. The editor has also caused an interlacing effect of black lines to run across the president's white shirt. For good measure, he has carefully stretched the screen lengthways in order to make Mr. Obama appear thin and gaunt."[25]

These subtle editing tweaks—clearly not the work of a novice—achieve the desired propaganda effect: an impression that the Islamic State has America on its heels, and Obama is beleaguered (the president's painful, "no strategy" dithering during ISIS's rapid rise in the summer of 2014 did nothing to dispel that impression). With America on the decline and the caliphate ascendant, why not hop on board the ISIS express and join the winning team? Heck, adopt the right look and just the right amount of demonic viciousness, and you may even become famous. As we'll see shortly, the exploits of individual ISIS fighters have enabled them to achieve rock star status among the global jihadist set. But before we meet a few of them, let's go inside the world of the alleged American mastermind behind ISIS's sophisticated multimedia offensive.

THE COMPUTER GEEK

"And so we have a huge common interest in dealing with this issue of poverty, which in many cases is the root cause of terrorism…."

That was Secretary of State John Kerry in January 2014, speaking after a meeting at the Vatican. His poverty-causes-terrorism comments mirrored similar remarks he had made a few months before about providing "economic opportunities for marginalized youth at risk" in order to combat terrorist recruitment.[26] Kerry reiterated those thoughts once again in September 2014, telling a global development forum, "[Jihadists] don't have a plan to create jobs or deliver opportunity. They don't have any of those things that people most want. But they do have a strategy to capitalize on the grievances of those who feel under-represented and left behind."[27]

Secretary Kerry, meet Ahmad Abousamra.

The alleged brain behind ISIS's cutting-edge social media and video operation was not raised in a dilapidated Afghan hut or a squalid Baghdad slum. Instead, Abousamra, a dual Syrian-American citizen, was reared in leafy Stoughton, Massachusetts, a highly desirable Boston suburb that boasts no shortage of affluent professionals—including Abousamra's own father, a leading endocrinologist at Massachusetts General Hospital. Opportunities abounded for the younger Abousamra, who made the honor roll at a prestigious Catholic high school and later the Dean's List at Northeastern University.[28]

Privileged, well-educated, and with a knack for computers, Abousambra, now in his early thirties, could have enjoyed a successful and lucrative career in the technology industry. Instead, in 2004, he chose to travel to Iraq in an attempt to join al Qaeda and kill U.S. troops. He did so not because of poverty—clearly—but because of jihadist ideology. The FBI believes Abousamra was self-radicalized with online resources and hooked up with another aspiring terrorist, fellow U.S. citizen Tarek Mahanna.[29] The pair helped run al Qaeda in Iraq's media operation until Mahanna was arrested on terrorism charges.[30] He was convicted in 2012 and sentenced to seventeen and a half years in prison for supporting al Qaeda.

Mahanna, it should be mentioned, was a pharmacist from the Boston suburbs—again, hardly the desperate, uneducated street urchin that Secretary Kerry imagines as the face of global jihad.

As for Abousambra, he fled the U.S. for Syria in 2006 after being questioned by the FBI and is currently wanted by U.S. authorities. If Abousambra is indeed the driving force behind ISIS's current multimedia blitz, he may have learned a few tricks of the trade from yet another American jihadist, Samir Khan. A Pakistani-American from Charlotte, North Carolina, Khan made his way to Yemen in 2009 and went on to head up the media wing of al Qaeda in the Arabian Peninsula (AQAP). He became editor and publisher of *Inspire* magazine, an online glossy geared toward young, English-speaking Muslims and including articles with charming titles like "How to Make A Bomb in the Kitchen of Your Mom."

Khan, who was killed in the same U.S. drone strike that took out American al Qaeda mouthpiece Anwar al-Awlaki in 2011, was young, clever, and plugged in to Western culture, qualities that made *Inspire* magazine a very effective propaganda tool. Yet as in the social media and video production realms, ISIS has once again outdone al Qaeda by producing its own online magazine—which Ahmad Abousambra ostensibly has a major hand in—called *Dabiq*.

The title of a *New Republic* article comparing *Dabiq* and *Inspire* summarized the new publication accurately: "ISIS's New Mag Looks like a New York Glossy—with Pictures of Mutilated Bodies." According to the piece, *Dabiq* is the far superior product. "Al Qaeda is like AOL"—outdated, unhip—while "The Islamic State is Google" and has replaced al Qaeda as "the go-to organization for young jihadists":

> "Dabiq" refers to a small town near Aleppo where the prophet
> Muhammad foretold that Muslims and the West would clash
> before the apocalypse. It follows that much of *Dabiq*'s content
> focuses on a coming apocalypse, while pulling out the same
> glossy stops that one would expect from an American

magazine.... Al Qaeda isn't selling the same vision. Articles in *Inspire* range from tutorials ... to Q&As with prominent Al Qaeda members and denunciations of Western culture, but don't call for the establishment of an Islamic State or elimination of all other religions.

"*Inspire* serves more as a how-to guide for individual attacks than an articulation of an overall religious, military, and political vision," writes Harleen Gambhir in a report by the Institute for the Study of War. Beyond that, *Inspire* lacks the sleek production values and religious justifications of Dabiq. "What you see with *Dabiq* is the combination of Islamic theological credentials with battlefield success," Clarke noted. "ISIS really takes great care to back up everything that it does with religious justification. That's one area where Al Qaeda got soft over time."

Most terrifyingly, *Dabiq* documents the lengths to which ISIS will go to achieve their goals. Its pages are littered with pictures of the mutilated corpses of "infidels," while their inaugural issue, "The Return of the Khilafah," featured a photoshopped image of Western troops engulfed in flames.

Ben Connable, the former head of the Marine Corps' cultural intelligence program and a senior analyst at the RAND Corporation, says that while "Al Qaeda has hesitated in some ways [with] statements against indiscriminate bombings and attacks," the Islamic State "has been less restrictive, and far more violent and willing to do just about anything to achieve their ends. That unrestricted behavior generates some excitement."[31]

Including amongst a group of psychopathic young Westerners with a taste for hardcore hip-hop.

THE RAPPERS

"Be prepared for the battle with the infidels.... Dirty Kuffar wherever you are; From Kandahar to Ramallah; OBL (Osama bin Laden) Crew be like a shining star; like the way we destroy them two tower, ha ha."

"Kuffar" refers to non-Muslims and the "two tower" reference—well, you get the picture. The above lyrics are from the song "Dirty Kuffar," released in 2004 by Sheikh Terra (or Terror) and the Soul Salah Crew, a London-based jihadi rap outfit. "Dirty Kuffar"—which features pro-al Qaeda boasts and violent threats against the West rhymed over a dancehall beat—has become a seminal work of the jihadi rap subculture, with millions of online downloads and views since its now decade-ago release (which was accompanied by an MTV-worthy video featuring al Qaeda leader Ayman al-Zawahiri shape-shifting into a lion and then-president George W. Bush turning into a chimpanzee).[32]

Without "Dirty Kuffar," we might never have been subjected to the lyrical stylings of one Abu Mansoor al-Amriki, formerly known as Omar Hammami. Al-Amriki, a U.S. citizen who grew up in sleepy Daphne, Alabama, turned to radical Islam in college and eventually traveled to Somalia in 2006, where he joined the al Qaeda–linked Somali terror organization al-Shabaab. Hammami rose through the ranks of al-Shabaab to become one of its commanders and chief propagandists before being killed in 2013 by the group after a falling-out over its direction.[33] Although designated a global terrorist by the U.S. government, al-Amriki was known more for his rapping than his battlefield exploits. He appeared in a series of YouTube videos in which he served up amateurish raps designed to recruit, in particular, young American Somalis to join al-Shabaab (and judging by the flow of Twin Cities Somalis overseas to wage jihad, he appears to have had some success). Songs such as "Blow by Blow" and "Make Jihad with Me," delivered clumsily by al-Amriki, were far from lyrical masterpieces.[34] Yet the American native was on to something: the use of hip-hop music—no stranger to violent imagery—to entice Western youths to join in the ultimate "Thug Life" of violent jihad.

Leave it to ISIS to take a nefarious idea and run with it. As we saw earlier in this chapter, Abdel-Majed Abdel Bary—the masked ISIS terrorist believed to have carried out the vicious beheadings of American journalists James Foley and Steven Sotloff and other Islamic State hostages—was once a London-based rapper. His songs (usually performed under the name L-Jinny), which can still be viewed on YouTube, featured the kind of violent, angry, and alienated lyrics typical of the genre.[35] In the videos, "L-Jinny" raps in a London street accent and is frequently clad in a hoodie and baseball cap with flat brim, much like his American rap counterparts.

As someone who listened to his fair share of hip-hop in high school and college in the 1990s (during what is considered a Golden Era for the genre), I can report that L-Jinny is a spectacularly bad rapper, both in lyrics and delivery. A notch above Abu Mansoor al-Amriki, to be sure, but let's just say the Grammys aren't going to come calling anytime soon. That said, Abdel Bary/L-Jinny, who alluded to himself as a misfit in his songs, clearly yearned for the spotlight. His quest for fame, combined with his obvious fondness for cold-blooded murder and his terrorist pedigree (Abdel Bary's father was an al Qaeda associate who is serving time in an American prison for his role in the 1998 Africa Embassy bombings), brought him to Syria in 2013, where he has gained notoriety for his graphic tweets and alleged skill at hacking off the heads of bound ISIS hostages. And he is not the only rapper whose career has taken a similar trajectory.

Denis Mamadou Cuspert, a German rapper who performed under the stage name "Deso Dogg," enjoyed the kind of recording success that Abdel Bary could only dream about. He released a trio of successful albums and toured with platinum-selling American rapper DMX before converting to Islam in 2010 and taking the name "Abou Maleeq." After his conversion, the tattooed former hip-hopper quickly gained the attention of German authorities with his anti-Western, pro-terror rhetoric and was found guilty of illegally possessing weapons.[36] He left Germany for Egypt and then moved on to Syria, where he eventually pledged allegiance to ISIS.

Reports swirled in April 2014 that Cuspert/Deso Dogg had been killed in a suicide bombing carried out by jihadist rivals in Syria.[37] As of this writing, that has not been confirmed. But dead or alive, Deso Dogg's propaganda value to ISIS is obvious, as a 2011 *New York Times* profile written while he still lived in Germany showed:

> German terrorism investigators see Mr. Cuspert, 35, as a threat who provokes young people angered by what they see as a Western campaign against Islam.... "After establishing rapport through music, he introduced radical ideology to an audience already receptive to him," said Raphael F. Perl, who runs the antiterrorism unit for the Organization for Security and Cooperation in Europe.... [His] message in videos posted on YouTube and jihadi Web sites ... have made Mr. Cuspert popular among Al Qaeda supporters in Europe and elsewhere. As evidence of his reach, a man who goes by the name Abu Bilal in the tribal areas in the Afghanistan-Pakistan border region said of Mr. Cuspert: "The brother's voice has reached the hearts of many people here, too." Mr. Cuspert gives speeches all over Germany, and young people are drawn to elements of his personal story, including his membership in Berlin street gangs—he said he used to be a "real bad boy"— and the notion that he finally found the "right way." ... Security officials say that young people who are clicking on his videos do not realize that what they are listening to has been inspired by a radical jihadist theology based on the fundamentalist Salafi branch of Islam.[38]

A former hip-hop star and gang-banger, Deso Dogg has tons of jihadi cool and street cred to spare. And in ISIS's frenzied, social media–centric world, image is everything.

THE HIPSTER

Those curls. Those glasses. That sword.

The image of Islam Yaken mounted on a horse, brandishing a curved scimitar as he let out a war cry recalled the earliest days of Islam, when it roared out of the Arabian desert to conquer everything in its path.

Yet the photo of Yaken—which quickly became iconic among global jihadists after it was posted to his Twitter account in the summer of 2014— had a very contemporary flavor. It wasn't just the rifle slung over his shoulder, or the storefronts in Raqqa, Syria, seen in the background. It was Yaken's look. His flowing, corkscrew curls and stylish, black-rimmed glasses looked more suited to a SoHo coffee shop than the battlefields of the Middle East. The jarring spectacle of a guy one step removed from skinny jeans riding on a horse and waving an Arabian sword provided major propaganda value for ISIS. Yaken perfectly epitomizes how the group has one foot planted in the seventh century and another in modern day popular culture: an irresistible combination for a growing number of adventure-seeking, tech-savvy Western extremists. ISIS killers will lop off your head and in the next moment tweet out a sardonic selfie on their iPhones.

Although Yaken is an Egyptian native who may have never even set foot in the West before traveling to Syria, his story is relevant here because it is so similar to those of an untold number of Muslims from Europe and the U.S. who have answered ISIS's call. Yaken reportedly attended a private high school in an upscale Cairo suburb and earned a law degree from Egypt's prestigious Ain Shams University in 2013.[39] Fluent in English, French, and Arabic, he was a bodybuilding enthusiast who posted shirtless photos of himself on social media sites and enjoyed popular music.[40] In a 2011 tweet, a still-secular Yaken wrote, "Kissing burns 6.4 calories a minute." Talk like that in the Islamic State and you'll be kissing your head goodbye.

It's unclear where the cosmopolitan Yaken took a turn for the sinister. He is said to have been a supporter of Egyptian president and Muslim

Brotherhood leader Mohammed Morsi prior to Morsi's ouster in 2013. Was Yaken radicalized, like so many young Muslims before him, by the Brotherhood's violent teachings of jihad and martyrdom? Did Yaken, like another fellow Egyptian native, al Qaeda leader Ayman al-Zawahiri, grow frustrated with the Brotherhood's slow-and-steady approach and their participation in the political process and yearn for violent confrontation and the immediate overthrow of non-Islamist Arab regimes?

If that was the case, he found what he was looking for in Syria, where ISIS was waging holy war not only against secular dictator Bashar al-Assad, but against anyone else—Muslim and non-Muslim alike—who refused to yield to the dark vision of ISIS.

"Islam Yaken's story is freaking scary," tweeted one former classmate of Yaken's after the sword-waving photo surfaced.[41]

No scarier than that of the similarly fresh-faced Tsarnaev brothers, perpetrators of the April 2013 Boston Marathon bombings that killed three people and wounded some 264 more. The young pair sported a Westernized look and appeared thoroughly assimilated—at least, on the surface. *Rolling Stone* magazine even featured a photo of the younger brother, Dhokthar—then nineteen years old—on the cover of its August 1, 2013, issue staring straight ahead in a dreamy rock star pose, sporting a thin moustache and goatee and long, curly hair that partially covered his face. "The Bomber," read the breathless caption beneath Tsarnaev's photo: "How a popular, promising student was failed by his family, fell into radical Islam and became a monster." *Rolling Stone*'s portrayal of a terrorist murderer as a sort of misunderstood, brooding teen pinup drew widespread outrage, including from Boston mayor Thomas Menino and several national pharmacy chains and New England–area grocery and convenience stores that refused to carry the magazine.[42]

How long before *Rolling Stone*—which has essentially become a leftist propaganda rag masquerading as a serious music journal—features a glam ISIS cover with Abdel Bary and Deso Dogg striking their naughtiest hip-hop poses? Think about it: whereas dreamy Dhoktar Tsarnaev possesses no known lyrical skills, the ISIS rappers were actual recording artists, which means *Rolling Stone* can even award their albums fawning five-star reviews! If you're eager to give Islamic jihadists the rock star treatment for your impressionable young readers, it doesn't get any more cutting edge than ISIS—masters of social media and thoroughly plugged in to the Millennial generation. From severed heads rolling to *Rolling Stone*: a natural progression for ISIS in today's morally depraved media climate. Sales of *Rolling Stone*'s Tsarnaev issue, by the way, were double the magazine's usual sales, despite boycotts from some national retail stores.[43] Memo to ISIS: jihadi cool sells here in what used to be known as Western civilization.

■   ■   ■

There is no shortage of young Muslims in Europe and North America who are being fed Islamist ideology in Muslim Brotherhood–connected mosques—and who will be eager for scimitar-ready jobs once they get bored with the MB's gradualist approach to reestablishing the caliphate. These are twisted, heavily indoctrinated young minds that are not repulsed, but turned on by the severed heads of innocents. They want jihad *right now*, and lots of it—and ISIS is capitalizing in a major way. As one Western security source told me:

> People now expect their news in 140 characters or less. They're seeking shorter YouTube, Snapchat, or Vine videos for entertainment. ISIS seems to understand this. While al-Qaeda is launching wordy publications like *Inspire* or announcing a new terrorist franchise in the subcontinent of India via a 55-minute video, ISIS is using Instagram and Twitter to deliver shorter punches and gain maximum exposure. Not many individuals

have watched an entire Osama Bin Laden movie, but nearly everyone in the United States has seen a tweet from ISIS.

So, too, have an untold number of young Muslims across Europe. ISIS has appealed to them through everything from "selfie" tweets taken by ISIS supporters in front of Spanish landmarks (vowing to reclaim Spain for the caliphate) to tweets featuring photos of its fighters holding jars of Nutella, the hazelnut spread so popular in Europe. *Come join us*, the photos seem to beckon.

Unless we join you first.

CHAPTER SIX

LONDON FALLING: THE BATTLE FOR BRITAIN

"I BELIEVE THERE WERE MANY POSITIVE OUTCOMES FROM 9/11...the legacy of that is what you see today in the Islamic state that has been established in Syria and in Iraq."

It was September 11, 2014, the thirteenth anniversary of the 9/11 attacks—and I was interviewing a man who has openly supported al Qaeda and called for sharia law to be imposed in every corner of the globe.

"I think the Muslims are defending themselves around the world," said Anjem Choudary, leader of the radical Islamist group al-Muhajiroun, banned by the British government under the UK's counterterrorism laws. "There is a giant that has woken up. The Sharia is being implemented. [Muslims] are getting rid of the dictators, which many of the Western regimes put in place—in Iraq, in Syria, in Libya, in Tunisia, in Egypt. And that is affecting the interests of the West.... Communism is dead. Capitalism is dying. Islam is the future, I believe, for mankind."

During our talk, Choudary prefaced Osama bin Laden's name with the honorific title, "Sheikh," and followed his mention of the deceased al

Qaeda leader with a heartfelt, "May Allah bless him." Coming from Choudary—whose al-Muhajiroun group once praised the 9/11 hijackers as "The Magnificent 19"—this veneration of history's most notorious terrorist was no surprise.[1]

Over the past few years, I've spent hours talking with Choudary, Great Britain's most notorious and outspoken radical Islamist. The previous two encounters, which I described in my books *The Terrorist Next Door* and *The Brotherhood* (2013), had been in person, on Choudary's London home turf. On those occasions, he always made sure to bring along some of his followers—a somber, bearded crew who looked like they had just stepped out of an al Qaeda recruitment video.

This time, however, there would be no such jihadi ambience. We were speaking long distance via Skype—and our discussion focused not so much on 9/11 as it did another date: 6/29. That would be June 29, 2014—the day ISIS leader Abu Bakr al-Baghdadi declared the establishment of a caliphate across a broad area of Syria and Iraq, in the process branding himself as "caliph," or leader, of all Muslims worldwide.

I was eager to get Choudary's thoughts on the Islamic State. After all, he was one of Europe's most visible Salafists and had long pined for the return of the caliphate. I figured that Choudary's take on ISIS would be a pretty good indicator of what the rest of Europe's ever-growing radical Salafist community felt about al-Baghdadi and his minions. As expected, "Great Britain's Most Hated Man" gave the new caliphate his enthusiastic endorsement.

"There are two types of people in the world today," said the long-bearded Choudary, clad in a skullcap and grinning confidently as the black flag of Islam loomed over his shoulder as a backdrop. "Those who believe in man-made law, the head of which is Barack Obama, and those who believe in [sharia] law, the head of which at the current time is Abu Bakr al-Baghdadi. And I believe these will fight each other economically, politically, militarily, ideologically... there is a war taking place, Erick."

To hear Choudary declare outright that the Islamic State and its ilk are at war with the West was striking. As we've seen in previous chapters, President Obama and his team can't seem to decide whether America is at war with ISIS or not—Secretary of State John Kerry, in particular, has mumbled and bumbled his way through many an awkward press conference and media interview when pressed on that very question. Perhaps it's all just an "Overseas Contingency Operation" against "Man-Caused Disasters"—to quote some of the administration's own cringe-worthy jargon regarding Islamic terror. The Obama administration has treated Islamic terrorists as common criminals, trying them in civilian courts rather than in military tribunals, always with an eye toward shutting down Guantanamo Bay prison. This does not exactly scream "war footing."

But according to our jihadist enemies, a war it most certainly is—whether we choose to fight it or not.

"I think it's fascinating that you acknowledge this is a war," I said to Choudary. "Because some Western leaders say, 'Look, this is all just a criminal action....'"

"There is a war taking place," he reiterated. "I was just reading...that there are up to one thousand people who are joining the Islamic State's army every single day. And these people look down the barrel of a gun and they see paradise. They love to die, the way that you and others love to live. You cannot defeat people like that."

Actually, history has shown that you can—but it takes strong leadership, an unwavering commitment to victory, and an acknowledgment that a nation is facing an existential, fanatical enemy bent on its destruction. Unfortunately for the United States, the current occupant of 1600 Pennsylvania Avenue does not fit the bill.

"I believe this [ISIS] army will grow much stronger," Choudary continued. "Because the regimes in Muslim countries are so weak. They are so unjust, they are implementing so much oppression, that I think [the caliphate] will spread very, very quickly. The Muslim world will be united very quickly. And then I think you will have a superpower unparalleled in the world. After that, I believe it will be easy to annex many other countries like China, and Russia, and even America one day."

"This is a long term vision?" I asked.

"Well, I think it's a short term vision, actually," replied Choudary. "I think these things will happen rapidly. Regime change is something that has become quite an easy phenomenon for those people under the Islamic State nowadays."[2]

There was a time not too long ago that the British media and political establishments heard Choudary's big claims and predictions and regarded him as little more than an annoying rabble-rouser. Sure, he and his supporters would hold fiery rallies around the country calling for the establishment of sharia law and harassing troops returning from Iraq and Afghanistan. Plus, Choudary would pop up on various talk shows praising acts of terrorism and slamming the British government for its supposed oppression of Muslims. But he was just a fringe, extremist loon with a tiny, inconsequential following—or so "enlightened" British elite thinking went.

Then reports started to trickle in of several of Choudary's followers being arrested for plotting attacks against the British homeland, or of traveling abroad to fight alongside the likes of the Taliban. As one British terrorism expert told me, Choudary's teachings take his disciples right up to the edge of violence—from that point, it's just a hop, skip, and a suicide belt away from jihad, if they so choose.

There was white convert Richard Dart, radicalized by Choudary and later convicted for planning to bomb the British military repatriation town of Royal Wootton Bassett.[3] Then there was Afsor Ali, former spokesman for another banned Choudary-led group, Muslims Against Crusades, sentenced to jail in August 2014 for possessing terrorist materials.[4] And of course, as we have already seen in chapter five, there was former Choudary follower Michael Adebolajo, who, along with an accomplice, nearly beheaded British soldier Lee Rigby in a horrifying terror killing on a London street in May 2013. The list goes on.

According to Breitbart London, Choudary's banned al-Muhajiroun group "has been linked to nearly one in five individuals convicted of terrorism offences in Britain over the last decade."[5] Likewise, the UK non-profit HOPE not hate—a leftist organization that is openly hostile to conservatives and opponents of Islamism—nevertheless issued an eye-opening report stating that at least seventy people who have been convicted of terrorism or terrorist-related offenses in the UK, or who had died overseas, have been linked to Choudary's al-Muhajiroun network: "Anjem Choudary's group now leads a network of hardline Islamist organisations across Europe. These include groups in Belgium, the Netherlands, France, Denmark and Italy. It is also closely linked to Islamist extremist groups in Germany, Norway and Finland. Together, they represent the largest extreme Islamist network in Europe linked to domestic or overseas terrorism."[6]

The same report found that "al-Muhajiroun-connected groups across Europe have sent between 200–300 people to Syria, making it the largest single recruiting network in Europe" for terrorist groups like ISIS. Given that the report was published in November 2013, months before ISIS recorded its biggest successes in Fallujah, Mosul, and elsewhere, that 200–300 figure has almost certainly grown.

In short, Anjem Choudary is a very dangerous man, a virtual jihadi pied piper. At this stage, only the most stubbornly naive would dismiss him as a non-threat—indeed, as can be seen in the report quoted above, even the far-left HOPE not hate group has recognized him as a national security menace. Yet, incredibly, except for a brief stint in jail in September 2014 for allegedly supporting terrorism (he made bail and promptly blasted the British government),[7] Choudary continues to walk the streets of London freely, spewing hatred and stirring up his followers—and collecting welfare benefits to boot. You read that right. Choudary is one of a number of radical Islamists who receive benefits from the very British government they openly mock and despise.[8] He likewise encourages his followers to avoid work and collect welfare, saying in one lecture, "the normal situation is for you to take money from the kuffar [non-Muslims]. So we take Jihad Seeker's Allowance. You need to get support."[9] The British government seems all too happy to oblige—allowing Choudary to avoid the distraction of a 9-to-5 job as he devotes his time and energy to talking up the fledgling Islamic State.

In August 2014, a loud group of pro-ISIS demonstrators handed out leaflets in London's busy Oxford Street tourist district extolling the new Islamic State. They were holding signs saying, "Khilafah [caliphate] the Dawn of a New Era" and one of the leaflets read:

> After many attempts and great sacrifices from the Ummah of Islam throughout the world, the Muslims with the help of Allah have announced the re-establishment of the Khilafah and appointed an Imam as Khaleef [Caliph].
>
> As Muslims around the world we all have many great responsibilities towards the success and spread of the Khilafah across the world.
>
> 1. **Pledge** our [Allegiance] to the Khaleef [Abu Bakr al-Baghdadi].
> 2. **Obey** the Khaleef according to the Shariah.
> 3. **Advise** the Khaleef if he does anything wrong.
> 4. **Dua** [Prayer]—Make dua to Allah to help and guide the Khaleef.
> 5. **Migrate**—Those that can migrate and resettle should migrate.
> 6. **Educate** Muslims and non-Muslims about the Khilafah.
> 7. **Expose** any lies and fabrications made against the Islamic state.[10]

A few days after the demonstration, Choudary admitted that the pro-ISIS agitators were his students, telling a radio interviewer, "Yes...I've known them for several years. They've attended many demonstrations…many lectures of mine. Very good chaps."[11]

Ah, very good chaps. Fish, chips, Khilafahs. All very English, you see.

Choudary—born in England to parents of Pakistani descent—is undeniably charismatic. A former solicitor, he's a witty fast-talker steeped in the intricacies of radical Salafist ideology. His Twitter feed, which he updates regularly, is one way he reaches his network of followers. The tweets, as reported by the Middle East Media Research Institute (MEMRI) are vintage Choudary: "They include calls for jihad; calls for shari'a law to replace democracy, including stoning to death and cutting off criminals' hands; for the conquest of the West; for non-Muslims to pay the *jizya* tax to Muslim rulers; support for terrorist attacks inside the U.S. and U.K.; he expresses his delight in manifestations of Allah's wrath against the West, such as 'tornados, floods, hurricanes, and earthquakes,' and calls for Western leaders, including President Obama and Prime Minister Cameron, to convert to Islam."[12]

Choudary's grievance-laden rants on Twitter and elsewhere have had an effect. An investigation by Britain's *Daily Star* newspaper found that a growing number of misguided "good chaps" have been led astray by Choudary's teachings and straight into the arms of ISIS:

> We can…reveal new links between young Muslims fighting for the ISIS group and preacher Anjem Choudary.
>
> Former followers of the terror sympathiser have been recruited to join the rebels fighting in Syria and Iraq.
>
> Choudary boasted that young men he has taught have joined Isis, an outfit notorious for beheadings, crucifixions and amputations.
>
> And the Kent-raised radical says it is "no shame" that extremists based in France, Belgium and even Australia and Indonesia share his dream of a global Islamic state.

We can reveal former members of Choudary-backed groups on the continent, including Sharia4Belgium and Sharia4France, are signing up for jihad after meeting the London cleric.

...an unrepentant Choudary, 47, told us: "Although we don't recruit people to send abroad we are not surprised if they want to go abroad and stand with their Muslim brothers and sisters who are being killed and whose land is being occupied. Surely it is a noble thing to want to liberate Muslim land? I have no shame whatsoever in saying these people were at times in some way or other affiliated with us."[13]

During our Skype interview, I pressed Choudary about the *Daily Star* report:

STAKELBECK: You have been accused in the British media of recruiting for ISIS and it's been reported that some of your followers have actually gone to Syria to join with this group. How do you respond to that?

CHOUDARY: Well, you know, nobody has actually gone to date to Syria or Iraq having informed me beforehand. I mean, I have discovered that there are some people there, and by all accounts the people who are there who I know are just living there as citizens. They have decided that they want to live under the Sharia. They want to experience the Islamic State. They want to bring up their children according to Islam.... after the establishment of the Khilafah, I think you will find people are flocking there because they want to live under the Sharia. Remember, you have, now, a state there. Millions of people are living there, Christians, non-Muslims, Jews, Muslims, Yazidis are living there.[14]

Yes, the Islamic State is just one big multi-religious utopia. The abundance of reports detailing how non-Muslims are being slaughtered and harassed by ISIS? The footage of Christians, Yazidis, and Kurds fleeing their homes in terror with nothing but the clothes on their backs in the face of ISIS advances? The endless images of beheadings and mass executions? Choudary told me it's all just Western propaganda driven by imperialist, anti-Muslim bigotry:

> The Christians, by all accounts, are now coming back to Mosul. They prefer to live under the Sharia...and you find in fact that the Muslims and the non-Muslims who are actually living...under the Islamic State are quite happy now. They are having their basic needs of food clothing and shelter provided. Their life, their honor, their wealth is protected...in terms of the Islamic State, their basic needs are being met. The structure is there in terms of the Caliph, his assistants, the governors in the areas, the judges—you know, you can see from many clips that they have completely eradicated all of the vices in that particular area. By all accounts, I cannot see any reason why the people would not accept Abu Bakr al-Baghdadi as the Caliph.[15]

I'm sure the supposedly sharia-loving Christians whom Choudary describes, along with the Yazidis who have seen their wives and daughters sold into sex slavery by ISIS, could come up with a few reasons why al-Baghdadi would not be welcome in their towns and villages.

Anyone with a shred of common sense scoffs, as I did, at Choudary's disinformation campaign, seeing through it as the shameless pro-ISIS propaganda that it is. Indeed, it was tough to keep a straight face during stretches of our interview. After all, a cursory Twitter search will turn up loads of photos of ISIS beheading, raping, and pillaging Muslims and non-Muslims alike—and these are tweets proudly posted not by U.S. government agencies, but by ISIS fighters and their supporters. Yet Choudary has a script and he's sticking to it—and he has the ears of hundreds, if not thousands, of radicalized Muslims across Europe who take what he says very seriously when he describes the Islamic State as he did to me during our interview:

> ...people are so happy. They have basic needs. They have free houses. Gas, electricity, water, etc. is free of charge. I mean, nobody in the world, really, has this at the moment. We are living in times in Britain and even in America, the countries with the largest GDP, where people don't even have security for their homes. Their whole life they just work...and their basic income does not meet their everyday living expenses. And yet, it is a completely different scenario [in the Islamic State]. I am very happy. I would like to live in a society like that.[16]

So, apparently, would many other Muslims who have left comfortable lives in Great Britain behind to travel to the Middle East and join ISIS's growing terrorist army.

■   ■   ■

There's a reason it has been called "Londonistan."

According to most estimates, around five hundred British Muslims have traveled to Syria or Iraq to join up with ISIS and other Islamic terrorist groups.[17] Others place the number as high as eight hundred British ISIS recruits, while one British MP has said that at least fifteen hundred Brits have trekked to the Middle East to join ISIS over the past few years.[18]

To put it in even starker terms, one out of every four Europeans fighting alongside ISIS hails from Great Britain.[19] Indeed, twice as many Muslims are now fighting for ISIS as for the UK military.[20] Many of these battle-tested British fighters have already returned home after completing their jihadi apprenticeships in Syria.[21] Their next move is anyone's guess—perhaps they'll join Anjem Choudary on Britain's welfare dole. Or maybe they'll use some of the tricks they learned fighting with ISIS to carry out attacks on British soil. The UK's Islamism problem is so acute—and such a threat to spill over into other Western countries—that the Obama administration, in a rare instance of being proactive, not reactive, in the face of the jihadist threat, reportedly sent a special unit of CIA officers to Britain to investigate. According to Britain's *Daily Mail*,

> It is unusual for the CIA to send a team to the UK: the agency usually relies on information passed to it by MI5 or MI6 or by its agents stationed at the American Embassy in London.
>
> ...Professor Anthony Glees, of the Centre for Security and Intelligence Studies at Buckingham University, said the mission...showed the level of concern in Washington over the issue, which he claimed was rooted in the UK's "lax" immigration policies.
>
> "The US is worried about the British situation. They fear there might be a knock-on effect for them," Prof Glees said.
>
> ..."The Americans regard the UK as a disaster because of our lax stance on immigration which has allowed this militancy to take hold."
>
> ...sources also admitted that the move revealed a growing lack of trust in Washington over MI5 and MI6's ability to provide a reliable assessment of the security threat presented by young Muslims under the sway of imams who are radicalised and then recruited to fight in religious wars around the globe.
>
> The Obama administration has become increasingly anxious that young American Muslims could follow the same pattern. There are strong links between British and American

radicals and the sources say the CIA feels British efforts to identify and unmask them have been inadequate.[22]

Don't look now, but America has its own problems with "lax immigration policies," not to mention a wide-open southern border that ISIS could drive a caravan of pickup trucks through. If things continue the way they're going, we'll get to where Britain is soon enough. And to put it bluntly, our cousin across the pond is a jihadi wonderland.

How bad are things in the UK? During my trips to Britain over the past few years, I've interviewed 1) An al Qaeda–linked, U.S.–designated global terrorist named Saad al-Faqih, 2) An al Qaeda–linked radical named Yasser al-Sirri who was wanted in the United States and Egypt on terrorism charges, 3) Noman Benotman, a former Libyan terrorist leader and associate of Osama bin Laden and Ayman al-Zawahiri, and 4) Anjem Choudary, who needs no introduction.[23] And that's not even mentioning the various Muslim Brotherhood types and Hamas supporters with whom I've shared a spot of tea.

Benotman, to his credit, has since disavowed al Qaeda. He has transformed his life and left Islamism behind and now works against jihadists. The others, however, remain hardcore Islamist radicals with documented ties to the global jihadist movement. Yet none of my face-to-face interviews with them were conducted behind prison walls. Rather, all of these men are living comfortable lives in London, moving about freely in the land of Churchill and Thatcher (who are likely turning in their graves as I write this). And even Abu Qatada, long considered al Qaeda's top spiritual leader in Europe, lived in London for years and collected welfare benefits before finally being deported to Jordan in 2013. British taxpayers were no doubt thrilled to see him go.

Great Britain circa 2015 is a place that Churchill would not recognize and that Thatcher fought doggedly to prevent. It's a place where Mohammed is the most popular name for male babies;[24] where soldiers are murdered on the streets in broad daylight by Islamic fanatics; where Anjem

Choudary shouts for sharia law while leeching off the very government he'd like to see overthrown; where some eighty-five fully functioning sharia courts operate in major British cities;[25] and where hostile Islamist enclaves have been established in London neighborhoods. As I wrote in my 2013 book, *The Brotherhood*:

> In Europe, many...areas become no-go zones for non-Muslims where sharia law is enforced and even police are hesitant to enter. The Tower Hamlets section of East London, in the shadow of London's financial district, is well on its way to no-go status. I've walked the streets of this area on numerous occasions, spent time in its outdoor bazaars, and observed the massive flow of South Asian immigrants in and out of Friday prayers at the vast East London Mosque—which serves as the de facto British base for Jamaat-e-Islami, considered the South Asian branch of the Muslim Brotherhood. It's a stunning experience to see thousands of predominantly Pakistani and Bangladeshi Muslims dressed in Islamic garb spill out of the mosque and swarm the streets of East London, giving the area a distinctly non-Western, Islamicized feel. In the summer of 2011, Islamists (reportedly in league with our old friend Anjem Choudary), put up posters around Tower Hamlets proclaiming it a "Sharia Controlled Zone" where "Islamic rules are enforced." They wasted no time in getting busy "enforcing." Harassment of non-Muslims—particularly homosexuals, women, and alcohol consumers—at the hands of self-proclaimed "Muslim London Patrols" has become a regular occurrence in East London.[26]

The same people who survived Hitler's blitzkrieg seventy-five years ago and were famous for their stiff upper lips now seem doomed to succumb to Islamization—led into it by the British elites:

All of this is happening against the will of native-born British citizens. According to a 2013 report by a London think tank, British Future, one out of three Brits sees the culture clash between immigrants and indigenous Brits as the primary cause of the country's problems. Seventy-five percent would like to see a reduction in immigration, with 51 percent desiring a large reduction. Granted, Britain gets immigrants from around the world, but it seems likely that Catholic Poles, French job seekers, or other Europeans are less difficult to assimilate than sharia-governed Muslims. Between 2001 and 2011, the Muslim population of the UK doubled—from 1.5 million to 2.7 million (and those numbers don't include the country's many undocumented Muslim immigrants). In only ten years, Muslims grew from 3 percent to nearly 5 percent of the British population. And there are no signs that British politicians have the will or desire to turn off the spigot.[27]

Is it any wonder, given how Britain has utterly failed to assimilate the waves of Muslim immigrants that have come to its shores, that British recruits to ISIS seem to be popping up everywhere? They're chopping heads, appearing in propaganda recruitment videos, tweeting prolifically, and yes, dying for the cause—as of this writing, about twenty British citizens have been killed fighting for ISIS and other jihadist groups in Syria.[28]

A trio of British jihadists even had responsibility for guarding high-value ISIS hostages (Westerners who could fetch a large ransom or be used for propaganda effect)—including American journalist James Foley. The London-accented threesome came to be known among the hostages as "The Beatles," with Foley's beheader dubbed "Jihadi John." Those who were lucky enough to be freed—thanks to ransoms paid—later said that their British captors were extraordinarily cruel and ruthless. As the *Daily Mail* reported, "Both [British hostage John] Cantlie and [James] Foley were 'water boarded'—an interrogation technique that simulates drowning, in which the victim is strapped down with their mouth and nose covered with cloth, before large quantities of water are poured over their faces. They were also given electric shocks, and shot with Tasers, stunguns which cause temporary paralysis, after being dragged from their cells to be 'punished' for any behaviour their captors deemed a breach of their rules."

Their British captors, "did the most appalling stuff in the world—they were psychopathic." They pitted their prisoners against each other in "some sick pastiche of the film Fight Club" forcing them to box against each other and then torturing the men who lost the boxing matches.

Even other ISIS members apparently thought the Britons were going too far. "But the British Islamists, who spoke with London accents, were too enthusiastic in their torture of the hostages for the taste of their fellow jihadis. It is understood they were at one point taken off the job of guarding the Westerners because of their brutality. 'The British jihadis got into trouble because they were considered to be so brutal,' the [*Daily Mail*'s] source said."[29]

In other words, these British ISIS jihadis were among the worst of the worst—a uniquely sadistic crew that stood out even among the most sadistic terrorist group in memory. In previous centuries, the British Empire exported Judeo-Christian values and Western civilization to some of the darkest corners of the world. How far the mighty have fallen. Britain today is a leading exporter not of the Gospel or Shakespearean literature but of Islamic terrorism—indeed, no fewer than twenty-eight countries have suffered jihadist attacks carried out by British citizens.[30] That is an astounding indicator of the depths to which British society has plunged in the twenty-first century. The widespread riots and coordinated street violence carried out by young toughs in cities and towns throughout Great Britain for several days in August 2011 recalled the nightmare vision of Anthony Burgess's *A Clockwork Orange*. The 1962 novel, which was later made into a controversial film—banned in Great Britain for its graphic violence—by director Stanley Kubrick, envisioned a nightmarish UK of the future when violent young thugs ran amok. However, neither Kubrick's film nor the book ever envisioned one crucial detail: that a large chunk of the derelicts of the future would be driven into a murderous frenzy not by drugs or alcohol but by Islamist ideology. Forget "Singin' in the Rain." Try "Allahu Akbar."

Great Britain today has lost its once-proud culture, its traditional Christian faith, and its pride, only to see the vacuum filled by a bleak mixture of Islam, left-wing political correctness, violent street gang culture, and hedonistic celebrity-worship (are you listening, America?). Is it any wonder, then, that products of this increasingly dark society are joining ISIS and gleefully torturing innocent people in a manner that makes the Droogs of *A Clockwork Orange* look like the Wiggles?

Shiraz Maher, a former British radical who left Islamism and now monitors ISIS's European—and specifically, British—foreign fighters, described for the *Wall Street Journal* the sort of "chaps" ISIS is attracting from every corner of the UK. As the *Journal* reports, "The typical British Islamic State terrorist is male, in his 20s and from a South Asian background. 'He usually has some university education and a history of Muslim activism,' Mr. Maher adds." Maher divides the British jihadists into three different "personality types": "The first is the adventure-seeker. 'They're in jihadist summer school or camp,' Mr. Maher says. '"I'm with my buddies, we're hanging out and we have these great weapons—AK-47s, RPGs."'" Members of this group have frequently been "involved with U.K. gangs or drugs, and they might consult *Islam for Dummies* before traveling to Syria." These are the guys who post selfies in which they're "eating fast food, swimming and playing soccer in Syria"—basically as a recruiting message to their friends in Britain, evidence that life with ISIS is better than their lives in London.

The second type are "the 'really nasty guys,' Mr. Maher says, 'the ones who will show off a severed head on Facebook and say, "Yeah, I just beheaded this son of a bitch.'" These guys, Mr. Maher adds, 'should definitely never come back.'"

Third is a category of "'what you might call idealistic or humanitarian jihadists for want of a better phrase,' Mr. Maher says," inspired by compassion for suffering Muslim populations. Unfortunately, as Maher points out, these fighters eventually "'become hardened'" by their experiences in ISIS and "'no longer mention the innocents they came to rescue. "The land belongs to Allah," they now say. "We're here to impose Islam.""'[31]

The Islamic State has drawn British Muslims from all backgrounds and walks of life. From twenty-year-old medical student Nasser Muthana to sixteen-year-old twin sisters Salma and Zahra Halane (who traveled to Syria to become "jihad brides" for ISIS)[32] to former National Health Service doctor Shajul Islam[33] to rapper (and beheader extraordinaire) Abdel-Majed Abdel Bary to a former British banker who explained his decision to join ISIS thus: "[The Islamic State is] the only place where the shari'a of Allah is applied fully. I hate democracy and the self-indulgence of the rich.... I hate inequality...I hate the corporations who are trying to destroy this world because of tyranny."[34]

Yes, better to destroy the world through the sharia-fied tyranny of ISIS—which, as we saw in chapter two, is raking in the dough at a pace that would make many of those mean old corporations blush. But since when does a committed Islamist let facts stand in the way of a revived caliphate?

That caliphate, as we've already seen, needs women in order to flourish—and leave it to Britain to answer the call. As of this writing, at least sixty British women between the ages of eighteen and twenty-four have reportedly traveled to the Middle East to join ISIS since 2013 alone, making Britain the leading European source of female jihadists in the fledgling Islamic State. Like their British male counterparts, they've earned a reputation for brutality, even overseeing brothels where ISIS fighters routinely rape non-Muslim Iraqi women and girls imprisoned as sex slaves.[35] In a sickening example of the utter depravity of these "women of ISIS," one of them, a British medical student named Mujahidah Bint Usama, took to Twitter and posted pictures of herself clad in a white doctor's jacket and holding up a severed head as a group of young children looked on. The message accompanying the gruesome image read, "Dream job, a terrorist doc."[36]

Mind you, this female doctor of death hails from the same country that once produced Florence Nightingale. Think the sun isn't setting on Great Britain?

■   ■   ■

The recruitment of British Muslims into ISIS's ranks has become such a widespread problem that British authorities seem perplexed as to how to handle it. London counterterror police have called on families, religious leaders, and the public to out the extremists in their midst.[37] But their plea for help is unlikely to move the majority of Britain's increasingly insular, radicalized Muslim population. Prime Minister David Cameron's proposed anti-terror legislation that would seize the passports of British citizens seeking to fight overseas with ISIS and bolster authorities' ability to track ISIS supporters on British soil is a belated step in the right direction. Nevertheless, investigators have their work cut out for them as "preachers, battle-hardened returning fighters and jihad sympathisers" work to recruit young Britons. According to the *Guardian*:

> Examples of on the ground recruitment have been seen in Cardiff and Birmingham—amid wider evidence that the UK is being specifically targeted by those with links to ISIS in Europe.
>
> …In Birmingham a leaked police report …. reveal[ed] that extremists are providing support and facilitation for those wishing [to] travel abroad to fight. The report, written

by former assistant chief constable Sharon Rowe ... says: "Influential extremists continue to operate in Birmingham, promoting extremist ideologies." Rowe said they were operating from locations including gyms, restaurants and cafes, which are "used to facilitate extremist activity by allowing key figures to operate and promulgate their message."[38]

As we've seen in the case of Anjem Choudary and his al-Muhajiroun network, some of this activity is happening right under UK authorities' noses. Take thirty-five-year-old "hate preacher" Abu Waleed—yet another Choudary crony—who was seen at an outdoor barbeque in Wales in June 2014 where the black flag of ISIS was flown and an attendee was spotted with the ISIS symbol emblazoned across his shirt.[39] Abu Waleed, who has been linked to at least three young Brits who have traveled to Syria to join ISIS, gave a January 2014 lecture that nicely summarized what life will look like for non-Muslims under the Islamic State: "If a Muslim comes out on the day of 'Eid and sees an infidel with nice clothes, the infidel has to take his clothes off and give them to the Muslim. When an infidel walks down the street, he has to wear a red belt around his neck, he has to have his forehead shaved, and he has to wear two shoes that are different from one another. He is not allowed to walk on the pavement. He has to walk in the middle of the road, and he has to ride on a mule.... So everyone is going to become Muslims. That, my dear brothers, is the Islamic state."[40]

In another lecture, Abu Waleed said Muslims want to "make sure David Cameron comes on his hands and knees, and gives us the jiziya [tax paid by non-Muslims in Islamic states]." He also vowed that in an Islamic society, Queen Elizabeth and Princess Kate Middleton—"the whore, the fornicator"—would be covered up in Islamic garb.[41]

Remember: these diatribes were delivered by a British citizen, on British soil—a citizen who (you guessed it) reportedly collects welfare benefits from the British government for himself, his wife, and his three disabled children.

The current state of recruitment to jihad was perhaps best described by a twenty-one-year-old British university student named Hamzah Parvez. The former London resident—who's now fighting alongside ISIS—recorded an Islamic State recruitment video aimed at UK Muslims in which he called our time, "the golden era for jihad."[42] Of course, if you're a young British Muslim in 2015 with a hankering for holy war, Parvez was merely repeating what you already knew.

■   ■   ■

While most clear-thinking citizens of the UK—Muslim and non-Muslim alike—are fully aware of which way the winds are blowing, I often speak to audiences in the United States that are stunned to learn that the nation that is closest to us culturally has descended into such an atrophied, Islamicized condition. They wonder if Great Britain, generally considered America's staunchest ally and a stalwart of Western civilization, can turn things around. I answer with sadness that I am not optimistic. Yes, British Prime Minister David Cameron talks tough, saying that multiculturalism has failed, promising to curb immigration, and proposing tough new anti-terror laws. Yet the flow of immigration from Muslim countries into the UK continues, seemingly unabated. Extremist preachers continue to openly ply their trade and radicalized young British Muslims are lining up to go to Syria and Iraq and join ISIS.

Also problematic is the fact that Cameron, like President Obama, likes to play armchair imam, refusing to honestly identify the enemy Britain faces and choosing rather to say, laughably, that ISIS jihadists are "not Muslims." He's also fond of repeating the standard "Islam is a religion of peace" platitude that has become so depressingly commonplace among clueless Western leaders who have never picked up a Koran, let alone read one.[43]

Then, there is this gem, courtesy of Al Jazeera: "Britain is set to the [sic] become the first non-Muslim nation to raise money by issuing a government bond-style 'Sukuk' compliant with Sharia law as part of a bid to transform London into a global capital of the Islamic finance industry."

Cameron "unveiled the scheme along with plans to launch an Islamic market index at the London Stock Exchange." As he told the World Islamic Economic Forum (WIEF), *"Already London is the biggest centre of Islamic finance outside the Islamic world, but today our ambition is to go further still.... I want London to stand alongside Dubai and Kuala Lumpur as one of the great capitals of Islamic finance anywhere in the world* [emphasis added]."[44]

Does this sound like a leader—or a nation—that is truly prepared to confront the Islamist threat, in all its nefarious forms?

"If we can't count on the Brits anymore, who can we count on?" discouraged American audiences ask me.

Other than the obvious answer, Israel, that is becoming an increasingly tough call. Unfortunately, Britain's suicidal obsession with multiculturalism, with tolerating the intolerant, and with distancing itself from its Judeo-Christian heritage, is far from an isolated case. Europe's elites have promoted policies that have led to isolated, self-segregating Muslim communities springing up across the Old Continent. Many disaffected young European Muslims living in these areas have noticed ISIS and the new caliphate it is building with interest.

And ISIS has noticed them.

CHAPTER SEVEN

AMSTERDAMNED: ISIS OVER EUROPE

"THE SITUATION HERE IS VERY GRIM."

Wim Kortenoeven was calling from The Hague, but the urgency in his voice made it seem like he was right beside me. I felt like I was standing next to him at his window, looking out over the carcass of an Islamicized Netherlands.

"We have reached the point of no return," he said of his country's struggle with Islamism. "And when you reach the point of no return, you withdraw. People are moving out of cities, leaving the country. And the political elites are ignoring the problem—because they made it happen through their policies."

Kortenoeven has been grappling with those same left-wing elites for decades, first as a journalist and activist and then as a member of the Dutch Parliament from 2010 to 2012. A longtime leader in Holland's counter-jihad and pro-Israel movements, he has been a tireless defender of Judeo-Christian values in one of the world's most liberal societies. Even

by the libertine standards of today's Western Europe, the Netherlands—
which in 2001 became the first country to legalize same-sex marriage—is
infamously permissive, with marijuana, prostitution, and euthanasia all
lawful and laissez-faire immigration policies that have seen its Muslim
population approaching 1 million, or 6 percent of the overall population
of 17 million.[1]

But Dutch uber-tolerance has created an atmosphere where the intolerant have run rampant. In July 2014, radical Islamists held Europe's first
public pro-ISIS rallies in The Hague, which is the seat of the Dutch government. Twice—on July 4 and then again on July 24—at least fifty ISIS supporters waved black Islamic State flags amid shouts of "Allahu Akbar" and
calls for "death to the Jews" as they marched through the Dutch capital.[2]
The left-wing mayor of The Hague, Jozias van Aartsen, was on vacation
during the rallies, and his deputy apparently saw no need to take action in
his absence. The stunning inaction by van Aartsen's office prompted calls
for his resignation. Upon his return from vacation, the mayor responded
to the criticism not by taking action against the city's genocidal ISIS supporters, but by banning a planned anti-ISIS rally, deeming it "too provocative." Van Aartsen's decree added insult to injury: an earlier anti-ISIS
rally had been broken up by Islamic State supporters who threw stones and
punches at the marchers.[3]

When most Americans think of the Netherlands, they envision wind-
mills and clogs, not burqas and hijabs. You'd think Amsterdam, with its
red-light districts and marijuana cafés, would be about as far from sharia
law as you can possibly get. But in October 2014, as reports continued to
surface about Dutch Muslims either traveling to Syria to join ISIS or agitat-
ing for the caliphate on Dutch soil, I reached out to Kortenoeven to get a
sense of what was happening on the ground in ultra-liberal Holland. The
former Dutch parliamentarian painted a bleak picture.

"The Hague incidents were very serious," he explained. "Gradually,
people are moving from all sorts of Islamist movements to the most

successful: ISIS. They will support the only movement that gets things done."

As of this writing, at least 130 Dutch Muslims have traveled to Syria to join ISIS.[4] Kortenoeven pointed out that most of these ISIS recruits were criminals, and that Dutch prisons are filled with Muslim men from Morocco, Egypt, Somalia, and other Islamic countries. His comments echoed those of another former Dutch politician, Mustapha Abbou, who told Dutch Public Radio 1 that many of the Netherlands' Moroccan youths have "no education, no prospects and are barely supervised. They are a ticking time bomb."[5] Given that the Netherlands is home to nearly four hundred thousand Moroccan immigrants, the Dutch may have a slight problem on their hands. One 2011 study found that in Dutch neighborhoods where Moroccans were a majority, the youth crime rate was 50 percent.[6]

"The caliphate gives them a chance at success," Kortenoeven said of the Netherlands' ever-expanding Muslim population. "With the Islamic State, they can go from being a pauper to a prince. The disenfranchised gain power… people will commit unthinkable atrocities because they want to be a part of something successful, something larger."

One ISIS fighter who goes by the name "Abudurahman" collected welfare benefits from the Dutch government for years before making his way to Syria, where he has appeared in YouTube videos posing proudly in front of severed heads.[7] Another Holland-bred jihadist, "Yilmaz," served in the Dutch army before quitting and relocating to Syria, where he has boasted on social media of training young British ISIS recruits in the finer points of jihad.[8]

Yilmaz is apparently the charismatic sort. A nineteen-year-old Dutch woman named Aicha who had converted to Islam saw him interviewed on TV and fell in love. She decided to travel to Syria and marry the terrorist, whom she saw "as a sort of Robin Hood." Quickly discovering that life in the Islamic State was a far cry from Sherwood Forest, Aicha contacted her mother and told her she wanted to come home. In a daring rescue mission straight out of a Hollywood movie (and against the advice of Dutch authorities), the mother donned a burqa and entered Syria to find her daughter.

Thankfully, the pair escaped over the Syrian border into Turkey and made their way back to the Netherlands.[9] As we saw in chapter four, however, there is no shortage of young Western women ready and willing to take Aicha's place in the Islamic State.

The Netherlands' struggle with Islamism is not a new one. In 2004, in an act foreshadowing the "one-man jihad" strategy of ISIS in the West today, an Islamic terrorist named Mohammed Bouyeri murdered filmmaker and TV host Theo van Gogh in broad daylight on an Amsterdam street. Van Gogh had recently directed a short film called *Submission* that highlighted Islam's oppression of women. On the morning of November 2, 2004, he was bicycling to work when Bouyeri emerged and shot him several times with a handgun. Van Gogh, seriously wounded, staggered across the street and fell to the ground, pursued by Bouyeri. He reportedly pleaded, "Can't we talk about this?" before Bouyeri shot him at close range and then slit his throat, nearly decapitating him. Bouyeri then plunged a large knife deep into van Gogh's chest and attached a note to the filmmaker's lifeless body threatening Ayaan Hirsi Ali, a former Muslim and Dutch politician who wrote the script for *Submission* and is known for her courageous public stand against Islamic supremacism.

Bouyeri, who is serving life in a Dutch prison for slaughtering van Gogh, was part of a terror cell called the Hofstad Network that planned to conduct additional attacks inside the Netherlands. Dutch authorities broke up the cell in 2006 and several of its members were sent to prison like Bouyeri. But according to an eye-opening report released by the Dutch intelligence service, the AIVD, the jihadist movement in the Netherlands is experiencing stunning growth once again today thanks in large part to the inspiration to jihad that is the Syrian Civil War. The report compares Dutch jihadism to a "swarm"—a network of loosely affiliated independent yet like-minded individuals that are all working toward the same end, and to great effect: "The increasing momentum of Dutch jihadism poses an unprecedented threat to the democratic legal order of the Netherlands.... Dutch jihadists are convinced that the caliphate is not some utopian dream but an achievable reality for Syria and other Muslim nations—and even for the Netherlands." Predictably, many are being drawn to the ISIS cause through social media, which the report says, "has changed the structure and cohesions of the jihadist movement."[10]

As of December 2014, the AIVD estimated that close to thirty Dutch jihadists had already returned home to Holland from the battlefields of Syria. It's unlikely that these newly returned veterans of Syria's hellish killing fields will spend their days lounging at cannabis cafés or paddling amiably along Amsterdam's canals. It is entirely likely that they will attempt to carry out attacks on Dutch soil. If they are successful, the simmering culture clash in the Netherlands could boil over in a nasty way.

"People are talking about civil war," Kortenoeven said. "The general population—and I'm not only talking about the Netherlands, but all over Europe—is fed up."

A major reason for their frustration is the glaring shortage of rational, forthright voices in the European political realm that are willing to take a stand against Islamist encroachment. Those who are, such as Dutch MP Geert Wilders, are branded as bigots and Islamophobes and in some cases even brought to trial for supposed "hate speech" against Islam. Like the rest of the Western world, the Netherlands' elite class and opinion shapers in government, media, and academia are overwhelmingly leftists who have enshrined politically correct multiculturalism as a virtual religion. This new religion is totalitarian to its core: ultra-secular, atheistic, socialistic, and openly hostile to Judeo-Christian Western civilization, yet fiercely protective of Islam and damning of its critics. Witness the aforementioned pro-ISIS rallies in The Hague getting a pass from the city's leadership while anti-ISIS rallies were deemed too incendiary.

When average citizens begin to feel like society is slipping out of their grasp—thanks largely to weak, out-of-touch leadership—desperation can creep in. With that sense of desperation comes a hunger for a voice—any voice—that articulates the frustrations of the people. History shows that the rush to embrace a political savior often ends in disaster: witness the rise of Hitler in post-Versailles Germany and the Muslim Brotherhood's ascension in Egypt in the wake of the so-called Arab Spring. Kortenoeven is concerned that a similar scenario could develop today if European governments, including that of the Netherlands, continue to appease their restless, radicalized Muslim communities.

"If right-wing extremists and Neo-Nazis are the only voices speaking out against Islamism, and the governments won't, then people will drift towards the extremists," he told me. "So, we have people who can destroy our countries from two sides—Islamists on one side and neo-Nazis on the other."

In the meantime, the Islamization of tiny Holland continues unabated, particularly in its largest cities. The Muslim population of Amsterdam is 24 percent, while Rotterdam—Holland's second-largest city—is 25 percent Islamic. The Hague boasts a Muslim population of 14 percent and Utrecht, 13 percent.[11]

These communities are fertile ground for ISIS recruitment. One 2014 study found "tremendous support" for the Islamic State among young Dutch Muslims of Turkish background. According to the study, 87 percent of Turkish-Dutch between the ages of eighteen and thirty-five believe that ISIS creates positive change in the Middle East, and 80 percent have no problem with Dutch jihadists returning from Syria and Iraq. Another study reportedly found that three quarters of Dutch Muslims regard those who have gone to fight in Syria as "heroes." The Dutch minister of social affairs called the results of these studies "alarming."[12]

During our conversation, Kortenoeven recounted a meeting he had during his days in Parliament with a former colleague who is now a Dutch government official. Kortenoeven warned him about the growing Islamist threat, only to be waved off as an alarmist. "'They are just a few idiots,'" Koretenoeven recalled the official saying. "'We are too strong for them. You are exaggerating.'" But what a difference a caliphate makes. Today, Kortenoeven said, that same politician says ISIS must be destroyed.

The prospect of ISIS supporters carrying out Theo van Gogh–style executions of infidels on Holland's streets was apparently enough to shake Kortenoeven's colleague out of a self-satisfied slumber. Unfortunately, other Dutch officials have chosen not only to ignore the ISIS threat but to act as outright apologists for Islamic State jihadists. Pieter Broertjes, the left-wing mayor of an affluent town called Hilversum, told a radio interviewer that Dutch Muslims should be permitted to travel to the Islamic State and join the jihad, comparing them, incredibly, to Jews who left for Israel after World War II. "It comes to adult humans," he sniffed. "The Dutch [Jews] also went to Israel after the war to fight against the British. We didn't stop them then either."[13] In other words, Broertjes believes that Jews fighting to establish a pro-Western democracy in their ancient homeland were no different from ISIS jihadists committing genocide to create a caliphate devoted to the West's destruction. Not to be outdone, Yasmina Haifi, a Dutch security official who worked for a department within the government's National Coordinator of Anti-Terrorism and Security, tweeted in August 2014 that "ISIS has nothing to do with Islam. It is a preconceived plan of Zionists who want to deliberately make Islam look bad." Haifi, who is of Turkish descent, was suspended from her post because of her anti-Semitic outburst.[14]

The notion that Israel is a greater threat to world stability than ISIS is not unique to the Netherlands. In fact, it is a commonly held view heard in cafés, newsrooms, and government chambers throughout Western Europe. Any American that is expecting a strong, confident Europe to stand shoulder-to-shoulder with the United States in the generational struggle against Islamism is in for a very unpleasant surprise. Uninterested in defense spending, dismissive of Christianity, rife with anti-Semitism, and beholden to their restive and growing Muslim populations, our European allies have passed the point of moral relativism and are well on their way to moral rot.

And jihadists are eagerly waiting in the wings.

■   ■   ■

In 2004, Princeton historian Bernard Lewis, one of the world's foremost scholars of Islam, told the German daily *Die Welt* that Europe would be Islamic by the end of the twenty-first century "at the very latest."[15] Lewis's statement may have come as a shock to Americans who had not been following the demographic trends in Europe during the latter half of the Cold War and during the 1990s. But to native Europeans who have witnessed whole neighborhoods transform into sharia enclaves where non-Muslims—including police—are unwelcome, Lewis was merely stating the obvious. From Spain to Sweden to Italy, towering minarets adorn newly built mosques that are overflowing with worshipers. Europe's churches, on the other hand, are old, empty, and lifeless; and its Jewish communities, as we'll see later in this chapter, are under siege and leaving. Further, indigenous Europeans simply do not reproduce; in country after country, their fertility rates are below the needed replacement level of 2.1 children per family. Conversely, Muslims reproduce above replacement levels in nearly every Western European nation. In France, for instance, Muslims have 2.8 children per couple, while non-Muslims have 1.9. In the United Kingdom, it's 3.0 children per Muslim couple and 1.9 for non-Muslim couples. The trend is the same across the continent.[16]

As of 2010, over 44 million Muslims lived in Europe, 6 percent of the total population. That number is estimated to rise by nearly one-third, to over 58 million, or 8 percent of the European population, by 2030.[17] France, with at least 5.5 million Muslims, or 8 to 10 percent of its total population, leads the way in Western Europe, followed by Germany, with over 4 million Muslims, Great Britain with nearly 3.1 million, Spain with 1.67 million, and Italy with 1.6 million.[18]

ISIS has found these burgeoning European Muslim communities, which are largely unassimilated and frequently radicalized, to be a sort of jihadi jackpot. As of this writing, at least three thousand European citizens, and counting, have traveled to the Middle East to join the Islamic State.[19] Neither Western airstrikes nor the increased scrutiny of European governments seems to have done much to stem the flow of European-born fighters to Syria and Iraq.[20] In June 2014, the Soufan Group, a respected global consulting firm, released a report on Syrian foreign fighters that included a comprehensive country-by-country breakdown.[21] Here are the numbers for Western Europe—which have undoubtedly increased since the report was published, perhaps significantly, given ISIS's higher profile and battlefield successes and the establishment of a caliphate in the summer of 2014. Australia and Canada are also included:

- **France**: The Soufan Group report had the number at 700, but the French interior minister upped that number in September 2014, telling an interviewer, "930 French citizens or foreigners usually resident in France are today involved in jihad in Iraq and Syria."[22]
- **United Kingdom**: The Soufan report had the number at 400. But as we saw in chapter six, other estimates range from anywhere between 500 and 1,500 British jihadists in Iraq and Syria.
- **Germany**: The Soufan report had the number at around 300, but in November 2014 the head of Germany's domestic intelligence service put the number at 550, adding, "About 60 people from Germany have died or killed themselves, at

least nine in suicide attacks." Some 180 German jihadists have already returned home from Syria and Iraq.[23]

- **Australia**: Around 250.
- **Belgium**: Around 250.
- **The Netherlands**: 120 (upped to 130 by Dutch intelligence).[24]
- **Austria**: No approximate number given in the Soufan report, but Austrian authorities put the number around 130.[25]
- **Denmark**: 100.
- **Spain**: 51.
- **Italy**: No approximate number given in the Soufan report, but Italian media reports put the number at 50, with Italy's interior minister confirming that "tens" of Italians have left for the Middle East to fight alongside ISIS.[26]
- **Norway**: Between 40 and 50.
- **Finland**: More than 30.
- **Canada**: The Soufan report put the number at 30, but more recent estimates have placed the number at 130 Canadian foreign fighters.[27]
- **Sweden**: Around 30.
- **Ireland**: Between 25 and 30.
- **Portugal**: No approximate number given in the Soufan report, but Portuguese authorities put the number at 12.[28]
- **Switzerland**: Around 10.
- **Luxembourg**: No approximate number.

These Euro-jihadis not only pose a threat to their home countries if and when they return from the Middle East. They can also enter the United States without a visa as part of a waiver program that the U.S.

shares with its Western European allies. This Visa Waiver Program creates a much greater chance that Mohammed from Germany, on his way back from his adventures with the caliphate, will decide to bypass Berlin or Hamburg and make an unpleasant little pit stop in New York City or Chicago, instead.

While jihadists from Western Europe pose the greatest threat to the United States, thanks mainly to the Visa Waiver Program, the Soufan Group report shows that no corner of Europe has been untouched by the gravitational pull of ISIS. Hungary, Poland, the Czech Republic, Bulgaria, Bosnia, Albania, Macedonia, and Ukraine have all seen Muslim citizens travel to the Islamic State, and the Russian Federation (including jihadist hotbeds Chechnya and Dagestan) has sent some 800 jihadists into ISIS's ranks.[29]

Texas Congressman Michael McCaul, a Republican who chairs the House Committee on Homeland Security, has described the pipeline from Europe to the Islamic State and back again as a "jihadi superhighway." In an op-ed for *Time*, he called out Turkey, the main transit point for foreign fighters looking to enter the Islamic State, for not doing enough to stem the flow of European jihadis. He added, "European Union security gaps are also a problem":

> EU law forbids member states from automatically running EU citizens against terror watch lists when they return to the continent's 26-country Schengen Area, a large swath of Europe in which its citizens can travel freely without border checks. As a result, only a fraction of EU citizens are screened against terror databases when they re-enter Europe. This vulnerability may allow European foreign fighters—many of whom can travel visa-free to the United States—to make it back to the West without drawing attention.
>
> Other EU security deficiencies can also make it easier for American extremists to travel back from the conflict zone,

including the lack of an advanced EU-wide air passenger information screening system and inadequate fraudulent document
detection capabilities.[30]

McCaul went on to note, "In all too many ways, Europe is in a pre-9/11
counterterrorism posture," citing barriers to cooperation between European law enforcement and intelligence agencies and the difficulties EU
member states face in prosecuting foreign fighters. McCaul's observation
that America's closest allies in the world outside of Canada and Israel
continue to have a pre-9/11 mindset—despite numerous Islamic terror
attacks and foiled plots on European soil over the past decade, plus the
ongoing ISIS foreign fighter bonanza—should be disquieting to every
American. And according to Soeren Kern, one of the world's foremost
experts on the Islamization of Europe, things aren't likely to improve any
time soon.

I caught up with Kern as he visited the United States in September
2014. He's a Senior Fellow at the Gatestone Institute—an international
policy think tank chaired by former UN ambassador John Bolton—and a
Senior Analyst for the influential Strategic Studies Group in Spain, where's
he's based. Kern travels widely, and no one has a better on-the-ground feel
for what's happening in Europe.

> STAKELBECK: How strong is ISIS in Europe?
> KERN: They are strong in Europe and becoming stronger.
>   Everything took on a new dimension after June [2014],
>   when ISIS declared a caliphate...ISIS is creating a new state
>   and that has strong appeal. A lot of European Muslims want
>   to support it financially—they may not travel there, but they
>   will support the caliphate financially and logistically. I'm
>   concerned that we could see an audacious attack by ISIS or
>   its supporters on European soil.... The Salafists are fear-
>   less—they have absolutely no respect for the West. They

hate the West and they hate democracy. They are becoming more bold and assertive—and as the Muslim population grows in Europe, we'll see more of that.

STAKELBECK: Talk about the assimilation problems in Europe's Muslim communities.

KERN: Most of the Islamists are second or third generation immigrants who have not been accepted into European society. There is a lot of prejudice. If your name is Mohammed, it isn't easy getting a job. Many Muslims don't feel like they have a home in Europe, yet many have never even been to their native lands like Algeria or Morocco. They are frustrated and angry and susceptible to the Salafist propaganda of [radical UK preacher] Anjem Choudary and other people. They have no hope—Salafist preachers give them new meaning in life. They can become jihadists in this world and secure life in the next world. There is no guarantee of salvation in Islam. Martyrdom is the only guarantee. Unlike Christianity, where belief in Jesus gets you to heaven, a Muslim is never quite sure. That is why jihad is so appealing.

STAKELBECK: Why aren't Europeans more resistant to the growth of Islamism in their midst?

KERN: I think it has something to do with the social welfare state. Europeans are provided for, from cradle to grave. People would rather enjoy today than plan for tomorrow. They don't want to have children, and the culture is very hedonistic. That attitude contributes to the atmosphere of Islamization. By rejecting the Judeo-Christian worldview, Europeans have created a huge spiritual vacuum—and Islam is filling it. Islam is very black and white—for people who are lost it is very appealing. It tells you what you can and can't do and provides clear direction.

STAKELBECK: Is there any way Europe can turn this around?

KERN: Multiculturalism is so ingrained in the European psyche that it is very difficult to reverse. Even if Europe's political class were made up entirely of conservative parties, it would still be very difficult to reverse because it is so ingrained.

ISIS actually owes Europe's craven political class a debt of gratitude. Think about it: without the suicidal policies enacted by European governments over the past half-century or so, particularly in regards to mass Muslim immigration, the Islamic State would not have thousands of ruthless, fanatical European fighters bolstering its ranks today.

Perhaps more important, it would not possess such a strong foothold on European soil.

■   ■   ■

Islam has a long track record of aggression in Europe. At various points throughout Islamic history, Muslims conquered and ruled over Spain, Sicily, the Balkans, Greece, Hungary, and Bulgaria. Muslim armies raided southern Italy, attacked Rome, and reached the gates of Vienna twice before being turned back. Had a Frankish army led by Charles Martel not defeated an invading Muslim force at the Battle of Tours in central France in 732 AD, all of Western Europe might have come under Islamic dominion.

Today, every jihadist group, including ISIS, wants to reclaim those European territories and reintegrate them into a revived caliphate. Ironically enough, Islam has indeed established a firm foothold in Europe once again, but not through the kind of military conquest favored by ISIS and the jihadist armies of centuries past. In a 1995 speech in Ohio, the Muslim Brotherhood's global spiritual leader, Sheikh Yusuf al-Qaradawi—who has since been banned from entering the United States—declared, "We will conquer Europe, we will conquer America! Not through [the] sword but through Da'wa [proselytization]."[31]

In the twenty-first century, Islamists—led by the Muslim Brotherhood—are putting al-Qaradawi's words into action, employing a sort of demographic jihad (the Brotherhood calls it "settlement jihad") that invariably includes the following steps: 1) Large numbers of Muslims migrate to a given European country. 2) Once settled in Europe, Muslims reproduce at higher rates than the indigenous, non-Muslim population. Additionally, native Europeans convert to Islam in small but steadily growing numbers. 3) Mosques are built at a rapid pace. Saudi, Qatari, and other Persian Gulf funding, as well as Turkish government money, flows into European Muslim communities and organizations, enabling the construction of sprawling "mega-mosques." 4) Muslims form self-segregating enclaves—cut off from the broader society at large and often centered on mosques—where non-Muslims are not welcome and European laws and culture are not respected. Many residents of these enclaves receive welfare benefits. They become an increasingly important constituency that is pandered to by liberal politicians. 5) Islamist pressure groups, working hand in glove with liberal governments and the mainstream media, attempt to silence critics of Islamism by tarring them as right-wing bigots, fascists, and "Nazis." Every new act of terrorism or foiled terror plot is dismissed by this triumvirate as having nothing to do with Islam. 6) Islamic anti-Semitism becomes more open and prevalent, particularly whenever Israel engages in military actions against Islamic terrorist organizations such as Hamas and Hezbollah. 7) Culture clashes increase, whole communities change, and average Europeans are left feeling angry, frustrated, and powerless to halt the transformation of their countries.

Does any of this sound familiar? It should. From immigration to mega-mosques to the government-media-Islamo-pressure group troika (the Council on American-Islamic Relations, anyone?), this seven-step process is already being repeated in the United States, albeit at a much slower pace than in Europe—no thanks to the Obama administration's full-on embrace of all things Islamic.

ISIS, for its part, is reaping the benefits of years of meticulous settlement jihad by the Muslim Brotherhood in Europe that dates back to the 1950s. Before the Islamic State even emerged, Europe already had plenty of radicalized mosques and immigrant communities filled with disenfranchised young Muslims looking for meaning and a cause. Then along came ISIS, conquering vast amounts of territory in the heart of the Middle East, declaring the return of the caliphate, chopping off head after head and chronicling it all on Twitter and Instagram. Scores of European Muslims in their teens and twenties were instantly smitten, and the great jihadi pipeline from Europe to Syria was open for business. Those who didn't join the exodus to the new caliphate simply chose to stay put and advance its cause in their own backyards.

In short, things couldn't have lined up any better for ISIS. It took advantage of already well-established jihad-friendly communities in Europe that were just waiting for a strong horse they could rally behind. ISIS has also benefited from the enthusiasm of European converts to Islam who are frequently drawn by what French scholar Dr. Mathieu Guidère calls "revolutionary appeal" rather than religious ideology: "There are people fighting with the Islamic State who don't even know how to correctly recite the Shahada," he says, referring to the Islamic declaration of faith. "They just want to fight the system, and to them jihadi groups have the same kind of appeal that radical left-wing terrorism used to have in the 1970s."[32]

We saw in chapter four how ISIS has appealed to men, women, blacks, whites, freaks, geeks, and every demographic in between, resonating with Westerners in a manner that is unprecedented for an Islamic terrorist group. For instance, it's estimated that converts to Islam make up some 60 percent of the French citizens fighting for the Islamic State, and 80 percent of ISIS's Italian *mujahideen*.[33]

■ An August 2014 poll found that 16 percent—or one out of every six—French citizens supports the Islamic State. The number rose to 27 percent for those between the ages of eighteen and twenty-four.[34] Given that France has the largest Muslim population in Western Europe and has seen more of its citizens join the Islamic State than any other European nation (with the possible exception of Great Britain), these poll results should come as no shock.

ISIS sees France as a gold mine of potential recruits and is making a concerted effort to woo more French citizens to its ranks. An increasing number of French fighters have appeared in ISIS propaganda videos, including one self-described former French paratrooper, a white convert who calls himself "Abu Qatada." In an April 2014 video, Qatada said, "I am French, of French origin, with French parents, and I used to be a paratrooper in the French army.... I have disavowed that army of tyrants, and now I am here in an army that is [the] opposite [of the French army].... Now I do not have comrades-in-arms, I have brothers. It is not the French flag that unites us, but rather Allah...."[35]

In another video, released in November 2014, three French ISIS fighters burned their passports and called on French Muslims to either conduct attacks inside France or migrate to the Islamic State. That same month, two French citizens, both converts, appeared in a gruesome video featuring a beheaded U.S. aid worker, Peter Kassig.[36]

As of this writing, at least 118 French ISIS fighters have already returned home—including one who was clearly not ready to abandon jihad: twenty-nine-year-old Mehdi Nemmouche, whom we have already met.[37] European intelligence services had their ultimate nightmare realized in May 2014, when Nemmouche, recently returned from Syria, gunned down four people at a Jewish museum in Brussels. How many more like Mehdi Nemmouche will return—or already have returned—to Europe after their jihadi apprenticeships inside the caliphate?

Then again, how many homegrown French radicals who have never even been to the Middle East are hell-bent on carrying out attacks on

French soil? Consider the carnage in France during one horrific three-day span in December 2014: 1) A man stabbed and wounded three police officers in central France while shouting "Allahu Akbar." 2) Another man rammed his car into a crowd of people in the eastern city of Dijon, injuring thirteen, while screaming, you guessed it, "Allahu Akbar." 3) Yet another man drove a van into a crowd of people at a Christmas market in the city of Nantes in western France, injuring at least ten people, one critically. An initial report claimed that the man screamed "Allahu Akbar" while mowing down pedestrians, but witnesses apparently said that he did not in fact use the infamous Islamic war cry.[38]

As we saw in chapter three, the steadily increasing number of jihadist attacks in France culminated in three days of horrific bloodshed between January 7 and 9 in and around Paris. Said and Cherif Kouachi, two brothers who had trained with al Qaeda in Yemen, stormed the Paris office of the satirical magazine *Charlie Hebdo* and slaughtered twelve people, including two police officers. Meanwhile, Amedy Coulibaly, an acquaintance of the Kouachis who had pledged allegiance to ISIS, murdered a French police officer and then slaughtered four more people after taking hostages at a Jewish deli in Paris. The Kouachis and Coulibaly were eventually killed by French security forces. Following the attacks, ten thousand French soldiers fanned out across the country, protecting "sensitive sites," including Jewish schools, synagogues, and businesses.[39]

■ I recounted in *The Brotherhood* how I was struck by the large number of hardcore Salafist Muslims, including many white converts, that I encountered on the streets of Cologne and Bonn during a June 2012 visit to Germany to investigate the country's growing Salafi scene. One German journalist described to me the steady flow of German Muslims to jihadi hotspots like Pakistan, Yemen, and Somalia and said that the problem was only going to get worse. Unfortunately, he was right. Germany's intelligence service, the BfV, believes that the number of radical Salafists in Germany practically doubled between 2011 and the end of 2014, to a total of nearly seven thousand.

Salafists are ultra-fundamentalist and frequently violent—they comprise ISIS's base. It's no wonder Germany's interior minister has warned that the terrorist threat in his country "is critical. The number of threatening individuals has never been as high as now."[40]

In the western German city of Wuppertal, Salafists led by a radicalized white convert named Sven Lau have dubbed themselves "Sharia Police" and taken to patrolling city streets at night to curb drinking and gambling, which are "un-Islamic" activities.[41] Predictably, Germany's growing ISIS problem, combined with incitement by Lau and other Salafi extremists, has created a backlash. Rival groups of German soccer hooligans have put aside their differences to start a new movement called "Hooligans Against Salafists." On October 26, 2014, close to five thousand hooligans gathered in Cologne to march against radical Islam. The protest began peacefully but soon descended into violence, with demonstrators battling German police.[42]

A few weeks before the hooligan rally, supporters of ISIS engaged in violent clashes with Kurdish opponents of the Islamic State on the streets of Hamburg, bringing a violent Middle East conflict to the heart of Europe.[43] Those clashes were a major reason behind the formation of a mass movement called Patriotic Europeans Against the Islamization of the West (PEGIDA) that has drawn thousands of protestors to weekly anti-Islamization rallies in the city of Dresden in eastern Germany (including seventeen thousand at one pre-Christmas event in December 2014).[44] German Chancellor Angela Merkel, in typical Euro-PC fashion, has condemned the rallies, saying PEGIDA leaders' "hearts are cold and often full of prejudice, and even hate."[45] Yet one poll showed that nearly one out of three Germans believed the marches were justified and one out of eight Germans would attend a PEGIDA march if one were held in their hometown.[46]

The growing popularity of PEGIDA and the hostilities in Cologne and Hamburg are merely harbingers of culture clashes to come. As of November 2014, a whopping three hundred ISIS supporters were facing trial in Germany.[47]

■ For most Americans, Scandinavia conjures images of blond-haired, blue-eyed Swedish bikini babes and Viking longships. Yet the most popular name for men and baby boys in the Norwegian capital, Oslo, is not Sven or Olaf, but Mohammed.[48] Meanwhile, in Sweden's third-largest city, Malmo, which is 20 percent Muslim, "Large enclaves…have earned the dread label 'no-go zone.' They are unsafe for non-Muslims, particularly women who do not conform to Islamist conventions of dress and social interaction. They are especially perilous for police, firefighters, and emergency-medical technicians."[49]

Denmark may be the smallest Scandinavian country, but when it comes to producing ISIS jihadists, the Danes punch well above their weight. Among Western nations, Denmark has sent the second-highest rate of foreign fighters per capita to the Islamic State, trailing only Belgium. At least twenty-eight of those Danish jihadists reportedly received welfare benefits from the Danish government—while they were still waging jihad on behalf of ISIS in Syria. But never fear: fifteen of them have been ordered to pay the government back.[50] I'm sure they'll hop right on it, being loyal Danish citizens and all.

That's precisely the attitude that Denmark, somewhat quixotically, seems to be counting on its wayward jihadi sons to adopt. Aarhus, Denmark's second-largest city, has chosen to treat its returning ISIS fighters not to prison time but to counseling sessions. According to the *Washington Post*,

> In Denmark, not one returned fighter has been locked up. Instead, taking the view that discrimination at home is as criminal as Islamic State recruiting, officials here are providing free psychological counseling while finding returnees jobs and spots in schools and universities. Officials credit a new effort to reach out to a radical mosque with stanching the flow of recruits.
>
> Some progressives say [the Danish city of] Aarhus should become a model for other communities in the United States

and Europe that are trying to cope with the question of what to do when the jihad generation comes back to town.[51]

Please Aarhus, don't give the Obama administration any more brilliant ideas.

While the Danish government—via Danish taxpayer dollars—is busy helping returning jihadists get in touch with their feelings, Aarhus's Grimhojvej mosque (which the *Washington Post* article described, charitably, as "one of the most polarizing houses of worship in Europe") is busy "openly back[ing] a caliphate in the Middle East" and "refus[ing] to offer a blanket denunciation of the Islamic State." And why would it? Danish authorities believe the "vast majority" of the some thirty Aarhus residents who left Denmark for the Islamic State had links to the mosque. It's easy to see why. A mosque spokesman told a Danish newspaper: "An Islamic state will always be what we Muslims yearn for, therefore we can not help but support the Islamic State, even though it comes with errors, so we must wait and see."[52]

While they're waiting, Aarhus officials will no doubt be more than happy to recommend a good shrink.

　　　　■　　　■　　　■

If anyone should have their heads examined, it's European government officials, who've created an atmosphere where returning ISIS terrorists are coddled while Jews are openly harassed in the streets in a vicious manner not seen since Hitler's heyday.

First, some background. One of the major stories of the summer of 2014 was Israel's fifty-day military operation against Hamas terrorists in Gaza. The Israeli military launched Operation Protective Edge to put a stop to the endless barrage of rocket fire by Hamas and Palestinian Islamic Jihad terrorists against Israeli civilian centers. The Israelis also aimed to dismantle an extensive network of heavily fortified underground tunnels dug by Hamas beneath the Gaza border and into Israeli territory. The Isralis learned from prisoners that they captured in this operation that Hamas was planning to use at least some of the tunnels to infiltrate Israeli communities and kill and kidnap Israeli civilians.[53]

In short, Israel was battling to eliminate a Palestinian jihadist threat competitive with ISIS in its remorseless desire to slaughter innocent men, women, and children. Like ISIS, Hamas despises the West and openly calls for its demise. And like ISIS, Hamas wishes to see the establishment of a global Islamic caliphate ruled by sharia law. Given these facts, it should have been a no-brainer for European governments to stand strong with Israel and support its efforts to vanquish a shared radical Islamic enemy. Only it didn't work out that way.

From Britain to Norway, from Spain to Italy to Belgium, European government officials blasted Israel's supposed use of "disproportionate force" in Gaza, with Britain's deputy prime minister, Nick Clegg, going so far as to say that Israel's "response appears to be deliberately disproportionate. It is amounting now to a disproportionate form of collective punishment."[54]

The fact that Hamas was using Palestinian civilians as human shields, leading to countless Palestinian deaths, didn't matter. Nor did the fact that Israel went to such extraordinary lengths to avoid civilian casualties that the former commander of Britain's forces in Afghanistan said, "No army in the world acts with as much discretion and great care as the IDF [Israel Defense Forces] in order to minimize [civilian] damage."[55] Despite all the international hand-wringing about civilian deaths, an exhaustive Israeli study showed that the majority of Palestinians killed during Operation Protective Edge were, in fact, terrorists.[56] But Europe's elites had long since made up their minds. From the meeting rooms of Brussels to the newsrooms of the BBC, Israel was cast as a militarized, oppressive bully and the Palestinians as noble, helpless victims.

Not surprisingly, the increasingly hostile, condemnatory view held by European politicians and media outlets toward Israel has trickled down to the European public, culminating in large, widespread anti-Israel rallies across the continent during Operation Protective Edge. Tens of thousands of anti-Israel protestors, composed mostly of an unholy alliance of Islamists, pro-Palestinian activists, and hard leftists, took to the streets of European capitals to castigate not just the Jewish State but the Jewish people—in some of the most audacious displays of anti-Semitism that Europe had seen in decades. Here is just a small sampling:

- On July 26, 2014, Metropolitan Police estimated that as many as forty-five thousand demonstrators gathered outside the Israeli embassy in London to protest against Israel's operation against Hamas.[57] The rhetoric at that march and similar ones around the country was replete with calls to genocide:

> In Britain, peaceful protests against the violence have been marred by vile placards including one declaring: "Hitler you were right!"
>
> At a Central London march, protesters confronted a Jewish woman with her two young children and told them: "Burn in hell." ...
>
> Activists and supporters of the Palestinian cause gathered outside the Israeli embassy in Kensington, west London, before marching towards Parliament Square.
>
> Carrying Palestinian flags and placards with slogans such as Stop the Killing and Free Palestine, the protesters chanted "Israel is a terror state", "Gaza don't you cry, we will never let you die" and "Allahu Akbar" (god is great).[58]

Over one hundred hate crimes were committed against Jews in Great Britain in July 2014, more than double the usual number.[59]

- A modern-day pogrom broke out in the "Little Jerusalem" section of Paris on July 27, 2014. Protestors chanted, "Gas the Jews" and "Kill the

Jews" while attacking Jewish-owned businesses and torching cars.[60] Similarly, in the Paris suburb of Sarcelles, a "400-strong mob" firebombed a synagogue and "smashed and looted" kosher stores. Chants of "Death to the Jews" and "Slit Jews' throats" filled the air, and similar murderous epithets adorned banners waved by members of the mob.[61] This type of Kristallnacht-like violence exploded across France, with no less than eight synagogues attacked throughout the country in the span of one week in July 2014.[62] France currently has Europe's largest Jewish population, at an estimated five hundred thousand. But Jews are now leaving France in droves thanks to rampant Muslim-driven anti-Semitism, with many making their way to Israel.[63]

■ You'd think that Germany, the country where Kristallnacht and the Holocaust were perpetrated not so long ago, would be especially vigilant in guarding against open displays of anti-Semitism. Yet during a series of large pro-Palestinian protests across Germany in July 2014, Israelis were compared to Nazis and Operation Protective Edge to the Holocaust. That was some of the tamer rhetoric. At one rally in Berlin, Muslim protestors pumped their fists in the air and chanted, "Jew, Jew, cowardly swine, come out and fight on your own!" Cries of "Hamas Hamas Jews to the gas!" were heard at demonstrations in Dortmund and Frankfurt, and one Berlin imam called on Allah to "destroy the Zionist Jews.... Count them and kill them, to the very last one."[64] These Hitler-esque outbursts set off alarm bells in Germany's Jewish community. Dieter Graumann, president of Germany's Central Council of Jews, told the *Guardian*, "These are the worst times [for Germany's Jews] since the Nazi era."[65]

European Muslims were the most sizable and vocal group at all of the above-mentioned anti-Semitic hatefests—including, no doubt, a high percentage of ISIS sympathizers. Anyone who watched the mass continent-wide rallies had to realize that Islam was in Europe to stay—and not a moderate, rational, Westernized Islam. No, this was radical Islamism: raw, unadulterated, and in-your-face. The recent emergence of ISIS has only intensified this troubling trend, which had been percolating in Europe for years.

In early 2009, as an earlier round of violent anti-Israel protests erupted in Europe during Israel's Operation Cast Lead in Gaza (an operation meant to—you guessed it—stop sustained barrages of Hamas rocket fire at Israeli civilian centers), I interviewed Cliff May, a former *New York Times* correspondent who is now president of the Foundation for Defense of Democracies in Washington, D.C.

"It's unclear whether there is a future for Jews in Europe—I would go that far," May told me. "But it's unclear whether there is a future for Europeans in Europe as well."

The future is looking quite bright, however, for ISIS and its radical adherents, who are multiplying daily across Europe.

CHAPTER EIGHT

AMERICA FIDDLES
AND THE WORLD BURNS

"FROM HERE, THEY COULD HIT BEN GURION AIRPORT."

I was standing on the mountains of Samaria—an area of Israel that the Obama administration and most of the world calls "the West Bank"— with an Israeli local who wanted to show me their strategic importance. It was early December 2012 and "Operation Pillar of Defense," a week-long Israeli military action against Hamas terrorists in Gaza, had just recently ended. The "international community" had a solution it was touting to prevent another round of hostilities—the same one it has been demanding for decades. Israel must hand over Samaria and the neighboring area of Judea to the Palestinians. And it must do so immediately.

"You can see Tel Aviv right there in the distance," said my Israeli guide as he motioned with his hand. "And of course, Ben Gurion Airport is there. If we hand Judea and Samaria over to the Palestinians, Hamas will move in. And instead of shooting rockets at Israel from Gaza, which is flat, they'll be able to move their rockets onto these mountains and have a perfect view of Israel below. Tel Aviv—and Ben Gurion—will then be hit with a barrage of rockets. There is no doubt."

Tel Aviv, Israel's second-largest city, with over four hundred thousand residents, lies on the coastal plain where some 70 percent of the total Israeli population is situated. Ben Gurion International, which is located in Tel Aviv, is Israel's lone commercial airport. Targeting Tel Aviv and forcing a shutdown of Ben Gurion Airport for any extended period of time would cripple the Israeli economy and ruin the country's vital tourism industry.

Hamas is already rapidly approaching the ability to do just that from its Gaza stronghold. During its summer 2014 war against Israel, the terror group fired long-range rockets out of Gaza that reached deep into Israeli territory, well beyond Tel Aviv. When one of the rockets fell a mile away from Ben Gurion Airport on July 22, 2014, the Obama administration and some European countries temporarily canceled commercial flights to Israel, citing safety concerns. Israeli government officials were furious— some called the flight bans a victory for terror. And they were right. Hamas and other regional terror groups now realized that firing rockets that fall even a full mile away from Ben Gurion Airport is enough to make Western governments essentially abandon Israel in its time of need. Talk about psychological jihad.

The flight ban decision was particularly inexplicable given that Israel's Iron Dome missile defense system had shot down about 90 percent of all the rockets Hamas had fired at civilian and strategic areas during the conflict.[1] And in any case, the Obama administration had never enacted a total ban on commercial flights—as it did with Israel—when it came to the airspace above hotspots such as North Korea, Syria, Yemen, Pakistan (the scene of attempted terrorist attacks on commercial airports in the months leading up to the Israel-Hamas war), Ukraine (where pro-Russian separatists shot a commercial flight out of the sky the *very same month* as the Israel flight ban), and Iraq. Warnings, yes—but not total bans. According to retired Naval Intelligence officer J. E. Dyer, "The prohibition on Ben Gurion is uniquely stringent, and inconsistent with FAA [Federal Aviation

Administration] practices elsewhere. It also had to be approved by Obama. Israel is an ally, one of America's closest partners in the world. Cutting off her commercial airport from U.S. carriers is inherently a presidential-level decision, and Obama is responsible whether he made it or not."[2]

So why would President Obama, who doggedly refused to ban commercial flights into the U.S. from Ebola-affected countries in Africa, approve the FAA's decision on Israel and defend it as "prudent"?[3] Could it have been retaliation for Israel's defiance of the Obama administration's demands that it reach a ceasefire with Hamas—the same Hamas that had already broken repeated ceasefires during the conflict and continued to fire rocket after rocket at Israeli population centers and kill Israeli soldiers? Was the Obama administration's move, as Republican Senator Ted Cruz suggested, tantamount to an "economic boycott" and a not-so-subtle message to Israel to fall in line and get with the Obama foreign policy program, which includes the establishment of a Palestinian state?[4] Cruz, who threatened to block all State Department appointees until he got answers regarding the Israel flight ban, also pointed out that the Obama administration had recently rewarded the Palestinians with a $47 million aid package—aid, he said, that was "in effect $47 million for Hamas."[5]

Rest assured that Hamas and other jihadists heard the administration's message loud and clear: America punishes its friends and rewards its foes. As a result, the enemies of Israel—and America—were emboldened yet again.

Israel also undoubtedly got the memo—and the delicious irony is that the Obama administration's flight ban made the Palestinian state that Obama, Europe, and the UN are demanding even less likely. After all, if one rocket out of Gaza that fell a mile from Ben Gurion International Airport can cause a commercial flight ban and harm the Israeli economy, what would thousands of rockets fired by Hamas and other Palestinian terror groups from the high ground of Judea and Samaria do? Israel, which is roughly the size of New Jersey, has seen the disastrous effects of past withdrawals from southern Lebanon and Gaza in the form of thousands of rockets rained down upon its cities by Hezbollah and Hamas, respectively. Needless to say, a new Palestinian terror state on the so-called West Bank is not a very appealing option.

Why would Israel hand over these strategically vital mountain areas to a Palestinian people (including Mahmoud Abbas's supposedly "moderate" Palestinian Authority, a hotbed of anti-Semitic, pro-terror incitement) that have shown no inclination toward peace and refuse even to recognize Israel's right to exist? Should not Jews have a right to live in the biblical heartland of Judea and Samaria, of all places, regions mentioned throughout the Old and New Testaments, where the Jewish patriarchs Abraham, Isaac, and Jacob lived—and where King David ruled (from Hebron, in Judea) before moving his capital to Jerusalem three thousand years ago? The three hundred fifty thousand–plus Jews currently living in Judea and Samaria are called "illegal settlers"—and yet their ancestors settled those same lands thousands of years ago.

The West's frequently condescending treatment of Israel—the only free, Western-style democracy in the Middle East and a standard-bearer for Judeo-Christian civilization in a sea of Muslim tyranny—is shortsighted and self-defeating. For years, Israel has literally been on the front lines of the struggle against the very same jihadists who have declared war against the United States and Europe. Islamic terror attacks like the ones in Paris, Ottawa, and Boston that have caused so much consternation in the West in recent years are a regular occurrence in Israel, where Palestinian terrorists practically invented the kind of "chip away," lone wolf jihadi assaults discussed in chapter three.

Americans and Europeans may be stunned by this jihadist barbarism, but Israel, sadly, has grown quite used to it and knows exactly how to deal with it—not with rosy "Islam is peace" platitudes and half measures but with force and steely resolve. Here's just a small sampling of what the state of Israel was experiencing at the same time that ISIS was surging across the Middle East and leaving a trail of severed heads in its wake during 2014:

- On June 12, 2014, Hamas operatives kidnapped and murdered three Israeli teenagers—including sixteen-year-old
Naftali Fraenkel, a U.S. citizen. The killings helped trigger
the third war between Israel and Hamas in a five-year span.
As we have seen, "Operation Protective Edge" was the
Israeli campaign designed to stop Hamas and Palestinian
Islamic Jihad rocket barrages against Israeli civilian centers
and to neutralize a vast network of underground "terror
tunnels" that Hamas had dug from Gaza into Israeli territory, some of which were reportedly designed to carry out
mass terror attacks against civilians in southern Israel.[6]
- On August 4, in Jerusalem, a Palestinian man driving a
tractor ran over and killed one Israeli pedestrian and
injured several more before crashing into a public bus and
overturning it. The terrorist was shot and killed by Israeli
police.[7]
- On October 22, a Palestinian in a car careened into a Jerusalem Light Rail station, killing two people—including a
three-month-old Israeli girl with dual American citizenship—and injuring several more before being shot and
killed by Israeli police.[8]
- On October 29, in an assassination attempt in Jerusalem, a
Palestinian man shot and critically wounded Rabbi Yehuda
Glick, an activist who advocates for Jews to be able to pray
on the Temple Mount, the holiest site in Judaism—which is
now the site of the Dome of the Rock, a Muslim shrine, and
the Al-Aqsa Mosque, the site from which Muslims believe
Mohammed ascended to heaven on his Night Journey.[9]
They believe this despite the fact that Jerusalem is never
mentioned in the Koran (while it is mentioned literally
hundreds of times in the Bible).

- On November 5, in Jerusalem, a Hamas operative plowed a van into a group of Israeli Border Patrol forces and pedestrians, killing one person and injuring at least fourteen more. He was shot and killed by police, but not before exiting the van and attempting to attack more pedestrians with a metal rod.[10]
- On November 10, a twenty-six-year-old woman waiting at a bus stop was run over and then stabbed to death by a Palestinian man in Gush Etzion, in Judea.[11]
- On November 18, two Palestinian men stormed into a Jerusalem synagogue and used a meat cleaver and a gun to murder five worshipers, including three dual U.S.-Israeli citizens, before being shot and killed by Israeli police.[12]

Israel has been suffering through these types of atrocities on a regular basis for *decades*, often at the hands of Hamas. Like ISIS, Hamas is a ruthless terrorist organization that revels in the slaughter of innocent men, women, and children. And although Hamas is focused, first and foremost, on wiping Israel off the map, it shares ISIS's goal of a global Islamic caliphate. Also like ISIS, Hamas is an avowed enemy of the United States and has murdered American citizens.[13] The fact is, Israel's enemies are the West's enemies—we face common foes.

Indeed, Israel is the prime target not just of Palestinian terrorist groups. It is also squarely in the crosshairs of ISIS and al Qaeda, the same global jihadist organizations that are devoted to America's destruction.

- As we saw in chapter two, Ansar Beit al-Maqdis, a jihadi group based in Egypt's Sinai Peninsula, along Israel's southern border, has pledged allegiance to the Islamic State and has a history of carrying out cross-border attacks against Israel.

- ISIS sympathizers are also active to Israel's north, in Lebanon, and to Israel's south, in Gaza—where some Palestinians are reportedly leaving Hamas to join what they view as the more extreme Islamic State.[14]
- In December 2014, three local jihadist groups based in southern Syria reportedly pledged allegiance to ISIS, meaning that "For the first time since the Syrian civil war began in early 2011, Islamic State...has gained a presence near the border with Israel on the Golan Heights."[15]
- Likewise, the al-Nusra Front, al Qaeda's affiliate in Syria, also controls territory along the Syrian side of the Golan Heights, on the Israeli border.[16]
- Israel also faces a growing number of ISIS sympathizers within its borders. In November 2014, Israeli authorities arrested three members of an ISIS-linked terror cell operating in the city of Hebron in Judea.[17] Israeli security services believe that over thirty Israeli Arabs have left the country to join ISIS.[18]

From ISIS to al Qaeda to Hamas to Hezbollah, tiny Israel is encircled by terrorist groups encamped on its borders and committed to its destruction. As we have seen, these existential enemies of Israel are also America's enemies, not to mention Europe's. You'd think that obvious fact—along with our shared Judeo-Christian heritage and democratic ideals—would be more than enough reason for Western governments to express solidarity with the Jewish State. Yet on November 18, 2014, just hours after the deadly attack by two Palestinian terrorists on worshipers in a Jerusalem synagogue, lawmakers in Spain's lower parliament voted overwhelmingly to recognize a Palestinian state—despite the Palestinians having proven again and again, through numberless acts of terror and incitement, that they are far from ready for, or deserving of, statehood.[19] Nevertheless, in a sign of naked antagonism toward Israel, the European Parliament and national legislatures in Britain, Ireland, France, and Sweden have joined Spain in recognizing the state of "Palestine."[20]

As for the Obama administration, it has at times shown the Israelis open hostility, culminating in December 2014 with reports that it was even considering sanctions against Israel for continuing to build homes in Jerusalem (in areas of the city that the White House believes should be part of a future Palestinian state).[21] Ordering Israelis not to build homes in Jerusalem—considered by the Jewish people to be their eternal capital for the past three thousand years—is like forbidding Americans from buying property in New York City or Washington, D.C.

But for the Obama administration, when something goes wrong in the Middle East—which is often, particularly since President Obama took office—it's invariably somehow Israel's fault. Incredibly, the administration has even found a way to blame Israel for the rise of ISIS. At a White House ceremony marking the Muslim holiday Eid al-Adha in October 2014, Secretary of State John Kerry suggested that the lack of a peace deal between Israel and the Palestinians was helping to fuel ISIS recruitment. "As I went around and met with people in the course of our discussions about [building a coalition against ISIS]," Kerry said, "…there wasn't a leader I met with in the region who didn't raise with me spontaneously the need to try to get peace between Israel and the Palestinians, because it was a cause of recruitment and of street anger and agitation that they felt they had to respond to."[22] In other words, America's top diplomat believes thousands of jihadists from around the world are flocking to Syria and Iraq and chopping off the heads of Christians, Yazidis, and Kurds partly because they're angry that there is no Palestinian state.

Kerry is far from the only administration official wallowing in ignorance when it comes to the ISIS threat. On June 29, 2011, CIA Director John Brennan—who at the time was a senior adviser to President Obama—

declared, "Our strategy is…shaped by a deeper understanding of al Qaeda's goals, strategy, and tactics. I'm not talking about al Qaeda's grandiose vision of global domination through a violent Islamic caliphate. *That vision is absurd, and we are not going to organize our counterterrorism policies against a feckless delusion that is never going to happen.* We are not going to elevate these thugs and their murderous aspirations into something larger than they are [emphasis added]."[23]

Except that al Qaeda's vision of a caliphate *did* happen. And ironically enough, as terrorism expert Thomas Joscelyn pointed out in the *Weekly Standard*, it all came to fruition on June 29, 2014—exactly "three years later to the day" after Brennan had said the revival of the caliphate was an "absurd" pipe dream.

Major General Michael K. Nagata, who commands U.S. Special Operations forces in the Middle East, convened a diverse panel of experts over the summer of 2014 to try to understand what makes ISIS so successful. His concern: "We do not understand the movement, and until we do, we are not going to defeat it. We have not defeated the idea. We do not even understand the idea."[24]

Nagata's admission was stunning. We're a full fourteen years from the 9/11 attacks, yet Nagata and other leaders and decision makers in the United States still don't understand "the idea" behind the Islamic State? A major reason for this lack of understanding is a knee-jerk refusal to acknowledge any connection between Islamic terror and Islam. President Obama leads the way (for once) in this regard with his repeated declarations that ISIS is "not Islamic." But he is far from alone on the political left. After Islamic terrorists with links to al Qaeda and ISIS slaughtered seventeen people in separate incidents over three days in France in January 2015, former Democratic National Committee chairman Howard Dean appeared on MSNBC (a fitting venue) and declared, "I stopped calling these people Muslim terrorists. They're about as Muslim as I am. I mean, they have no respect for anybody else's life, that's not what the Koran says…. I think

ISIS is a cult. Not an Islamic cult. I think it's a cult."[25] Thus sayeth Howard Dean, professor of Islamic Studies and Koranic expert (not). This is a man whose religious knowledge is so profound that he once said his favorite book in the New Testament was the Book of Job. (Only, the Book of Job is found in the Old Testament.)[26]

In completely disassociating acts of Islamic terrorism from Islamic teachings, Dean, President Obama, and their far left, progressive ilk not only violate the first rule of war—know your enemy—they take things a dangerous step further by refusing even to identify who the enemy is. For example, in the wake of the jihadist attacks in Paris, President Obama announced plans to hold a "Summit on Countering Violent Extremism" in February 2015. The title of the event perfectly encapsulates the West's head-in-the-sand approach to the problem. "Violent extremists" have not declared war on the United States—Islamic jihadists have. Being able to admit that fact is a start. Getting around to educating the American people about the jihadist threat and preparing them for a difficult struggle against it would be the next step, because if you don't understand your enemy—its strengths, weaknesses, and ideology—you cannot defeat it. Uniting the American people and laying out a clear strategy to defeat jihadism would follow. It's called leadership. Unfortunately, that's a quality currently in very short supply in Washington, D.C.

On January 11, 2014, over forty world leaders, including British Prime Minister David Cameron, German Chancellor Angela Merkel, King Abdullah II of Jordan, and Israeli Prime Minister Benjamin Netanyahu, gathered in Paris to join French President Francois Hollande and well over one million French citizens (seven million including other locations nationwide) in a massive solidarity march against Islamic terrorism.[27] Yet the man who is supposed to be the Leader of the Free World was conspicuous by his absence. President Obama not only skipped the Paris rally—he didn't even bother to send a top administration official such as Vice President Joe Biden or Secretary of State John Kerry to represent the

United States (Attorney General Eric Holder was actually in Paris during the event yet did not attend).[28] Sending a high-level American official to the march would have been a forceful statement by the president that America fully realizes that the West is locked in a generational struggle against the rapidly growing threat of radical Islam—and a declaration that the most powerful country in the world will stand together in solidarity with its allies to defeat the jihadist enemy, no matter the cost. Instead, President Obama and his cabinet were glaringly, embarrassingly MIA. It's not hard to figure out why.

For starters, any rally that spotlighted the menace that Islamic terrorism—not "violent extremism"—posed to the world didn't pass the president's "Islam is peace/the terrorists are not Muslims" test. Obama had spent years assuring us that al Qaeda was decimated, that Iraq was pacified, and that the world was, in his words, "less violent" and more stable, safe, tolerant, and peaceful than it has ever been.[29] He had even given a speech at the National Defense University in May 2013 declaring that the "Global War on Terror" was essentially over.[30] Besides, it was his second term—meaning he only had a short time left to focus on domestic issues and complete the task of "fundamentally transforming the United States of America," something he vowed to do before being elected in 2008.[31] Then along came the ISIS juggernaut, a resurgent al Qaeda, and a steady wave of deadly jihadist attacks on Western soil. All of a sudden, it was painfully clear that the president had been wrong all along. The Islamic terrorist threat was not receding—it was metastasizing in every corner of the globe, thanks in part to his policies. And he had no coherent strategy—and worse, no desire—to lead the fight against it. In other words, forget Paris.

■　　　■　　　■

"I say and repeat again that we are in need of a religious revolution."

Coming from the Muslim head of state of the most populous and influential Arab nation, the words were nothing less than earth shattering. On January 1, 2015, at a prestigious, high profile venue that some have called the "Muslim Vatican," Egyptian President Abdel Fattah al-Sisi gave one of the most courageous and visionary speeches in recent memory. The event at Cairo's famed al-Azhar University commemorated the birthday of Islam's prophet Mohammed. Al-Sisi used the occasion to directly challenge Egypt's top Islamic authorities, who were in attendance, to lead what the civilized world (including some secular Muslims) has been calling for ever since 9/11—a reformation of Islam:

> I am referring here to the religious clerics. We have to think hard about what we are facing—and I have, in fact, addressed this topic a couple of times before. It's inconceivable that the thinking that we hold most sacred should cause the entire umma [Islamic world] to be a source of anxiety, danger, killing and destruction for the rest of the world. Impossible!
>
> That thinking—I am not saying "religion" but "thinking"—that corpus of texts and ideas that we have sacralized over the centuries, to the point that departing from them has become almost impossible, is antagonizing the entire world. It's antagonizing the entire world!
>
> Is it possible that 1.6 billion people [Muslims] should want to kill the rest of the world's inhabitants—that is 7 billion—so that they themselves may live? Impossible!
>
> I am saying these words here at Al Azhar, before this assembly of scholars and ulema—Allah Almighty be witness to your truth on Judgment Day concerning that which I'm talking about now.
>
> All this that I am telling you, you cannot feel it if you remain trapped within this mindset. You need to step outside

of yourselves to be able to observe it and reflect on it from a more enlightened perspective.

I say and repeat again that we are in need of a religious revolution. You, imams, are responsible before Allah. The entire world, I say it again, the entire world is waiting for your next move...because this umma is being torn, it is being destroyed, it is being lost—and it is being lost by our own hands.[32]

Finally. A prominent Muslim leader, caretaker of what is arguably the most prominent Muslim nation, stands up and tells the unvarnished truth about the state of his religion. And he does so in front of a roomful of powerful imams and Islamic religious scholars at al-Azhar University, considered the most influential educational institution in the Muslim world (and a hotbed of anti-Western and anti-Semitic thought).

Islam expert Raymond Ibrahim, an Egyptian-American Coptic Christian, explained the significance of al-Sisi's statements: "...one must appreciate how refreshing it is for a top political leader in the heart of the Islamic world to make such candid admissions that his Western counterparts dare not even think let alone speak. And bear in mind, Sisi has much to lose as opposed to Western politicians. Calls by the Muslim Brotherhood and other Islamists that he is an apostate are sure to grow more aggressive now."[33]

To label someone an "apostate" in the Islamic world is to mark him for death. Al-Sisi, a practicing Muslim, knows this. He has already drawn the eternal ire of Egypt's Islamists for his sweeping crackdown on the Muslim Brotherhood. But that hasn't stopped him from smashing the Brotherhood, working closely with Israel, cracking down on Hamas's smuggling tunnels along the Gaza-Egypt border, and calling for the aforementioned Islamic reformation. Just days after his groundbreaking speech at al-Azhar, al-Sisi again made history—and angered Islamists everywhere—by becoming the first Egyptian president to attend mass at a Coptic Christian church. His appearance alongside the Coptic Pope came as Egypt's Copts were celebrating their Christmas Eve. Al-Sisi told the congregation, "It's important for the world to see this scene, which reflects true Egyptian unity, and to confirm that we're all Egyptians, first and foremost. We truly love each other without discrimination, because this is the Egyptian truth."[34]

Sounds like the kind of Muslim leader the West has been waiting for, right? Bold, reasonable, and forthright. Yet the mainstream media in the United States virtually ignored al-Sisi's al-Azhar speech for days. And the Obama administration, instead of holding up al-Sisi's statements as a model for Muslims everywhere to emulate, had not a word to say about it, at least publicly. Because the Obama White House does not like al-Sisi one bit. It balked when al-Sisi led a popular coup against Mohammed Morsi's Muslim Brotherhood regime in July 2013—despite the fact that Morsi was clearly taking the country in a disastrous Islamist direction, and that some thirty million Egyptians were in the streets demanding his ouster. And the administration has decried al-Sisi's subsequent harsh crackdown on the Brotherhood, which has seen the Islamist movement crippled in its Egyptian birthplace thanks to mass arrests and trials of its members by the al-Sisi government.

You'd think a U.S. president would consider the weakening of the Muslim Brotherhood—an anti-American, anti-Semitic organization that spawned al Qaeda, Hamas, and the entire modern jihadist movement—a good thing. The Obama White House, however, has made clear that it is deeply unhappy with al-Sisi's moves against the Brotherhood, to the point that it suspended much-needed military aid to Egypt—aid that would have been used, no doubt, to bolster the Egyptian military's fight against terrorism on its soil, including the jihadist hotbed of Sinai.[35] As of this writing, it appeared that the aid would be restored by Congress.[36] But the damage to the U.S.-Egypt relationship has been done. I've spent time with Egyptian officials who are perplexed by the Obama administration's continued defense of the Muslim Brotherhood. Why, they wonder, is President Obama going to the mat for a caliphate-craving organization that hates America and whose ideology has inspired terrorism throughout the world? It's tough to find an answer. Rest assured, without the creation of the Muslim Brotherhood in Egypt in 1928, there would be no ISIS today. And while al-Sisi may not be a Western-style democrat, he's clearly the best option, by far, in a chaotic Egypt, and a man with whom the West—and Israel—can do business.

Still, one gets the distinct feeling that the Obama administration would be thrilled to see Mohammed Morsi—who, as of this writing, was awaiting trial in Egypt for murder and other charges—back in power.[37] As I documented extensively in my 2013 book, *The Brotherhood*, the Obama administration has been advised by radical Islamist organizations including the Council on American-Islamic Relations (CAIR) and the Islamic Society of North America (ISNA), which have been tied to the Muslim Brotherhood by federal prosecutors.[38] In November 2014, CAIR, along with another U.S-based Brotherhood front, the Muslim American Society, were named terrorist organizations by the United Arab Emirates, ostensibly for their ties to the Brotherhood (which the UAE also designated as a terror organization).[39] The Obama administration, predictably, decried the move and pressured the UAE to reverse it.[40] After all, it doesn't look good for the president when Islamic groups whose members have been frequent visitors to the White House are branded terrorist organizations—and by a Muslim nation, to boot.[41]

Then there are Turkey and Qatar, the world's two biggest backers of the Muslim Brotherhood—and, incidentally, two of the Obama administration's closest allies in the Middle East. Turkey's Islamist president (formerly prime minister) Recep Tayyip Erdogan has demanded that Morsi be put back in power—no surprise, given that Erdogan's ruling Justice and Development Party (AKP) is essentially the Turkish Muslim Brotherhood.[42] And prior to Morsi's ouster, Qatar was seen as the Brotherhood's biggest cheerleader and backer in the region. Both Turkey and Qatar have also been staunch supporters of the Brotherhood's Palestinian branch,

Hamas. Qatar has been the terror group's main financier and played host to its political leadership[43] while Turkey has given safe haven to top Hamas operative Salah al-Arouri—who has allegedly directed Hamas terror attacks against Israeli civilians from his Turkish safe haven.[44]

As of this writing, there are signs that Qatar, which has seen the Muslim Brotherhood movement severely weakened throughout the region since 2013, may be changing its tune and distancing itself from the Brothers while attempting a rapprochement with its Gulf neighbors and al-Sisi's Egypt.[45] How a potential Qatari realignment will turn out remains to be seen. What is clear, however, is that Turkey remains unrepentant and continues to openly embrace Hamas.[46]

But Hamas isn't the only reason a bipartisan group of two dozen members of the U.S. Congress have called for Turkey and Qatar to be sanctioned over support for terrorism.[47] Both countries have also poured untold amounts of money (and in Turkey's case, arms) into Syria to help rebel groups fighting against the Assad regime. Some of the reported recipients of that Turkish and Qatari assistance are terrorist groups—the al Qaeda–affiliated al-Nusra Front chief among them.[48] And ISIS may also be benefiting. According to the *Wall Street Journal*, "The U.S. Treasury [Department]...has increasingly voiced concerns about the alleged flow of Qatari money to Mideast militants, including Islamic State, Nusra Front and al Qaeda.... The Obama administration hasn't publicly charged Qatar's government of directly making these payments, but rather says it has been lax in regulating the finances of Qatari nationals, charities and Islamic organizations. Treasury officials allege one wealthy Qatari businessman late last year transferred $2 million to a senior Islamic State commander in Syria who was in charge of recruiting foreign fighters."[49]

Nevertheless, "The Obama administration has made Qatar one of its closest diplomatic partners" in the Middle East."[50] Ditto for Turkey, which, along with Qatar, was the Obama administration's preferred mediator (despite Israel's strenuous objections and Turkey's clear pro-Hamas sympathies) to broker a ceasefire between Israel and Hamas during the summer of 2014.[51] To say that Turkey, a NATO member, is also playing a problematic role in the fight against ISIS would be an understatement. An extensive November 2014 report by the Foundation for Defense of Democracies called "Bordering on Terrorism: Turkey's Syria Policy and the Rise of the Islamic State" laid out the ugly details:

> The IS [Islamic State] crisis has put Turkey and the U.S. on a collision course. Turkey refuses to allow the coalition to launch military strikes from its soil. Its military also merely looked on while IS besieged the Kurdish town of Kobani, just across its border. Turkey negotiated directly with IS in the summer of 2013 to release 49 Turks held by the terrorist group. In return, Ankara reportedly secured the release of 180 IS fighters, many of whom returned to the battlefield. Meanwhile, the border continues to serve as a transit point for the illegal sale of oil, the transfer of weapons, and the flow of foreign fighters. Inside Turkey, IS has also established cells for recruiting militants and other logistical operations. All of this has raised questions about Turkey's value as an American ally, and its place in the NATO alliance.[52]

With friends like these, who needs enemies? In the upside down world of President Obama, fire-breathing, terror-sponsoring radical Islamists like Turkey's President Erdogan can be reasoned with and allied with to fight *against* terrorism.

It's a strange principle, but how else to explain the Obama administration's receptivity to the world's number one state sponsor of terrorism pitching in to help battle ISIS in Iraq? Yes, Iran has undergone quite the image rehabilitation during President Obama's time in office. Mind you, the Iranian regime continues to brazenly support U.S.-designated terrorist groups of all shapes and sizes, from its chief proxy Hezbollah to Hamas to Palestinian Islamic Jihad to al Qaeda and the Taliban.[53] Tehran's support for Islamic jihadists worldwide stretches across the Sunni-Shia divide and bridges any ideological or theological differences for the greater "good" of destroying the "Little Satan," Israel, and the "Great Satan," the United States—goals to which Iran remains rabidly committed. To drive that point home, an Iranian general said in January 2015, "Our ideal is not [nuclear] centrifuges but the destruction of the White House and the annihilation of Zionism [Israel]."[54] As for the said centrifuges, Iran also refuses to relinquish its nuclear program, which has placed the terror regime on the threshold of acquiring a nuclear bomb.[55]

The Obama administration's response to this Iranian intransigence has been not only to give Iran repeated, undeserved extensions in ongoing nuclear talks with the P5+1 nations (the U.S, Britain, France, China, Russia, and Germany) but to raise hopes that Iran—which is clearly buying time and hoodwinking the West as it inches ever closer to nuclear weapons capability—can be a responsible actor on the world stage, despite every indication to the contrary. In a December 2014 interview with National Public Radio, President Obama said of the possibility of re-opening a U.S. embassy in Tehran, "I never say never, but I think these things have to go in steps." He then went a step further, stating, "[The Iranians] have a path to break through that isolation and they should seize it. Because if they do, there's incredible talent and resources and sophistication . . . inside of Iran, and it would be a very successful regional power that was also abiding by international norms and international rules, and that would be good for everybody."[56]

Yes, I'm sure that the Israelis—not to mention Saudi Arabia, Jordan, and Egypt—believe that having (unapologetically genocidal, jihadist) Iran as a "very successful regional power" would be just grand. Don't look now, but that's exactly the reality the Obama administration seems determined to create—to the point that it has tacitly accepted an Iranian role in the fight against ISIS. According to the *Washington Post*, "the two nations' arms-length alliance against the Islamic State is an uncomfortable reality":

Iranian military involvement has dramatically increased in Iraq…as Tehran has delivered desperately needed aid to Baghdad in its fight against Islamic State militants, say U.S., Iraqi and Iranian sources. In the eyes of Obama administration officials, equally concerned about the rise of the brutal Islamist group, that's an acceptable role—for now.… A senior Iranian cleric with close ties to Tehran's leadership, who spoke on the condition of anonymity to discuss security matters, said that since the Islamic State's capture of much of northern Iraq in June, Iran has sent more than 1,000 military advisers to Iraq, as well as elite units, and has conducted airstrikes and spent more than $1 billion on military aid.[57]

Iran is not opposed to the Islamic State out of any sort of noble indignation over ISIS's brutality or tactics (Iran itself executed 852 people during one recent eleven-month span).[58] Rather, Iran sees ISIS as a direct challenge to its goal of regional supremacy—particularly since ISIS is hell-bent on removing any trace of Iran's Shia brand of Islam from the Middle East. Iran, just like ISIS, desires to lead a confederation of Islamic nations (in Iran's case an "Imamate," or Shia-style caliphate, led by the Iranian Supreme Leader) that would confront Israel and the West. At the end of the day, ISIS and Iran, despite profound differences in some areas, are both notorious purveyors of terrorism that essentially want the same exact thing. Yet the Obama administration, by employing an all-carrot-and-no-stick strategy with Iran that would make Neville Chamberlain blush, has in effect decided to hand the keys of the Middle East over to the terror masters in Tehran—while conceding whatever territory Iran doesn't gobble up to what has become Washington's chief ally in the region, the Muslim Brotherhood. The MB movement across the region has unquestionably taken massive hits since 2013, and it is on life support in Egypt. But like jihadi vampires, the Brothers, throughout their bloody history, have always seemed to find a way to rise from the dead.

And the Obama administration's policies may one day help them to do exactly that.

■   ■   ■

President Obama's isolation of Israel and Egypt and embrace of Turkey, Qatar, and Iran is instructive as we consider the future of ISIS. If the United States, under the Obama administration, cannot distinguish between the enemies of Islamic terrorism and its supporters, little promises to change before the president leaves office in 2016. Indeed, the ISIS crisis—and the broader assault by global jihadists against the West—promises only to intensify in President Obama's remaining years in office. Unfortunately, as we've seen repeatedly on the president's watch, when it comes to matters of national and global security, a great amount of damage, some of it irreversible, can be inflicted in a short amount of time.

Here are some trends to watch for in the near future as ISIS continues its march across the Middle East—and its supporters multiply here in the West:

- "Lone wolf" jihadi terrorism carried out by ISIS and al Qaeda sympathizers will remain a persistent and deadly problem for Western democracies. At the same time, Western citizens who have trained with ISIS in Syria and Iraq could very well return home under the direction of their terror overlords and conduct increasingly professional attacks against soft civilian targets as well as harder targets, including law enforcement and the military. The January 2015 terror attacks in France—carried out, in part, by two brothers who had trained with al Qaeda in

Yemen—is a frightening glimpse of what could be in store. Following those attacks, ISIS embarked on a wide-ranging social media campaign glorifying the carnage in France and calling on each Muslim in the West "to act as a 'city wolf' and kill co-workers and fellow commuters."[59] In other words, random attacks against random civilians in Western cities. Clearly, the eventual goal of the jihadists is nothing less than a full-scale guerilla war on Western soil.

- If, as seems probable, terrorism in Europe increases and European governments continue to refuse to take the necessary steps to combat it, European citizens will become increasingly outraged. The culture clash between Europe and Islam could, in some cases, descend into violence between Europe's large Muslim immigrant communities and the indigenous populations. Anti-Semitic violence in Europe will also continue to worsen, much of it at the hands of Muslim immigrants. And as European leaders show a lack of will to combat this ancient poison, Jews will leave the continent in increasing numbers. The exodus from France has already begun.

- ISIS, while consolidating most of the areas already under its control, will continue to explore ways to expand its caliphate. Look for continued incursions into Lebanon and probing along the Jordanian and Saudi borders (which, as we saw in chapter two, is already happening). Jordan and Saudi Arabia would be tough nuts for ISIS to crack, and they can count on strong support from the U.S. (and Israel, in Jordan's case) were the Islamic State to make serious moves inside their territory. Yes, even the impotent Obama administration would have no choice but to intervene (with no ground troops, of course) to stave off an ISIS advance if Jordan or Saudi Arabia were threatened. After all, the Democrats have an election to win in 2016.

- Again, especially if ISIS continues to stall in northern Iraq, look for it to embark on new adventures elsewhere, whether in Lebanon, Saudi Arabia (Mecca, Medina, and all that Saudi crude would suit the caliphate just fine), Jordan (all that separates ISIS from Israel), and Syria (as of this writing, ISIS continues to advance around Damascus and near the Israeli border). In addition, ISIS's fierce battle to control Iraq's Anbar province could be crucial in its plans to eventually turn its sights on Baghdad. In October 2014, ISIS made it within 15.5 miles of the Baghdad International Airport before being turned back[60]—and it promises to continue to soften up the Iraqi capital through a campaign of shelling and suicide bombings.

- Iran and the Iraqi Shia militias under its sway would fiercely resist any ISIS encroachment on the historic city, and they could count on heavy U.S. air support. Baghdad, needless to say, would be another very tough nut for ISIS to crack. But given the recent history of the Middle East, "never say never" is a good rule of thumb. It's a safe bet that no one— save a gaggle of "experts" inside the Beltway—will be completely shocked if the black flag of ISIS was one day flying above Baghdad.

- Look for ISIS to make a concerted effort to target U.S. forces in Iraq and shoot down Coalition planes in an attempt to nab hostages for propaganda value. As of this writing, ISIS was holding a Jordanian pilot whose plane had been shot down above Syria.[61]

- As the Obama administration withdraws U.S. troops from Afghanistan, it's a good bet that the country will descend into Iraq-style chaos, with jihadists running amok. Ominously, in January 2015 a group of Pakistani and Afghan jihadists who formerly belonged to the Taliban beheaded a captured Afghan soldier in a gruesome video in which they pledged allegiance to the Islamic State.[62] As of this writing, ISIS supporters had also reportedly made inroads in southern Afghanistan's Helmand province.[63] As we saw in chapter two, declarations of loyalty in diverse places around the world enable ISIS to establish caliphate satellites outside of its primary sphere of influence in Iraq and Syria. And as ISIS continues to achieve success, more followers will come.

- The cyber-jihad against the West will intensify, especially as ISIS and other jihadi groups continue to draw in tech-savvy Western recruits. On January 12, 2015, ISIS sympathizers were apparently able to hack into social media accounts of the U.S. military's Central Command, "posting threatening messages and propaganda videos, along with some military documents," including "contact information for senior military personnel."[64]

- The intensity and savagery of Islamic terrorism will descend to increasingly demonic depths. ISIS's audaciously violent emergence has seemingly inspired other Islamic terror groups to engage in greater and more shocking acts of carnage, including the Pakistani Taliban's slaughter of 150 schoolchildren in December 2014 and the Nigerian terror group Boko Haram's murder of some two thousand people in attacks across northern Nigeria in early January

2015.[65] Jihadists clearly do not believe in limited rules of engagement.

The strategies we should be implementing against ISIS and the global jihadist movement—both at home and abroad—remain depressingly similar to the solutions I suggested in the conclusion to my 2013 book, *The Brotherhood*, with some obvious updates. One thing has not changed: the extreme unlikelihood of any of these changes being enacted prior to President Obama's leaving office. Nevertheless, it's important for well-informed and patriotic Americans to resolve to take the steps we must eventually take if the global jihad embodied today by ISIS is to be defeated:

- Completely destroy ISIS militarily in Iraq and Syria so that it can never pose any semblance of a threat ever again. This would not only eliminate the most powerful terrorist movement in history—it would send a clear message to jihadists everywhere that the United States was through pulling punches and playing nice. I am not a military strategist. What I do know is that every credible military strategist I have spoken to, both on and off the record, over the past two years has told me unequivocally that ISIS cannot be totally defeated militarily without some level of involvement from U.S. ground forces—and in more than just an "advisory role." Whatever it takes.
- Educate the American people about jihadism and the nature of the threat ISIS poses and why it is absolutely crucial for America to defeat this movement at any cost. Start by naming the enemy—Islamic terrorism—and then take it from there.
- Revoke not only the passport but the citizenship of any American who fights for ISIS or any other terrorist group overseas so that he is never able to reenter the United States.

- Secure America's borders, particularly the egregiously porous southern border, which is like an E-ZPass for criminal elements who wish to enter the United States, including terrorists.
- Review and revise America's Visa Waiver program with Western European countries that have become hotbeds of Islamic terrorists.
- Bolster cooperation with Europe, Canada, Australia, Israel, Egypt, Jordan, and any other nation—Muslim or non-Muslim—that shows a sincere and committed desire to root out Islamic extremism.
- Isolate and pressure supposed "allies" that do not share that commitment—Turkey, Qatar, and Pakistan chief among them. Dishonorable mention goes to the Palestinian Authority and Saudi Arabia, whose help in the fight against ISIS and global jihadists should not be welcomed until they renounce their own shameful ongoing legacies of supporting terrorism when it suits their interests. I'm not holding my breath waiting for that unlikely day to come, and neither should you.
- Make clear to the Iranian regime that it is not an ally or friend, in the fight against ISIS or anywhere else. Actively work to foster regime change in Iran, the world's number one state sponsor of terrorism, through a variety of overt and covert means. And stop Iran from acquiring a nuclear weapon by any means necessary.
- Stand proudly and unflinchingly with Israel and the Jewish people worldwide, and with the persecuted, beleaguered Christians and other religious minorities of the Middle East, now besieged by Islamic jihadists.
- Stringently review all current U.S. immigration and student visa polices when it comes to Muslim nations.

- Ban all Muslim Brotherhood–connected groups operating on U.S. soil and neutralize any influence they have over American policy. The Brotherhood's ideology of martyrdom and jihad in pursuit of a caliphate has served as the gateway drug for far too many Islamic terrorists. Work to counter and de-glamorize that same jihadist ideology in American Muslim communities—ideally, with help from eloquent, patriotic Muslim moderates. I say that, however, with a very serious caveat: except for a few notable and courageous individuals, such as Dr. Zuhdi Jasser and former Egyptian Islamist Dr. Tawfik Hamid, moderate Muslims have just not spoken out publicly and forcefully in any significant numbers, despite the continuing jihadist onslaught. For example, why has no moderate Muslim activist organized a Million Muslim March against terrorism on the National Mall in the fourteen years that have passed since 9/11? Fear of retribution from their co-religionists is undoubtedly one major factor. Another problem is that the Obama administration has completely ignored moderate voices like those of Jasser and Hamid and instead given access and influence to jihad-supporting Muslim Brotherhood front groups.

- So we should support and encourage genuine Muslim reformers like Jasser and Hamid that want no part of jihad or sharia—while, at the same time, realizing that any sort of widespread, serious Muslim reformation remains a major long shot for the foreseeable future. If 9/11, London, Madrid, Fort Hood, Boston, Ottawa, Sydney, Paris, and the rise of ISIS weren't enough to bring millions of outraged Muslims into the streets in widespread anti-terrorism marches around the world, then what will be?

We have reached a tipping point in the battle against radical Islam. Future generations will look back on this period in history, much as we now look back on the Cold War and World War II, and judge us on how we confront the existential challenge of Islamic jihadism that has already changed the Western way of life in profound ways.

It's up to us whether our children and grandchildren will write the history of the first half of the twenty-first century as free men and women, or as slaves under a brutal system that shows no mercy, gives no quarter, and regards the very concepts of "freedom" and "democracy" with scorn.

ACKNOWLEDGMENTS

WRITING THREE BOOKS IN THE SPAN OF FOUR YEARS IS NO EASY task—especially when the subject matter is as dark as radical Islam and terrorism. Fortunately for me, I have been surrounded by an amazing group of people who have supported and loved me through all the ups and downs of putting together this "epic trilogy" on jihad, culminating in *ISIS Exposed*.

My beautiful wife, Lori, has once again been a rock, selflessly sacrificing and never complaining even though I was on a tight deadline with this book and life often intruded. Baby, your love, loyalty, and support through all the ups and downs of books—and life—are an endless blessing to me. There's no one else I would rather have by my side on this crazy journey. Thank you.

Every time I would wrap up another session writing about the horrors of ISIS, I would emerge from my office, a bit down, and have my lovely daughters Juliana and Leah eagerly waiting to pick me up and remind me that beauty, pure goodness, innocence, joy, and unconditional love still exist in this upside down world. Girls, you are the light of my life and my pride and joy. Thank you so much for your patience and understanding with Daddy's book writing. I thank God every day for both of you.

My researcher, Matthew Nieminski, was the perfect choice to work on this book. Matt's superior knowledge of the subject matter, combined with his relentless research and attention to detail, was simply invaluable and I am truly indebted. Every challenging research task Matt was given, he tackled enthusiastically, quickly, and without complaint, all while juggling other pressing commitments. His future is bright.

It is always a pleasure and an honor working with the team at Regnery Publishing. Marji Ross, Harry Crocker, and the team are approachable, patient, creative, and encouraging—for a writer, it doesn't get any better. I am extremely grateful. Special thanks go to my superb editor on this project, Elizabeth Kantor, who was always available for advice and insights and whose hard work, tweaks, and improvements on the book were irreplaceable. Thanks also go to Maria Ruhl for her contributions.

Eternal thanks go, as always, to my Mom, Agnes, my brother, Fred, and my sister, Judy, for their prayers, encouragement, support, and love during the writing of this book and throughout my life. Dad is very happy as he looks down on us.

A big thank you to CBN News' news director, Rob Allman, and Washington, D.C., bureau chief, Robin Mazyck, for their longtime friendship, guidance, and support, and the creative freedom they have given me on this and every other project I have pursued.

Thank you to Dr. Pat Robertson, Gordon Robertson, and Michael Little for the opportunity to work at an organization like CBN News that exposes radical Islam without apology. Thanks also to the CBN Partners for their love, prayers, and support of our vital work.

Thanks to the entire CBN News team in Washington, D.C., Virginia Beach, and Jerusalem: I am honored to work with such an incredible group of dedicated journalists who are also dear friends and prayer warriors.

Thanks also to Ian Rushing of Toy Box Productions, my frequent partner in crime in exposing the bad guys around the world.

Many thanks to Ryan Mauro, Wim Kortenoeven, Soeren Kern, Brian Fairchild, Bob Fletcher, and many others who can't be named for the invaluable insights they shared for this book.

Thanks to my good friend, Willem Griffioen and his lovely wife Kathy for their friendship, fellowship, and for always lending a helping hand.

Thanks to the entire team at the Israel Allies Foundation for their tireless work in support of Israel and for giving me an opportunity to sound the alarm about terror organizations such as ISIS that wish to wipe the Jewish people off the map.

Thanks also to Fox News and Christians United for Israel (CUFI) for giving me a regular opportunity to talk about these pressing issues for a wide audience.

Thanks to Carrie and Zeke and also to Stephanie Reis—you are dear friends, and I appreciate your prayers and wise counsel. Thanks also to Carrie for her insights into Israel's security situation.

To all the voices for freedom in the Middle East, especially the region's persecuted Christians: thank you for your boldness, courage, and resilience. You are an inspiration.

To all of my friends in Fox Chase: I was forged in the iron of Philadelphia, and no matter where I go, I never forget. Thank you as always.

To the reader: if you are a bit down after taking in the very heavy subject matter in this book, don't be. Here's the good news: as the world feels like it is going to hell and evil is on the march, God still sits on the Throne.

Check out this passage from Psalm 37, which I kept reminding myself of while writing this book:

"The wicked plot against the righteous and gnash their teeth at them; but the Lord laughs at the wicked, for He knows their day is coming. The wicked draw the sword and bend the bow to bring down the poor and needy, to slay those whose ways are righteous. But their swords will pierce their own hearts, and their bows will be broken."

One day, hopefully soon, ISIS will be defeated. And goodness will prevail. You can take it to the bank.

God keeps His promises and is always faithful. Thank you, Lord. For everything.

Erick Stakelbeck
Washington, D.C.
January 16, 2015
Psalm 91
Isaiah 54:17

NOTES

PROLOGUE: THE ISLAMIC STATE OF MINNESOTA

1. Jamie Yuccas, "Minneapolis Has Become Recruiting Ground for Islamic Extremists," CBS News, August 27, 2014, http://www.cbsnews.com/news/minneapolis-has-become-recruiting-ground-for-islamic-extremists/.

2. Gary Strauss, Donna Leinwand Leger, and Kevin Johnson, "Somalis in U.S. Condemn Kenyan Mall Attack," *USA Today*, September 24, 2013, http://www.usatoday.com/story/news/nation/2013/09/23/potential-somali-american-involvement-in-kenyai-mall-attack-setting-off-fears-in-us/2856553/.

3. E. A. Torriero, "They're 100% American, and Pro-Hezbollah: U.S. Scrutiny Resented in Dearborn," *Chicago Tribune*, July 27, 2006, http://articles.chicagotribune.com/2006-07-27/news/0607270148_1_hezbollah-israeli-terrorist-organization.

4. David Johnston, "Militants Drew Recruit in U.S., F.B.I. Says," *New York Times*, February 23, 2009, http://www.nytimes.com/2009/02/24/washington/24fbi.html?_r=0.

5. Paul McEnroe and Allie Shah, "Sept. 7: Federal Grand Jury Targets Local Terrorist Pipeline," *Star Tribune*, September 20, 2014, http://www.startribune.com/local/minneapolis/274233901.html.

6. Holly Yan, Sonia Moghe, and Greg Botelho, "Douglas McAuthur McCain: From American Kid to Jihadi in Syria," CNN, September 3, 2014, http://www.cnn.com/2014/08/27/us/who-was-douglas-mccain/.

7. Meg Wagner, "Minnesota Dad-of-Nine Abdirahmaan Muhumed Killed Fighting for ISIS in Syria: Report," *New York Daily News*, August 28, 2014, http://www.nydailynews.com/news/world/american-isis-terrorist-killed-syria-id-report-article-1.1919877.

8. Michael Zennie, "Somali-American Who Died Fighting for ISIS Cleaned Planes for Delta Airlines at Minneapolis Airport before He Joined Terrorist Group," *Daily Mail*, September 3, 2014, http://www.dailymail.co.uk/news/article-2742206/Somali-American-died-fighting-ISIS-cleaned-planes-Delta-Airlines-Minneapolis-airport-joined-terrorist-group.html.

9. Bob Fletcher, in interview with the author, September 16, 2014.

10. McEnroe and Shah, "Sept. 7: Federal Grand Jury Targets Local Terrorist Pipeline."

11. Ibid.

12. Tom Lyden, "Exclusive: Man Booted from Minn. Mosque an ISIS Recruiter or FBI Mole?," Fox 9 News (Minneapolis-St. Paul), October 5, 2014, http://www.myfoxtwincities.com/story/26469968/man-booted-from-minn-mosque-an-isis-recruiter-or-fbi-mole.

13. Fletcher, interview.

14. Omar Jamal, in interview with the author, September 16, 2014.

15. Kate Raddatz, "Homeland Secretary Visits Mpls. to Discuss Somali Terror Recruitment," CBS Minnesota, November 7, 2014, http://minnesota.cbslocal.com/2014/11/07/homeland-secretary-visits-mpls-to-discuss-somali-terror-recruitment/.

16. Ludovica Iaccino, "Isis and Jihadi Terrorists 'Post 90 Tweets Every Minute' to Spread Propaganda," International Business Times, November 4, 2014, http://www.ibtimes.co.uk/isis-jihadi-terrorists-post-90-tweets-every-minute-spread-propaganda-1473064.

17. Naina Bajekal, "ISIS Mass Beheading Video Took 6 Hours to Film and Multiple Takes," *Time*, December 9, 2014, http://time.com/3624976/isis-beheading-technology-video-trac-quilliam/.

18. Erika Solomon, "ISIS Fighters Crave Snacks and Gadgets of the West They Disdain," *Financial Times*, November 28, 2014, http://www.ft.com/intl/cms/s/0/5298d716-758a-11e4-a1a9-00144feabdc0.html#axzz3Ld2iJloI.

19. Ryan Mauro, "ISIS Releases 'Flames of War' Feature Film to Intimidate West," Clarion Project, September 21, 2014, http://www.clarionproject.org/analysis/isis-releases-flames-war-feature-film-intimidate-west.

20. Joseph A. Carter, Shiraz Maher, and Peter R. Neumann, "#Greenbirds: Measuring Importance and Influence in Syrian Foreign Fighter Networks," International Centre for the Study of Radicalisation and Political Violence, 2014, http://icsr.info/wp-content/uploads/2014/04/ICSR-Report-Greenbirds-Measuring-Importance-and-Infleunce-in-Syrian-Foreign-Fighter-Networks.pdf.

21. M. L. Nestel and Rachael Levy, "ISIS Supporters in America: The Jihadis Next Door?," Vocativ, October 1, 2014, http://www.vocativ.com/usa/nat-sec/isis-america-jihadi-next-door/?page=all.

22. Carter, Maher, and Neumann, "#Greenbirds."

23. Nestel and Levy, "ISIS Supporters in America."

24. Matt Zapotosky, "Virginia Woman Accused of Attempting to Aid Islamic State," *Washington Post*, November 17, 2014, http://www.washingtonpost.com/local/crime/va-woman-accused-of-attempting-to-support-isis/2014/11/17/060c250c-6e8b-11e4-893f-86bd390a3340_story.html.

CHAPTER ONE: THE CALIPHATE RETURNS

1. John Hall, "Western Aid 'Is Funding ISIS Fighters' because Jihadists Are Demanding Huge Bribes to Let Trucks Carrying Supplies Reach Desperate Families, Official Claims," *Daily Mail*, October 20, 2014, http://www.dailymail.co.uk/news/article-2800100/western-aid-funding-isis-fighters-jihadists-demanding-huge-bribes-let-trucks-carrying-supplies-reach-desperate-families-official-claims.html.

2. George Packer, "The Common Enemy," *New Yorker*, August 25, 2014, http://www.newyorker.com/magazine/2014/08/25/the-common-enemy.

3.   Janine di Giovanni, Leah McGrath Goodman, and Damien Sharkov, "How Does ISIS Fund Its Reign of Terror?," *Newsweek*, November 6, 2014, http://www.newsweek.com/2014/11/14/how-does-isis-fund-its-reign-terror-282607.html.

4.   Spencer Ackerman, "Foreign Jihadists Flocking to Iraq and Syria on 'Unprecedented Scale'—UN," *Guardian*, October 30, 2014, http://www.theguardian.com/world/2014/oct/30/foreign-jihadist-iraq-syria-unprecedented-un-isis.

5.   Greg Miller, "Airstrikes against Islamic State Do Not Seen [sic] to Have Affected Flow of Fighters to Syria," *Washington Post*, October 30, 2014, http://www.washingtonpost.com/world/national-security/airstrikes-against-the-islamic-state-have-not-affected-flow-of-foreign-fighters-to-syria/2014/10/30/aa1f124a-603e-11e4-91f7-5d89b5e8c251_story.html.

6.   Athena Yenko, "ISIS Is World [sic] Richest Terrorist Group in History," *International Business Times*, November 13, 2014, http://au.ibtimes.com/articles/572651/20141113/isis-forbes-israel-list-ten-richest-terrorist.htm#.VIoNryfQlJk.

7.   Martin Chulov, "ISIS: The Inside Story," *Guardian*, December 11, 2014, http://www.theguardian.com/world/2014/dec/11/-sp-isis-the-inside-story.

8.   Rachel Avraham, "Hezbollah's War against ISIS," Foreign Policy Association, August 31, 2014, http://foreignpolicyblogs.com/2014/08/31/hezbollahs-war-against-isis/.

9.   "ISIS Allegedly Issues 'Caliphate' Passport," Al Arabiya News, July 5, 2014, http://english.alarabiya.net/en/News/middle-east/2014/07/05/ISIS-allegedly-issues-caliphate-passport.html; Cheryl K. Chumley, "Islamic State Touts $250M Year-End Budget Surplus; Opens Bank," *Washington Times*, January 5, 2015, http://www.washingtontimes.com/news/2015/jan/5/islamic-state-touts-250m-year-end-budget-surplus-o/; Associated Press, "ISIS Says It Will Create Its Own Currency," *New York Post*, November 14, 2014, http://nypost.com/2014/11/14/isis-says-it-will-create-its-own-currency/.

10. Raf Sanchez, "Does the Islamic State Have a Scud Missile?," *Telegraph*, June 30, 2014, http://www.telegraph.co.uk/news/worldnews/middleeast/syria/10936926/Does-the-Islamic-State-have-a-Scud-missile.html.

11. Jeremy Bender, "As ISIS Routs the Iraqi Army, Here's a Look at What the Jihadists Have in Their Arsenal," Business Insider, July 8, 2014, http://www.businessinsider.com/isis-military-equipment-breakdown-2014-7?op=1#ixzz3LnUTdS3D.

12. David Majumdar, "U.S. Fighter Jocks Pray the 'ISIS Air Force' Rumors Are True," Daily Beast, October 21, 2014, http://www.thedailybeast.com/articles/2014/10/21/u-s-fighter-jocks-pray-the-isis-air-force-rumors-are-true.html.

13. Thomas Gibbons-Neff, "Islamic State Has a Guide to Shoot Down Apache Helicopters with MANPADS," *Washington Post*, October 28, 2014, http://www.washingtonpost.com/news/checkpoint/wp/2014/10/28/islamic-state-has-a-guide-to-shoot-down-apache-helicopters-with-manpads/.

14. Ted Thornhill, "ISIS Arming Themselves with US-Made Military Hardware to Wage Jihad across the Middle East after Seizing Weapons from Syrian Rebels and Iraqi Soldiers," *Daily Mail*, September 9, 2014, http://www.dailymail.co.uk/news/article-2749197/ISIS-arming-US-military-hardware-wage-jihad-Middle-East-seizing-weapons-Syrian-rebels-Iraqi-soldiers.html.

15. Nabih Bulos, Patrick J. McDonnell, and Raja Abdulrahim, "ISIS Weapons Windfall May Alter Balance in Iraq, Syria Conflicts," *Los Angeles Times*, June 29, 2014, http://www.latimes.com/world/middleeast/la-fg-iraq-isis-arms-20140629-story.html#page=1.

16. Ibid.

17. Bill Hutchison, "ISIS Seizes Chemical Weapons Depot Near Baghdad, May Have Access to Deadly Sarin Gas Rockets," *New York Daily News*, July 9, 2014, http://www.nydailynews.com/news/world/isis-seizes-chemical-weapons-depot-baghdad-sarin-gas-rockets-article-1.1859934.

18. Matt Schiavenza, "ISIS Captures Iraqi Chemical Weapons Facility," International Business Times, June 19, 2014, http://www.ibtimes.com/isis-captures-iraqi-chemical-weapons-facility-1606450.

19. Loveday Morris, "Islamic State Militants Allegedly Used Chlorine Gas against Iraqi Security Forces," *Washington Post*, October 23, 2014, http://www.washingtonpost.com/world/middle_east/islamic-state-militants-allegedly-used-chlorine-gas-against-iraqi-security-forces/2014/10/23/c865c943-1c93-4ac0-a7ed-033218f15cbb_story.html.

20. Alexander Smith, "Nuclear Experts Play Down Threat of Uranium Stolen by ISIS," NBC News, July 10, 2014, http://www.nbcnews.com/storyline/iraq-turmoil/nuclear-experts-play-down-threat-uranium-stolen-isis-n152926.

21. Adam Kredo, "Report: Islamic State Claims 'Radioactive Device' Now in Europe," Washington Free Beacon, December 8, 2014, http://freebeacon.com/national-security/report-islamic-state-claims-radioactive-device-now-in-europe/.

22. Noah Shachtman, "Hidden Horrors: Western Intelligence Suspects Assad Has a Secret Chemical Stockpile," Daily Beast, May 1, 2014, http://www.thedailybeast.com/articles/2014/05/01/western-intelligence-suspects-assad-has-a-secret-chemical-stockpile.html.

23. Annabel Grossman, "ISIS Using Bombs Containing Live Scorpions in Effort to Spread Panic, in Tactics Used 2,000 Years Ago against Romans," *Daily Mail*, December 16, 2014, http://www.dailymail.co.uk/news/article-2875968/ISIS-using-bombs-containing-live-SCORPIONS-effort-spread-panic-tactic-used-2-000-years-ago-against-Romans.html.

24. Fred Lucas, "Obama Has Touted al Qaeda's Demise 32 Times since Benghazi Attack," CNS News, November 1, 2012, http://cnsnews.com/news/article/obama-touts-al-qaeda-s-demise-32-times-benghazi-attack-0.

25. David Remnick, "Going the Distance: On and Off the Road with Barack Obama," *New Yorker*, January 27, 2014, http://www.newyorker.com/magazine/2014/01/27/going-the-distance-2?currentPage=all.

26. Marc A. Thiessen, "Obama vs. the Generals," *Washington Post*, September 15, 2014, http://www.washingtonpost.com/opinions/marc-thiessen-obama-overrules-his-generals-in-fight-against-islamic-state/2014/09/15/0cff59a0-3ce1-11e4-9587-5dafd96295f0_story.html.

27. Terence P. Jeffrey, "Flashback—Obama: 'We're Leaving behind a Sovereign, Stable and Self-Reliant Iraq,'" CNS News, June 12, 2014, http://cnsnews.com/news/article/terence-p-jeffrey/flashback-obama-we-re-leaving-behind-sovereign-stable-and-self.

28. Jonathan Karl, "3 Times Obama Administration Was Warned about ISIS Threat," ABC News, September 29, 2014, http://abcnews.go.com/Politics/times-obama-administration-warned-isis-threat/story?id=25843517.

29. Ibid.

30. Ibid.

31. Jeffrey, "Flashback—Obama."

32. Brendan Bordelon, "Former Iraq Ambassador: Obama 'Warned by Everybody' about ISIS, but 'Did Almost Nothing,'" National Review Online, October 29, 2014, http://www.nationalreview.com/corner/391398/former-iraq-ambassador-obama-warned-everybody-about-isis-did-almost-nothing-brendan.

33. James Franklin Jeffrey, "Behind the U.S. Withdrawal from Iraq: Negotiations Were Repeatedly Disrupted by Obama White House Staffers' Inaccurate Public Statements," *Wall Street Journal*, November 2, 2014, http://www.wsj.com/articles/james-franklin-jeffrey-behind-the-u-s-withdrawal-from-iraq-1414972705.

34. Mary Anne Weaver, "The Short, Violent Life of Abu Musab al-Zarqawi," *Atlantic*, July 1, 2006, http://www.theatlantic.com/magazine/archive/2006/07/the-short-violent-life-of-abu-musab-al-zarqawi/304983/.

35. "ISIS: Portrait of a Jihadi Terrorist Organization," Meir Amit Intelligence and Terrorism Information Center, November 2014, http://www.terrorism-info.org.il/Data/articles/Art_20733/101_14_Ef_1329270214.pdf.

36. Weaver, "The Short, Violent Life."

37. "ISIS: Portrait of a Jihadi Terrorist Organization."

38. Janine di Giovanni, "Who Is ISIS Leader Abu Bakr al-Baghdadi?," *Newsweek*, December 8, 2014, http://www.newsweek.com/2014/12/19/who-isis-leader-abu-bakr-al-baghdadi-290081.html.

39. Ruth Sherlock, "How a Talented Footballer Became World's Most Wanted Man, Abu Bakr al-Baghdadi," *Telegraph*, November 11, 2014, http://www.telegraph.co.uk/news/worldnews/middleeast/iraq/10948846/How-a-talented-footballer-became-worlds-most-wanted-man-Abu-Bakr-al-Baghdadi.html.

40. Chulov, "ISIS: The Inside Story."

41. Sherlock, "How a Talented Footballer."

42. Di Giovanni, "Who Is ISIS Leader Abu Bakr al-Baghdadi?"

43. Chulov, "ISIS: The Inside Story."

44. Bill Sanderson, "Iraq Insurgency Leader: 'I'll See You in New York,'" *New York Post*, June 14, 2014, http://nypost.com/2014/06/14/iraq-insurgency-leader-ill-see-you-in-new-york/.

45. "Profile: Abu Bakr al-Baghdadi," BBC, July 5, 2014, http://www.bbc. com/news/world-middle-east-27801676.

46. Di Giovanni, "Who Is ISIS Leader Abu Bakr al-Baghdadi?"

47. "US State Department Wants IS Leader Abu Bakr Al-Baghdadi, Offering $10 Million Reward," news.com.au, September 26, 2014, http://www. news.com.au/world/us-state-department-wants-is-leader-abu-bakr-albaghdadi-offering-10-million-reward/story-fndir2ev-1227071497608.

48. "ISIS Leader al-Baghdadi: 'Erupt Volcanoes of Jihad,'" NBC News, November 13, 2014, http://www.nbcnews.com/storyline/isis-terror/isis-leader-al-baghdadi-erupt-volcanoes-jihad-n247801.

49. "ISIS: Portrait of a Jihadi Terrorist Organization."

50. Michael S. Schmidt, "434 People Killed in Iraq Since U.S. Pulled Out," *New York Times*, January 27, 2012, http://www.nytimes.com/2012/01/28/ world/middleeast/suicide-bomber-attacks-funeral-procession-in-iraq. html?_r=0.

51. "ISIS: Portrait of a Jihadi Terrorist Organization."

52. Jessica Lewis, "Al Qaeda in Iraq's 'Breaking the Walls' Campaign Achieves Its Objectives at Abu Ghraib—2013 Iraq Update #30," Institute for the Study of War, July 28, 2013, http://iswiraq.blogspot.com/2013/07/ al-qaeda-in-iraqs-breaking-walls.html.

53. Michael Knights, "ISIL's Political-Military Power in Iraq," Combating Terrorism Center at West Point, August 27, 2014, https://www.ctc.usma. edu/posts/isils-political-military-power-in-iraq.

54. AFP, "Syria Death Toll Now Exceeds 200,000: Monitor," Al Arabiya News, December 2, 2014, http://english.alarabiya.net/en/News/middle-east/2014/12/02/Syria-death-toll-now-exceeds-200-000-monitor-.html.

55. Richard Barrett, "The Islamic State," Soufan Group, November 2014, http://soufangroup.com/wp-content/uploads/2014/10/TSG-The-Islamic-State-Nov14.pdf.

56. "ISIS: Portrait of a Jihadi Terrorist Organization."

57. Barrett, "The Islamic State."

58. Paula Astih, "Lebanon Braces for Attacks from ISIS and al-Nusra Front," *Asharq Al-Awsat*, December 18, 2014, http://www.aawsat.net/2014/12/ article55339612.

59.   Aaron Y. Zelin, "Jihad 2020: Assessing al-Qaida's 20-Year Plan," *World Politics Review*, September 11, 2013, http://www.worldpoliticsreview. com/articles/13208/jihad-2020-assessing-al-qaida-s-20-year-plan.

CHAPTER TWO: HELL AWAITS: WELCOME TO THE ISLAMIC STATE

1.   Steven Nabil, in telephone interview with the author, September 24, 2014.

2.   Phil Mattingly, "The Phases of Obama's Iraq War," Bloomberg, November 11, 2014, http://www.bloomberg.com/politics/articles/2014-11-11/the-phases-of-obamas-iraq-war; "Obama: Iraq Has to Solve Its Own Problems," Al Jazeera, June 14, 2014, http://www.aljazeera.com/news/americas/2014/06/obama-iraq-solve-own-problems-201461316139782530.html.

3.   "Obama: Iraq Has to Solve Its Own Problems."

4.   Rebecca Collard, "Why Iraq Is So Desperate to Retake Mosul Dam from ISIS," *Time*, August 16, 2014, http://time.com/3126423/iraq-isis-mosul-dam-airstrikes/.

5.   Fazel Hawramy, "Kurdish Pershmerga [sic] Forces Prepare Escape Route for Yazidis Trapped in Sinjar," *Guardian*, December 19, 2014, http://www.theguardian.com/world/2014/dec/19/kurdish-pershmerga-yazidis-safe-escape-route-sinjar-isis.

6.   Loveday Morris, "Iraqi Yazidis Stranded on Isolated Mountaintop Begin to Die of Thirst," *Washington Post*, August 5, 2014, http://www.washingtonpost.com/world/iraqi-yazidis-stranded-on-isolated-mountaintop-begin-to-die-of-thirst/2014/08/05/57cca985-3396-41bd-8163-7a52e5e72064_story.html.

7.   Haroon Siddique, "20,000 Iraqis Besieged by ISIS Escape from Mountain after US Air Strikes," *Guardian*, August 10, 2014, http://www.theguardian.com/world/2014/aug/10/iraq-yazidi-isis-jihadists-islamic-state-kurds.

8.   "Obama Says Militant Siege Broken—but Iraq Mission Not over Yet," Fox News, August 14, 2014, http://www.foxnews.com/politics/2014/08/14/obama-us-has-broken-iraqi-militant-siege-rescue-effort-not-needed/; Hawramy, "Kurdish Pershmerga [sic] Forces Prepare Escape Route."

9. Mark Landler and Eric Schmitt, "ISIS Says It Killed Steven Sotloff after U.S. Strikes in Northern Iraq," *New York Times*, September 2, 2014, http://www.nytimes.com/2014/09/03/world/middleeast/steven-sotloff-isis-execution.html?_r=0.

10. Ashley Killough, "Strong Reaction to Obama Statement: 'ISIL Is Not Islamic,'" CNN, September 11, 2014, http://www.cnn.com/2014/09/10/politics/obama-isil-not-islamic/.

11. Charlie Spiering, "Obama: ISIS Beheadings 'Represent No Faith, Least of All the Muslim Faith," Breitbart, November 17, 2014, http://www.breitbart.com/big-government/2014/11/17/obama-isis-beheadings-represent-no-faith-least-of-all-the-muslim-faith/.

12. Barack Obama, "Remarks by the President on a New Beginning," WhiteHouse.gov, June 4, 2009, http://www.whitehouse.gov/the-press-office/remarks-president-cairo-university-6-04-09.

13. Barack Obama, "Remarks by the President to the UN General Assembly," WhiteHouse.gov, September 25, 2012, http://www.whitehouse.gov/the-press-office/2012/09/25/remarks-president-un-general-assembly.

14. Yoel Natan, "164 *Jihad* Verses in the *Koran*," Answering Islam, 2004, http://www.answering-islam.org/Quran/Themes/jihad_passages.html.

15. Daniel Pipes, "How Many Islamists?," Daniel Pipes Middle East Forum, January 26, 2013, http://www.danielpipes.org/blog/2003/10/how-many-islamists; Nathan Lean, "Stop Saying 'Moderate Muslims.' You're Only Empowering Islamophobes," *New Republic*, June 25, 2014, http://www.newrepublic.com/article/118391/troubling-phrase-moderate-muslims-only-empowers-islamophobes.

16. Jeremy Diamond, "Poll: Most Americans Believe ISIS Serious Threat," CNN, November 24, 2014, http://www.cnn.com/2014/11/24/politics/isis-november-poll/.

17. Mark Murray, "Poll: Americans Want Boots on the Ground against ISIS," MSNBC, October 15, 2014, http://www.msnbc.com/msnbc/isis-poll-americans-want-boots-on-the-ground.

18. "Obama Warns Defeating ISIS Won't Be Quick," NBC News, August 26, 2014, http://www.nbcnews.com/storyline/iraq-turmoil/obama-warns-defeating-isis-wont-be-quick-n189356.

19. Dave Boyer, "Obama Confesses: 'We Don't Have a Strategy Yet' for Islamic State," *Washington Times*, August 28, 2014, http://www.washingtontimes.com/news/2014/aug/28/obama-admits-isil-dilemma-we-dont-have-strategy-ye/?page=all.

20. "Presidential Daily Briefs: A Time-Based Analysis," Government Accountability Institute, September 2014, http://www.g-a-i.org/wp-content/uploads/2014/09/GAI-Report-PDB-Update-9.29.2014.pdf.

21. Wynton Hall, "Report: Obama Has Missed Over Half His Second-Term Daily Intel Briefings," Breitbart, September 29, 2014, http://www.breitbart.com/national-security/2014/09/29/report-obama-has-missed-over-half-his-second-term-daily-intel-briefings/.

22. Jennifer Epstein, "Barack Obama's Long Walks Spoiled," Politico, August 24, 2014, http://www.politico.com/story/2014/08/barack-obama-criticism-110296.html.

23. Missy Ryan and Erin Cunningham, "U.S. Advisers in Iraq Stay Out of Combat but See Fighting Edging Closer," *Washington Post*, January 1, 2015, http://www.washingtonpost.com/world/national-security/us-advisers-in-iraq-stay-out-of-combat-but-see-fight-edge-nearer/2015/01/01/6da57c3a-9038-11e4-ba53-a477d66580ed_story.html.

24. Ibid.

25. Nicholas Watt, "Defeat of ISIS Cannot Be Achieved without Ground Troops, Says Tony Blair," *Guardian*, September 21, 2014, http://www.theguardian.com/politics/2014/sep/22/blair-defeat-isis-ground-troops.

26. Ryan and Cunningham, "U.S. Advisers in Iraq."

27. "US Flies Roughly 85 Percent of Airstrikes against Islamic State, in Complex Mix of Tactics, Politics," Fox News, November 30, 2014, http://www.foxnews.com/politics/2014/11/30/us-outpaces-allies-in-airstrike-in-iraq-syria/.

28. Josh Rogin and Eli Lake, "Iran-Backed Militias Are Getting U.S. Weapons," Bloomberg, January 8, 2015, http://www.bloombergview.com/articles/2015-01-08/iranbacked-militias-are-getting-us-weapons-in-iraq.

29. Martha Ann Overland, "U.S. Strikes Have Killed 1,100 ISIS Fighters and Cost $1 Billion," NPR, December 24, 2014, http://www.npr.org/blogs/thetwo-way/2014/12/24/372168736/u-s-strikes-have-killed-1-100-isis-fighters-and-cost-1-billion.

30. Hollie McKay, "Iraq's Peshmerga Desperate for US Arms in Fight against ISIS," Fox News, January 3, 2015, http://www.foxnews.com/world/2015/01/03/iraq-peshmerga-desperate-for-us-arms-in-fight-against-isis/.

31. Agence France-Presse, "Kurdish Peshmerga Forces Launch Offensive to Retake ISIS Held Areas," *Guardian*, December 17, 2014, http://www.theguardian.com/world/2014/dec/17/kurds-peshmerga-offensive-isis-sinjar-territory-mosul.

32. Agence France Presse, "Kurds Push Back ISIS in Syria's Kobani: Activists," *Daily Star* (Lebanon), January 5, 2015, http://www.dailystar.com.lb/News/Middle-East/2015/Jan-05/283114-kurds-push-back-isis-in-syrias-kobani-activists.ashx.

33. Reuters, "'Islamic State Seeking Bases inside Lebanon,'" *Jerusalem Post*, January 3, 2015, http://www.jpost.com/Arab-Israeli-Conflict/Islamic-State-seeking-bases-inside-Lebanon-386552.

34. Erin Banco, "ISIS Destroys at Least Six Border Control Stations on Jordan-Iraq Border," International Business Times, December 16, 2014, http://www.ibtimes.com/isis-destroys-least-six-border-control-stations-jordan-iraq-border-1759922.

35. Alessandria Masi, "ISIS Claims Attack on Saudi Arabian Border, Signals Strategy Change in Militant Infiltration," International Business Times, January 5, 2015, http://www.ibtimes.com/isis-claims-attack-saudi-arabia-border-signals-strategy-change-militant-infiltration-1773754.

36. Damien Sharkov, "Saudi Arabia Constructing 600-Mile Wall to Keep Out ISIS," *Newsweek*, January 15, 2015, http://www.newsweek.com/saudi-arabia-constructing-600-mile-long-wall-keep-isis-out-299664.

37. John Hall, "ISIS Signs Up More than 6,000 New Recruits Since American Airstrikes Began, As France Makes Ruling on Groups [sic] Name and Says It Will Start Calling Them Derogatory 'Daesh Cutthroats,'" *Daily Mail*, September 18, 2014, http://www.dailymail.co.uk/news/article-2760644/ISIS-signs-6-000-new-recruits-American-airstrikes-began-France-says-start-calling-group-derogatory-Daesh-cutthroats.html.

38. Greg Miller, "Airstrikes against Islamic State Do Not Seen [sic] to Have Affected Flow of Fighters to Syria," *Washington Post*, October 30, 2014,

http://www.washingtonpost.com/world/national-security/airstrikes-against-the-islamic-state-have-not-affected-flow-of-foreign-fighters-to-syria/2014/10/30/aa1f124a-603e-11e4-91f7-5d89b5e8c251_story.html.

39. Laura Dean, "Allegiance to ISIS: Egypt's Ansar Beit al-Maqdis Pledges Support," NBC News, November 12, 2014, http://www.nbcnews.com/storyline/isis-terror/allegiance-isis-egypts-ansar-beit-al-maqdis-pledges-support-n246741.

40. Ibid; "Video Shows Beheading of Four Egyptians in Sinai," Al Arabiya News, August 28, 2014, http://english.alarabiya.net/en/News/middle-east/2014/08/28/Sinai-militants-claim-beheading-of-4-Egyptians.html.

41. Mirco Keilberth, Juliane von Mittelstaedt, and Christoph Reuter, "The 'Caliphate's' Colonies: Islamic State's Gradual Expansion into North Africa," *Spiegel*, November 18, 2014, http://www.spiegel.de/international/world/islamic-state-expanding-into-north-africa-a-1003525.html.

42. Ibid.

43. Reuters, "Algeria Says It Killed Leader of ISIS-Linked Group behind French Tourist's Beheading," NBC News, December 23, 2014, http://www.nbcnews.com/news/world/algeria-says-it-killed-leader-isis-linked-group-behind-french-n273666.

44. "Pakistan Taliban Sack Spokesman Shahidullah Shahid for IS Vow," BBC October 21, 2014, http://www.bbc.com/news/world-asia-29640242?ns_mchannel=social&ns_campaign=bbc_news_asia&ns_source=twitter&ns_linkname=news_central.

45. Ryan Mauro, "Exclusive: Terror Org. Harbored by Pakistani Gov't Now Backs ISIS," Clarion Project, December 29, 2014, http://www.clarionproject.org/analysis/exclusive-terror-org-harbored-pakistani-govt-now-backs-isis.

46. Tim Arango, "Escaping Death in Northern Iraq," *New York Times*, September 3, 2014, http://www.nytimes.com/2014/09/04/world/middleeast/surviving-isis-massacre-iraq-video.html?_r=1.

47. Meg Wagner, "'I Had a Great Will to Live': Lone Survivor of ISIS Massacre That Killed as Many as 560 Played Dead to Escape Terrorists," *New York Daily News*, September 4, 2014, http://www.nydailynews.com/news/world/lone-survivor-isis-massacre-played-dead-report-article-1.1927471.

48. Ivan Watson, "'They Would Torture You': ISIS Prisoners Reveal Life inside Terror Group," CNN, October 28, 2014, http://www.cnn.com/2014/10/28/world/meast/syria-isis-prisoners-watson/index.html?iid=article_sidebar.

49. "Islamic State Executed Nearly 2,000 People in Six Months: Monitor," Reuters, December 28, 2014, http://www.reuters.com/article/2014/12/28/us-mideast-crisis-casualties-idUSKBN0K60EK20141228.

50. Sam Greenhill, "'There Are Hundreds of Bodies with Their Heads Cut Off... They Put Their Heads on Display to Scare Us': Survivors of Kobane Massacre Reveal the Brutality of ISIS Rampage in Syrian Border Town," *Daily Mail*, October 12, 2014, http://www.dailymail.co.uk/news/article-2790296/blood-curdling-screams-headless-bodies-siege-town-mail-man-sam-greenhill-reports-frontline-jihadi-squads-lie-wait-western-hostages.html.

51. Richard Barrett, "The Islamic State," Soufan Group, November 2014, http://soufangroup.com/wp-content/uploads/2014/10/TSG-The-Islamic-State-Nov14.pdf.

52. Ibid.

53. Duncan Gardham, "Exclusive: Grinning ISIS Commander Who Recruits Jihadis from Home Counties Taunts Britain 'from beyond the Grave,'" *Daily Mail*, updated November 21, 2014, http://www.dailymail.co.uk/news/article-2839307/Grinning-ISIS-commander-recruits-jihadis-Home-Counties-taunts-Britain-grave.html.

54. Cheryl K. Chumley, "Islamic State Touts $250M Year-End Budget Surplus; Opens Bank," *Washington Times*, January 5, 2015, http://www.washingtontimes.com/news/2015/jan/5/islamic-state-touts-250m-year-end-budget-surplus-o/.

55. Karen Leigh, "ISIS Makes Up to $3 Million a Day Selling Oil, Say Analysts," ABC News, August 2, 2014, http://abcnews.go.com/International/isis-makes-million-day-selling-oil-analysts/story?id=24814359.

56. S. B., "Where Islamic State Gets Its Money," *Economist*, January 4, 2015, http://www.economist.com/blogs/economist-explains/2015/01/economist-explains.

57. Rukmini Callimachi, "Paying Ransoms, Europe Bankrolls Qaeda Terror," *New York Times*, July 29, 2014, http://www.nytimes.com/2014/07/30/world/africa/ransoming-citizens-europe-becomes-al-qaedas-patron.html?_r=0&gwh=95C631B187E675A4006B7E85996AC BFA&gwt=pay&assetType=nyt_now.

58. Matthew Levitt and Lori Plotkin Boghardt, "Funding ISIS (Infographic)," Washington Institute, September 12, 2014, https://www.washington institute.org/policy-analysis/view/funding-isis-infographic.

59. S. B., "Where Islamic State Gets Its Money."

60. Cathy Otten, "Last Remaining Christians Flee Iraq's Mosul," Al Jazeera, July 22, 2014, http://www.aljazeera.com/news/middleeast/2014/07/last-remaining-christians-flee-iraq-mosul-201472118235739663.html.

61. Sharona Schwartz, "This Is Not a One-Eyed Smiley Face, It's a Symbol of Frightening Things Happening to Middle East Christians," TheBlaze, September 24, 2014, http://www.theblaze.com/stories/2014/09/24/this-is-not-a-one-eyed-smiley-face-its-a-symbol-of-frightening-things-happening-to-middle-east-christians/.

62. Perry Chiaramonte, "ISIS Reportedly Selling Christian Artifacts, Turning Churches into Torture Chambers," Fox News, December 23, 2014, http://www.foxnews.com/world/2014/12/22/isis-reportedly-selling-christian-artifacts-turning-churches-into-torture-159616450 9/?intcmp=trending.

63. Tera Dahl, "After 2,000 Years, the Last Christian Is Forced to Leave Mosul," Breitbart, July 20, 2014, http://www.breitbart.com/national-security/2014/07/20/after-2-000-years-the-last-christian-is-forced-to-leave-mosul/.

64. Chris Mitchell, "Before Being Killed, the Children Told ISIS: 'No, We Love Yeshua,'" CBN News, November 6, 2014, http://blogs.cbn.com/jerusalemdateline/archive/2014/11/06/before-being-killed-the-children-told-isis-no-we-love.aspx.

65. "17-Year Old Boy Crucified by ISIS in Raqqa," Clarion Project, October 20, 2014, http://www.clarionproject.org/news/islamic-state-crucifies-17-year-old-boy-raqqa.

66. "Video: Father Helps ISIS Militants Stone Daughter as per Sharia," Clarion Project, October 21, 2014, http://www.clarionproject.org/news/video-islamic-state-stones-young-woman-accused-adultery#.

67. Ivan Watson, "'Treated like Cattle': Yazidi Women Sold, Raped, Enslaved by ISIS," CNN, October 30, 2014, http://www.cnn.com/2014/10/30/world/meast/isis-female-slaves/.

68. Aki Peritz and Tara Maller, "The Islamic State of Sexual Violence," *Foreign Policy*, September 16, 2014, http://foreignpolicy.com/2014/09/16/the-islamic-state-of-sexual-violence/.

69. Nick Squires, "Yazidi Girl Tells of Horrific Ordeal as ISIL Sex Slave," *Telegraph*, September 7, 2014, http://www.telegraph.co.uk/news/worldnews/middleeast/iraq/11080165/Yazidi-girl-tells-of-horrific-ordeal-as-Isil-sex-slave.html.

70. "French, British IS Fighters Discuss Use of Yazidi Women as Sex Slaves," MEMRI (Special Dispatch No. 5833), September 3, 2014, http://www.memri.org/report/en/print8135.htm.

71. Dov Lieber, "ISIS Published Female Sex Slave Handbook," *Jerusalem Post*, December 13, 2014, http://www.jpost.com/Middle-East/ISIS-published-female-sex-slave-handbook-384510.

72. Sharona Schwartz, "Islamic State Fighters Accused of Raping 'Thousands of Women' and Girls as Young as Age Nine," TheBlaze, September 23, 2014, http://www.theblaze.com/stories/2014/09/23/islamic-state-fighters-accused-of-raping-thousands-of-women-and-girls-as-young-as-age-9/.

73. Omar Abdullah, "ISIS Teaches Children How to Behead in Training Camps," ABC News, September 6, 2014, http://abcnews.go.com/International/isis-teaches-children-behead-training-camps/story?id=25303940.

74. Jennifer Newton, "Forced to Watch Crucifixions, Stonings, and Beheadings and Taught to Fire Machine Guns as Big as They Are: How Islamic State Training Camps for Children Are Swelling Its Ranks with Junior Jihadis," *Daily Mail*, August 30, 2014, http://www.dailymail.co.uk/news/article-2738469/Forced-watch-crucifixions-stonings-beheadings-taught-fire-machine-guns-big-How-Islamic-State-training-camps-children-swelling-ranks-junior-jihadis.html.

75.   Mangala Dilip, "ISIS Releases Jihadi Mothers' Handbook on How to Raise Terrorists," International Business Times, January 1, 2015, http://www.ibtimes.co.in/isis-releases-jihadi-mothers-handbook-how-raise-terrorists-618978.

CHAPTER THREE: TARGET AMERICA: WHY YOU SHOULD CARE ABOUT ISIS

1.   Greg Botelho and Jim Sciutto, "Slain ISIS Jihadi among More than 100 Americans Fighting with Militants in Syria," CNN, August 28, 2014, http://edition.cnn.com/2014/08/26/world/meast/syria-american-killed/.

2.   Maggie Ybarra, "Intel Believes 300 Americans Fighting with Islamic State, Posing Threat to U.S.: American Militants Could Commit Terrorist Attacks with Skills Acquired in Iraq, Syria," *Washington Times*, August 26, 2014, http://www.washingtontimes.com/news/2014/aug/26/us-citizens-joining-islamic-state-pose-major-threa/?page=all.

3.   David Chazan, "Brussels Museum Shooting Suspect 'Beheaded Baby,'" *Telegraph*, September 7, 2014, http://www.telegraph.co.uk/news/worldnews/middleeast/syria/11080079/Brussels-museum-shooting-suspect-beheaded-baby.html.

4.   "The American Face of Foreign Terror Recruits," Anti-Defamation League, September 5, 2014, http://blog.adl.org/extremism/american-recruits-to-terror-abroad-isis.

5.   "FBI Director: We Know the Americans Fighting in Syria," CBS News, October 3, 2014, http://www.cbsnews.com/news/fbi-director-james-comey-we-know-the-americans-fighting-in-syria/.

6.   Zeke J. Miller, "Some Americans Fighting with Terror Groups Have Returned to the U.S., Obama Administration Says," *Time*, September 22, 2014, http://time.com/3418455/isis-isil-barack-obama-us/.

7.   "FBI Director: We Know the Americans."

8.   Adam Goldman and Greg Miller, "American Suicide Bomber's Travels in U.S., Middle East Went Unmonitored," *Washington Post*, October 11, 2014, http://www.washingtonpost.com/world/national-security/american-suicide-bombers-travels-in-us-middle-east-went-unmonitored/2014/10/11/38a3228e-4fe8-11e4-aa5e-7153e466a02d_story.html.

9.   Adam Kredo, "Dem Rep: 40 American ISIL Fighters Have Already Returned to the United States: These Individuals under Surveillance, 'Being Tracked' by the FBI," Washington Free Beacon, September 19, 2014, http://freebeacon.com/national-security/dem-rep-40-american-isil-fighters-have-already-returned-to-the-united-states/.

10. Brian Fairchild, in e-mail interview with the author, October 2, 2014.

11. Erick Stakelbeck, *The Terrorist Next Door: How the Government Is Deceiving You about the Islamist Threat* (Washington, DC: Regnery Publishing, 2011), 49–50.

12. Rukmini Callimachi, "Terrorists Used New Tactic to Spare Some Muslims," Associated Press, September 29, 2013, http://bigstory.ap.org/article/terrorists-used-new-tactic-spare-some-muslims.

13. "Sydney Siege: Two Hostages and Gunman Dead after Heavily Armed Police Storm Lindt Cafe in Martin Place," ABC News, December 16, 2014, http://www.abc.net.au/news/2014-12-16/sydney-siege-gunman-two-hostages-dead/5969162.

14. Chris Spargo, "ISIS Urges Muslims to 'Kill Disbelievers' and Calls Secretary of State John Kerry an 'Old Uncircumcised Geezer' in Latest Audio Release," *Daily Mail*, September 22, 2014, http://www.dailymail.co.uk/news/article-2764736/ISIS-urges-Muslims-kill-disbelievers-calls-Secretary-State-John-Kerry-old-uncircumcised-geezer-latest-audio-release.html.

15. Jana Winter, "Law Enforcement Bulletin Warned of ISIS Urging Jihad Attacks on US Soil," Fox News, September 18, 2014, http://www.foxnews.com/world/2014/09/17/law-enforcement-bulletin-warned-isis-urging-jihad-attacks-on-us-soil/.

16. Jessica Zuckerman, Steven P. Bucci, and James Jay Carafano, "60 Terrorist Plots since 9/11: Continued Lessons in Domestic Counterterrorism," Special Report #137 on Terrorism, The Heritage Foundation, July 22, 2013, http://www.heritage.org/research/reports/2013/07/60-terrorist-plots-since-911-continued-lessons-in-domestic-counterterrorism.

17. Eric Owens, "Don't Be Alarmed but Some Arab Guy Walked into a High School Asking 'Suspicious' Questions," Daily Caller, October 2, 2014,

http://dailycaller.com/2014/10/02/dont-be-alarmed-but-some-arab-guy-walked-into-a-high-school-asking-suspicious-questions/.

18. Ibid.

19. Meg Wagner, "Australian Police Kill Teen Terror Suspect Who Stabbed Officers, Foiling Plot to Behead Cops, Wrap Bodies in ISIS Flag: Officials," *New York Daily News*, September 24, 2014, http://www.nydailynews.com/news/world/australian-police-kill-teen-terror-suspect-wanted-behead-cops-report-article-1.1950841.

20. AP and AFP, "IS Ordered 'Demonstration Killings' in Australia, Says PM," Times of Israel, September 18, 2014, http://www.timesofisrael.com/australian-pm-is-ordered-demonstration-killings-in-country/.

21. Stewart Bell, "Soldier Dies after Being Run Down in Suspected Terror Attack Near Montreal: Martin 'Ahmad' Rouleau Killed after High-Speed Chase," *National Post* (Canada), October 20, 2014, http://news.nationalpost.com/2014/10/20/driver-who-ran-into-canadian-soldiers-near-montreal-was-known-to-counter-terrorism-officials-rcmp/.

22. Tristin Hopper, "What Exactly Happened When Martin Rouleau Was Lying in Wait to Run CF Members Over?," *National Post* (Canada), October 21, 2014, http://news.nationalpost.com/2014/10/21/what-exactly-happened-when-martin-rouleau-was-lying-in-wait-to-run-cf-members-over/.

23. Jon Williams et al., "Canada PM Calls Parliament Shooting a 'Terrorist' Act," ABC News, October 22, 2014, http://abcnews.go.com/International/canada-pm-calls-parliament-shooting-terrorist-act/story?id=26372013&page=2.

24. Les Whittington and Joanna Smith, "Cpl. Nathan Cirillo of Hamilton Identified as Soldier Gunned Down in Ottawa Attack," *Toronto Star*, October 22, 2014, http://www.thestar.com/news/canada/2014/10/22/one_person_shot_at_war_memorial_in_ottawa_police_say.html.

25. Brandon Darby, "Exclusive Leak: FBI Report Warns of Potential Homegrown ISIS Attacks against Law Enforcement in US," Breitbart, October 23, 2014, http://www.breitbart.com/Breitbart-Texas/2014/10/23/FBI-Report-Warns-of-Potential-Homegrown-ISIS-Attacks-Against-Law-Enforcement-in-US.

26. Jonathan Dienst, "Bratton: Hatchet Attack on Cops Was a Lone Wolf 'Act of Terror,'" NBC New York, October 29, 2014, http://www. nbcnewyork.com/news/local/Motive-Hatchet-Attack-NYPD-Zale-Thompson-Ax-Queens-Motive-280312192.html.

27. Olivier Guitta, "Stopping the Lone Jihadi," *National Post* (Canada), October 30, 2014, http://fullcomment.nationalpost.com/2014/10/30/olivier-guitta-stopping-the-lone-jihadi/.

28. Ashley Fantz, Pamela Brown, and Aaron Cooper, "Police: Seattle Man's Hatred of U.S. Foreign Policy Motivated Killings," CNN, September 16, 2014, http://www.cnn.com/2014/09/16/justice/ali-brown-charges-killing-spree/.

29. Fred Fleitz, "The Tevlin Murder: Another Sign of the President's Denial of the Radical Islamist/Sharia Threat," Center for Security Policy, September 15, 2014, http://www.centerforsecuritypolicy.org/2014/09/15/the-tevlin-murder-another-sign-of-the-presidents-denial-of-the-radical-islamistsharia-threat/.

30. "Yemeni al-Qaeda Claims French Magazine Attack," Al Jazeera, January 10, 2015, http://www.aljazeera.com/news/europe/2015/01/yemeni-al-qaeda-claims-french-magazine-attack-201511073656841867.html.

31. Simon Tomlinson, "More Questions Emerge over How Paris Jihadists Were Able to Operate amid Revelations Deli Killer Was on U.S. Watch List," *Daily Mail*, January 13, 2015, http://www.dailymail.co.uk/news/article-2907921/Further-questions-raised-Paris-jihadists-able-operate-s-revealed-Paris-deli-killer-U-S-terror-watch-list.html.

32. Rose Troup Buchanan, "Amedy Coulibaly Shot Dead by French Police in Hail of 40 Bullets during Paris Kosher Market Siege," *Independent* (UK), January 12, 2015, http://www.independent.co.uk/news/world/europe/amedy-coulibaly-shot-dead-by-french-police-in-hail-of-40-bullets-during-paris-kosher-market-siege-9971694.html.

33. Julian Borger, "Paris Gunman Amedy Coulibaly Declared Allegiance to ISIS," *Guardian*, January 11, 2015, http://www.theguardian.com/world/2015/jan/11/paris-gunman-amedy-coulibaly-allegiance-isis; Rowan Scarborough, "Islamic State Launches Social Media Campaign to Unleash 'City Wolves,'" *Washington Times*, January 13, 2015, http://www.washingtontimes.com/news/2015/jan/13/islamic-state-launches-new-jihad-kill-westerners-h/.

34.   Dan Bilefsky and Maïa de la Baume, "In a Video, ISIS Fighters Call for Attacks in France," *New York Times*, November 20, 2014, http://www. nytimes.com/2014/11/21/world/europe/video-shows-french-isis-fighters-calling-for-attacks-in-france.html?_r=1; Rowan Scarborough, "Islamic State Launches Social Media Campaign to Unleash 'City Wolves,'" *Washington Times*, January 13, 2015, http://www.washingtontimes.com/news/2015/jan/13/islamic-state-launches-new-jihad-kill-westerners-h/.

35.   Paul Cruickshank, Mariano Castillo, and Catherine E. Shoichet, "Belgian Operation Thwarted 'Major Terrorist Attacks,' Kills 2 Suspects," CNN, January 15, 2015, http://www.cnn.com/2015/01/15/world/belgium-anti-terror-operation/.

36.   Patrick Poole, "'Lone Wolf' or 'Known Wolf'? The Ongoing Counter-Terrorism Failure: An Extensive Report Shows How U.S. Law Enforcement Missteps and Dangerous Policies Keep Getting People Killed," PJ Media, October 24, 2014, http://pjmedia.com/blog/lone-wolf-or-known-wolf-the-ongoing-counter-terrorism-failure/?single page=true.

37.   Neil Munro, "Border Meltdown: Obama Delivering 290,000 Illegals to U.S. Homes," Daily Caller, July 5, 2014, http://dailycaller.com/2014/07/05/border-meltdown-obama-delivering-290000-illegals-to-u-s-homes/.

38.   Edwin Mora, "474 Illegals from Terrorism-Linked Countries Apprehended in 2014 Alone," Breitbart, September 19, 2014, http://cdn. breitbart.com/Big-Peace/2014/09/18/474-Aliens-From-Terrorism-Linked-Countries-Apprehended-in-2014-Alone.

39.   Eric Bradner, "Top Homeland Security Official: ISIS Hasn't Crossed Border into U.S.," CNN, October 8, 2014, http://www.cnn.com/2014/10/08/politics/jeh-johnson-duncan-hunter-isis/.

40.   Rebecca Kaplan, "Homeland Security Says Terrorists Haven't Crossed U.S.-Mexico Border," CBS News, October 9, 2014, http://www.cbsnews. com/news/homeland-security-says-terrorists-havent-crossed-us-mexico-border/.

41.   "GOP Rep: ISIS, Mexican Drug Cartels Are 'Talking to Each Other,'" Breitbart, August 20, 2014, http://www.breitbart.com/Breitbart-TV/2014/08/20/GOP-Rep-ISIS-and-Mexican-Drug-Cartels-Are-Talking-to-Each-Other.

42. Ashley Killough, "Rick Perry: It's Possible ISIS Has Crossed Southern Border," CNN, August 21, 2014, http://politicalticker.blogs.cnn.com/2014/08/21/rick-perry-its-possible-isis-has-crossed-southern-border/.

43. Terence P. Jeffrey, "Joint Chiefs Chair, 'Open Borders and Immigration Issues' Make ISIL 'Immediate Threat,'" CNS News, August 22, 2014, http://cnsnews.com/news/article/terence-p-jeffrey/joint-chiefs-chair-open-borders-and-immigration-issues-make-isil.

44. "EXCLUSIVE: Hezbollah Uses Mexican Drug Routes into U.S.," *Washington Times*, March 27, 2009, http://www.washingtontimes.com/news/2009/mar/27/hezbollah-uses-mexican-drug-routes-into-us/?page=all.

45. Jessica Vaughan, "ICE Enforcement Collapses Further in 2014," Center for Immigration Studies, October 2014, http://cis.org/ICE-Enforcement-Collapses-Further-2014.

46. Fairchild, e-mail interview.

47. Dale Hurd, "Chemical ISIS? New Photos Tell Disturbing Story," CBN News, October 15, 2014, http://www.cbn.com/cbnnews/world/2014/October/Photos-Suggest-ISIS-May-Have-Chemical-Weapons/.

48. Harald Doornbos and Jenan Moussa, "Found: The Islamic State's Terror Laptop of Doom: Buried in a Dell Computer Captured in Syria Are Lessons for Making Bubonic Plague Bombs and Missives on Using Weapons of Mass Destruction," *Foreign Policy*, August 28, 2014, http://www.foreignpolicy.com/articles/2014/08/28/found_the_islamic_state_terror_laptop_of_doom_bubonic_plague_weapons_of_mass_destruction_exclusive.

CHAPTER FOUR: HEARTLAND HORROR: THE AMERICAN RECRUITS

1. Jenny Deam, "Colorado Woman's Quest for Jihad Baffles Neighbors," *Los Angeles Times*, July 25, 2014, http://www.latimes.com/nation/la-na-high-school-jihadi-20140726-story.html#page=1.

2. Ibid.

3. Ibid.

4. Kirk Mitchell, "Arvada Teen Jihadist 'Wannabe' Pleads Guilty to Terror Charge," *Denver Post*, September 10, 2014, http://www.denverpost.com/news/ci_26504683/arvada-jihadist-wannabe-set-plead-guilty-terror-charge.

5. Anna Nemtsova, "Inside the Minds of Russia's Black Widows," Daily Beast, August 26, 2013, http://www.thedailybeast.com/witw/articles/2013/08/26/a-mother-s-despair-chechen-and-dagestani-mothers-radicalize-after-losing-sons-and-husbands-to-war-with-russia.html.

6. Deam, "Colorado Woman's Quest."

7. Bill Chappell, "4-Year Prison Term for Colorado Woman over Plot to Join ISIS," NPR, January 23, 2015, http://www.npr.org/blogs/thetwo-way/2015/01/23/379466005/4-year-prison-term-for-colorado-woman-over-plot-to-join-isis.

8. Mitchell, "Arvada Teen Jihadist 'Wannabe.'"

9. Associated Press, "Denver Teens Encouraged to Join ISIS by 'Online Predator', Friends Say," *Guardian*, October 23, 2014, http://www.theguardian.com/us-news/2014/oct/23/denver-teens-isis-online-predator.

10. Alessandria Masi, "ISIS Female Recruitment Campaign Could Have Inspired Three American Teenage Girls to Join ISIS in Syria," International Business Times, October 21, 2014, http://www.ibtimes.com/isis-female-recruitment-campaign-could-have-inspired-three-american-teenage-girls-join-1709185.

11. Alistair Bell, "Female Jihadists from U.S. Heartland Join ISIS," Reuters/Al Arabiya News, September 15, 2014, http://english.alarabiya.net/en/News/middle-east/2014/09/15/Female-jihadists-from-U-S-heartland-join-ISIS.html.

12. Bob Fletcher, in interview with the author, September 16, 2014.

13. Harriet Sherwood et al., "Schoolgirl Jihadis: The Female Islamists Leaving Home to Join ISIS Fighters," *Guardian*, September 29, 2014, http://www.theguardian.com/world/2014/sep/29/schoolgirl-jihadis-female-islamists-leaving-home-join-isis-iraq-syria.

14. Ibid.

15. Natasha Culzac, "ISIS: British Women Led by Aqsa Mahmood 'Running Sharia Police Unit for Islamic State in Syria,'" *Independent* (UK), September 8, 2014, http://www.independent.co.uk/news/world/middle-east/isis-british-women-running-sharia-police-unit-for-islamic-state-in-syria-9717510.html.

16. "UK Female Jihadists Run ISIS Sex-Slave Brothels," Al Arabiya News, September 12, 2014, http://english.alarabiya.net/en/variety/2014/09/12/UK-female-jihadists-run-ISIS-sex-slave-brothels.html.

17. Sherwood et al. "Schoolgirl Jihadis."

18. Ibid.

19. "ISIS Fighters Open 'Marriage Bureau,'" Al Arabiya News, July 28, 2014, http://english.alarabiya.net/en/variety/2014/07/28/Marry-me-ISIS-fighters-open-marriage-bureau-.html.

20. Elizabeth Kulze and Gilad Siloach, "ISIS Opens a Jihadi Finishing School for Women," Vocativ, October 17, 2014, http://www.vocativ.com/world/isis-2/isis-opens-jihadi-finishing-school-women/.

21. Ibid.

22. Chris Perez, "Pregnant Austrian Teens in ISIS: We've Made a Huge Mistake," *New York Post*, October 10, 2014, http://nypost.com/2014/10/10/pregnant-teen-girls-who-joined-isis-weve-made-a-huge-mistake/.

23. Ibid.

24. Chris Perez, "Teen Who Joined ISIS: 'Here I Can Really Be Free,'" *New York Post*, October 27, 2014, http://nypost.com/2014/10/27/austrian-teen-who-joined-isis-here-i-can-really-be-free/.

25. Nick Squires, Rome, and agencies, "Austrian Teenage Girl Jihadist 'Killed in Syria,'" *Telegraph*, September 15, 2014, http://www.telegraph.co.uk/news/worldnews/europe/austria/11098039/Austrian-teenage-girl-jihadist-killed-in-Syria.html.

26. AFP, "Austria Stops School Girls Going to Syria," Al Arabiya News, September 10, 2014, http://english.alarabiya.net/en/News/world/2014/09/10/Austria-stops-school-girls-going-to-Syria-.html.

27. Graeme Wood, "The Three Types of People Who Fight for ISIS: A Breakdown of the Most Evil Group on the Planet," *New Republic*, September 10, 2014, http://www.newrepublic.com/article/119395/isiss-three-types-fighters.

28. Erick Stakelbeck, *The Terrorist Next Door: How the Government Is Deceiving You about the Islamist Threat* (Washington, DC: Regnery Publishing, 2011), 114–15.

29. Ibid., 114–16.

30. Patrick Howley, "'Sharia Law Is Coming!!!!' Oklahoma Beheader Celebrated Terrorists, Disparaged Non-Muslims on Facebook," Daily Caller, September 26, 2014, http://dailycaller.com/2014/09/26/sharia-law-is-coming-oklahoma-beheader-celebrated-terrorists-disparaged-non-muslims-on-facebook/.

31. John Sexton, "Alton Nolen's Facebook Page Depicted Beheading a Month before Release from Probation," Breitbart, September 26, 2014, http://www.breitbart.com/Big-Government/2014/09/26/Alton-Nolens-Facebook-Page-Included-Image-of-Beheading-and-Jihadists-Abroad.

32. Lydia Warren et al., "Fired Muslim Convert Store-Worker Who Beheaded Female Colleague after Losing His Job Was 'Shouting Islamic Phrases' as He Carried Out His Bloody Rampage," *Daily Mail*, September 27, 2014, http://www.dailymail.co.uk/news/article-2771940/Fired-Muslim-convert-store-worker-beheaded-female-colleague-lost-job-argument-stoning-women.html.

33. Abby Ohlheiser, "What We Know about Alton Nolen, Who Has Been Charged with Murder in the Oklahoma Beheading Case," *Washington Post*, September 30, 2014, http://www.washingtonpost.com/news/post-nation/wp/2014/09/30/what-we-know-about-alton-nolen-who-has-been-charged-with-murder-in-the-oklahoma-beheading-case/.

34. Michael Daly, "No Purple Hearts: Nidal Hassan's Murders Termed 'Workplace Violence' by U.S.," Daily Beast, August 6, 2013, http://www.thedailybeast.com/articles/2013/08/06/nidal-hasan-s-murders-termed-workplace-violence-by-u-s.html.

35. Katharine Lackey, "Fort Hood Shooter Asks to Be 'Citizen' of Islamic State," *USA Today*, August 29, 2014, http://www.usatoday.com/story/news/nation/2014/08/29/fort-hood-shooter-islamic-state/14790297/.

36. Jason Howerton, "Oklahoma Beheading Suspect Uttered Arabic Words during Attack, Had 'Infatuation' with Beheadings: Prosecutor," TheBlaze, September 30, 2014, http://www.theblaze.com/stories/2014/09/30/oklahoma-beheading-suspect-uttered-arabic-words-during-attack-had-infatuation-with-beheadings-prosecutor/.

37. Ohlheiser, "What We Know about Alton Nolen."

38. Simon Sebag Montefiore, *Jerusalem: The Biography* (New York: Vintage Books, 2011), 129.

39. Eliza Shapiro, "Heavy History: Is Tamerlan Tsarnaev Named after a Brutal Warlord?," Daily Beast, April 19, 2013, http://www.thedailybeast.com/articles/2013/04/19/is-tamerlan-tsarnaev-named-after-a-brutal-warlord.html.

40. Ishaan Tharoor, "Saudi Arabia, Key to Obama's Strategy, Beheaded at Least 8 People Last Month," *Washington Post*, September 11, 2014, http://www.washingtonpost.com/blogs/worldviews/wp/2014/09/11/saudi-arabia-key-to-obamas-strategy-beheaded-at-least-8-people-last-month/.

41. "New York TV Exec Gets 25 Years to Life for Wife's Beheading," CNN, March 9, 2011, http://www.cnn.com/2011/CRIME/03/09/new.york.beheading/.

42. Jeff Pegues, "Gruesome Double Murder, Men Decapitated," WABC-TV New York, February 11, 2013, http://7online.com/archive/8989357/.

43. Ben Morgan et al., "Woman Beheaded: 'Muslim Convert' Known as Fat Nick Suspected of Slaughtering Grandmother Pictured for First Time," *London Evening Standard*, September 5, 2014, http://www.standard.co.uk/news/crime/woman-beheaded-first-picture-of-muslim-convert-nicknamed-fat-nick-suspected-of-murdering-82yearold-9714057.html.

44. Dave Urbanski, "Another Oklahoma Man, Reportedly a Muslim, Arrested after He Allegedly Threatened to Cut Off Coworker's Head: 'This Is Just What We Do,'" TheBlaze, September 28, 2014, http://www.theblaze.com/stories/2014/09/28/another-oklahoma-man-reportedly-a-muslim-arrested-after-he-allegedly-threatened-to-cut-off-coworkers-head-this-is-just-what-we-do/.

45. Richard Engel, James Novogrod, and Michele Neubert, "Exclusive: American Extremist Reveals His Quest to Join ISIS," NBC News, September 3, 2014, http://www.nbcnews.com/storyline/isis-terror/exclusive-american-extremist-reveals-his-quest-join-isis-n194796.

46. Ibid.

47. Ibid.

48. Rick Jervis, "Suspected American Militant Held after Airport Arrest," *USA Today*, August 11, 2014, http://www.usatoday.com/story/news/nation/2014/08/11/kennedy-airport-arrest/13889915/.

49. Associated Press, "NY Man 'Tried to Aid ISIS,'" *New York Post*, September 17, 2014, http://nypost.com/2014/09/17/upstate-ny-man-allegedly-tried-to-aid-isis/.

50. Greg Botelho, "Feds: NY Store Owner Plotted to Send Jihadists to Syria, Kill U.S. Troops Himself," CNN, September 17, 2014, http://www.cnn.com/2014/09/16/justice/suspected-isis-supporter-ny/.

51. Associated Press, "NY Man."

52. "Halal Mojoes Chicken & Pizza, 1193 North Clinton Avenue, Rochester, NY 14621—Restaurant Inspection Findings and Violations," City-Data. com, http://www.city-data.com/ny-state-restaurants/HALAL-MOJOES-CHICKEN-PIZZA.html.

53. Amy Young, "Former Employee Says Not Surprised by Elfgeeh's Arrest," RochesterHomepage.net, June 2, 2014, http://www.rochesterhomepage. net/story/d/story/former-employee-says-not-surprised-by-elfgeehs-arr/20415/H-4mUYmfNUOoW7cFfGjmiQ.

54. Botelho, "Feds: NY Store Owner."

55. Mike Brunker, "Illinois Teen Charged with Trying to Travel to Mideast to Join ISIS," NBC News, October 6, 2014, http://www.nbcnews.com/ storyline/isis-terror/illinois-teen-charged-trying-travel-mideast-join-isis-n219511.

56. Mark Guarino, "US Teen from Suburban Illinois Charged with Attempting to Join ISIS," *Guardian*, October 6, 2014, http://www. theguardian.com/us-news/2014/oct/06/us-teen-charged-isis-chicago-airport.

57. "Feds: Bolingbrook Teen Tried to Go to Syria to Join ISIS," CBS Chicago, October 6, 2014, http://chicago.cbslocal.com/2014/10/06/teen-terror-suspect-arrested-at-ohare/.

58. Associated Press, "Two Teenage Siblings Were Arrested with Would-Be Isis Recruit at Chicago Airport," *Guardian*, November 3, 2014, http:// www.theguardian.com/world/2014/nov/03/teenage-siblings-arrested-isis-recruit-chicago-mohammed-hamzah-khan.

59. "Motorist with ISIS Flag Makes Bomb Threat against Police," CBS Chicago, August 28, 2014, http://chicago.cbslocal.com/2014/08/28/ motorist-with-isis-flag-makes-bomb-threat-against-police/.

60. Devlin Barrett, "Ohio Man Charged with Plotting ISIS-Inspired Attack on U.S. Capitol," *Wall Street Journal*, January 14, 2015, http://www.wsj. com/articles/ohio-man-charged-with-plotting-isis-inspired-attack-on-u-s-capitol-1421272998.

61. Mike Conneen, "ISIS Graffiti in Northwest D.C. Puts FBI on Alert," ABC 7, October 8, 2014, http://www.wjla.com/articles/2014/10/isis-graffiti-in-northwest-d-c-puts-fbi-on-alert-107912.html.

62. Jeff Schogol, "Possible ISIL Leaflets Found Near Quantico Marine Base," *USA Today*, November 2, 2014, http://www.usatoday.com/story/news/nation/2014/11/01/possible-isil-leaflets-found-near-quantico-marine-base/18336375/.

63. Ryan Mauro, "Video: Houston Man Pledges Allegiance to ISIS in Front of Cop," Clarion Project, October 15, 2014, http://www.clarionproject.org/analysis/video-houston-man-pledges-allegiance-isis-front-cop.

64. See Erick Stakelbeck, "America Ripe for Muslim Brotherhood's Agenda?," CBN News, July 8, 2013, http://www.cbn.com/cbnnews/us/2013/July/America-to-Become-Brotherhoods-Fifth-Column/.

65. Shane Harris, "Lady al Qaeda: The World's Most Wanted Woman," *Foreign Policy*, August 26, 2014, http://foreignpolicy.com/2014/08/26/lady-al-qaeda-the-worlds-most-wanted-woman/.

66. See Erick Stakelbeck, "Muslim Brotherhood Gains Foothold in Boston," CBN News, June 6, 2013, http://www.cbn.com/cbnnews/us/2013/June/Muslim-Brotherhood-Gains-Foothold-in-Boston/.

67. Ibid.

68. Timothy M. Phelps, "Justice Department to Ban Profiling by Federal Law Enforcement," *Los Angeles Times*, September 26, 2014, http://www.latimes.com/nation/la-na-0927-holder-profiling-20140927-story.html; Pete Williams, "Holder Unveils Revisions to Limits on Profiling by Federal Law Enforcement," NBC News, December 8, 2014, http://www.nbcnews.com/news/us-news/holder-unveils-revisions-limits-profiling-federal-law-enforcement-n263661.

69. Steven Emerson, "New Details about the Threat and Operation of the New Islamic State," Investigative Project on Terrorism, September 6, 2014, http://www.investigativeproject.org/4559/emerson-on-fox-news-justice-with-judge-jeanine#.

70. Mordechai Kedar and David Yerushalmi, "Shari'a and Violence in American Mosques," *Middle East Quarterly* 18, no. 3 (summer 2011): 59–72, http://www.meforum.org/2931/american-mosques.

71. Ihsan Bagby, "The American Mosque 2011: Basic Characteristics of the American Mosque, Attitudes of Mosque Leaders," Report Number 1 from the US Mosque Study 2011, January 2012, http://faithcommunities today.org/sites/faithcommunitiestoday.org/files/The%20American%20Mosque%202011%20web.pdf.

72. See Erick Stakelbeck, *The Brotherhood: America's Next Great Enemy* (Washington, DC: Regnery Publishing, 2013), 222–23.

73. Chuck Ross, "Obama Official Praises Mosque of Oklahoma Beheader Alton Nolen," Daily Caller, October 5, 2014, http://dailycaller.com/2014 /10/05/obama-official-praises-mosque-of-oklahoma-beheader-alton-nolen/.

74. Kelly File, "Chilling: Man Who Attended Okla. Beheading Suspect's Mosque Reveals Radical Teachings," Fox News, October 1, 2014, http:// insider.foxnews.com/2014/10/01/chilling-man-who-attended-okla-beheading-suspect%27s-mosque-reveals-radical-teachings.

75. Ludovica Iaccino, "ISIS and Jihadi Terrorists 'Post 90 Tweets Every Minute' to Spread Propaganda," International Business Times, November 4, 2014, http://www.ibtimes.co.uk/isis-jihadi-terrorists-post-90-tweets-every-minute-spread-propaganda-1473064.

CHAPTER FIVE: JIHADI COOL: HIP-HOPPIN' AND HEAD-CHOPPIN'

1. Erick Stakelbeck, *The Terrorist Next Door: How the Government Is Deceiving You about the Islamist Threat* (Washington, DC: Regnery Publishing, 2011), 44–45.

2. "Anjem Choudary and the al-Muhajiroun Network," HOPE not hate, http://www.hopenothate.org.uk/al-muhajiroun/summary/.

3. "Return of the Islamic State?," Islamic Thinkers Society, http:// islamicthinkers.com/welcome/?p=1236&page=2.

4. Dominik Lemanski and Neil Doyle, "New Links Found between Isis Fighters and Preacher Anjem Choudary," Daily Star, June 15, 2014, http://www.dailystar.co.uk/news/latest-news/383905/New-links-found-between-Isis-fighters-and-preacher-Anjem-Choudary.

5. Russell Myers, "British Boxing Champion Anthony Small Defends IS Beheading James Foley," *Mirror*, September 2, 2014, http://www.mirror. co.uk/news/uk-news/steven-sotloff-beheading-british-boxing-4153714.

6. Jessica Best, "Radical Islamist Preacher Anjem Choudary 'Proud' of Lee Rigby Killer Michael Adebolajo," *Mirror*, December 20, 2013, http:// www.mirror.co.uk/news/uk-news/radical-islamist-preacher-anjem-choudary-2945584.

7. John Hall, "'Chillin' with My Homie or What's Left of Him': British Rapper Turned ISIS Jihadist Poses with Severed Head as They Seize More Key Towns Close to Syrian Border with Turkey," *Daily Mail*, August 13, 2014, http://www.dailymail.co.uk/news/article-2723659/ISIS-militants-seize-key-towns-villages-close-Syrian-border-Turkey.html.

8. Scott Shane and Ben Hubbard, "ISIS Displaying a Deft Command of Varied Media," *New York Times*, August 30, 2014, http://www.nytimes.com/2014/08/31/world/middleeast/isis-displaying-a-deft-command-of-varied-media.html?_r=0.

9. Alexander Trowbridge, "Jihadists on the Move in Iraq with Weapons, Hashtags," CBS News, June 16, 2014, http://www.cbsnews.com/news/isis-jihadists-on-move-in-iraq-using-weapons-and-twitter-hashtags/.

10. John Hall, "'How Is Democracy Treating You Guys?' ISIS Militants Take to Social Media to Encourage Ferguson Protesters to Embrace Islamic Extremism," *Daily Mail*, August 19, 2014, http://www.dailymail.co.uk/news/article-2728624/How-democracy-treating-guys-ISIS-militants-social-media-encourage-Ferguson-protesters-embrace-Islamic-extremism.html.

11. Adelle Nazarian, "#NapaQuake: ISIS Hijacks Napa Earthquake Hashtags to Spread Terror," Breitbart, August 26, 2014, http://www.breitbart.com/Breitbart-California/2014/08/26/NapaQuake-Islamic-Militants-Hijack-Napa-Earthquake-Hashtags-to-Spread-Message-of-Terror.

12. Simon Tomlinson and Amy White, "'This Is Our Football, It's Made of Skin #WorldCup,': After Posting Sickening Beheading Video of Iraqi Policeman, ISIS Boast of Slaughtering 1,700 Soldiers," *Daily Mail*, June 13, 2014, http://www.dailymail.co.uk/news/article-2656905/ISIS-jihadists-seize-two-towns-bear-Baghdad-U-S-tanks-helicopters-stolen-fleeing-western-trained-Iraqi-forces.html.

13. Jim Hoft, "ISIS Uses Kidnapped Reporter in Brutal New Twitter Campaign #StevensHeadInObamasHands," Gateway Pundit, August 25, 2014, http://www.thegatewaypundit.com/2014/08/isis-uses-kidnapped-reporter-in-brutal-new-twitter-campaign-stevensheadinobamashands/.

14. John Dodge, "Chicago a Top Terror Target: Ominous Tweet Connects ISIS Threat in City," CBS Chicago, August 22, 2014, http://chicago.cbslocal.com/2014/08/22/ominous-tweet-connects-isis-threat-in-chicago/.

15. Jamie Weinstein, "ISIS Threatens America: 'We Will Raise the Flag of Allah in the White House,'" Daily Caller, August 8, 2014, http://dailycaller.com/2014/08/08/isis-threatens-america-we-will-raise-the-flag-of-allah-in-the-white-house/.

16. Josiah Ryan, "ISIS Supporters Reportedly Post Photo of the Group's Black Flag with an Ominous Message in Front of the White House," TheBlaze, August 11, 2014, http://www.theblaze.com/stories/2014/08/11/isis-supporters-reportedly-post-photo-of-the-groups-black-flag-with-an-ominous-message-in-front-of-the-white-house/.

17. Nathaniel Zelinsky, "ISIS Sends a Message: What Gestures Say about Today's Middle East," *Foreign Affairs*, September 3, 2014, http://www.foreignaffairs.com/articles/141956/nathaniel-zelinsky/isis-sends-a-message.

18. Perry Chiaramonte, "ISIS T-shirts, Gear Help Terror Group Spread Murderous Message," Fox News, August 18, 2014, http://www.foxnews.com/world/2014/08/18/bootleg-isis-t-shirts-helping-terror-group-to-spread-fear-campaign/.

19. Ryan Mauro, in e-mail interview with the author, September 8, 2014.

20. Sophia Rosenbaum, "'Jumanji'-Loving Jihad Supporter Mourns Robin Williams," *New York Post*, August 13, 2014, http://nypost.com/2014/08/13/jumanji-loving-jihad-supporter-mourns-robin-williams/.

21. Alexander Smith, "28,000 Pro-ISIS Twitter Accounts Created Since James Foley Murder," NBC News, September 4, 2014, http://www.nbcnews.com/storyline/isis-terror/28-000-pro-isis-twitter-accounts-created-james-foley-murder-n195401.

22. Rachael Levy, "ISIS Tweets Call for Assassination of Twitter Employees: Extremists Linked to ISIS Tell 'Lone Wolves' to Target Employees of the Social Network," Vocativ, September 8, 2014, https://www.vocativ.com/world/syria-world/isis-threatens-twitter-employees/.

23. Guy Adams, "Five Minutes of Savagery and a Video as Slick as It Is Sickening," *Daily Mail*, August 20, 2013, http://www.dailymail.co.uk/news/article-2730354/Five-minutes-savagery-video-slick-sickening.html.

24. Scott Shane and Ben Hubbard, "ISIS Displaying a Deft Command of Varied Media," *New York Times*, August 30, 2014, http://www.nytimes.com/2014/08/31/world/middleeast/isis-displaying-a-deft-command-of-varied-media.html?_r=0.

25. David Blair, "How ISIL Doctored the Image of Obama, Making Him Appear Haggard in Videos: The Terrorist Group Carefully Manipulate Their Videos to Make the US President Look as Tired and Weary as Possible, Demonstrating Its Technical Prowess," *Telegraph*, September 3, 2014, http://www.telegraph.co.uk/news/worldnews/barackobama/11073769/How-Isil-doctored-the-image-of-Obama-making-him-appear-haggard-in-videos.html.

26. Jeryl Bier, "Kerry: 'Root Cause of Terrorism' Is Poverty: 'In Many Cases…'," *Weekly Standard*, January 15, 2014, http://www.weeklystandard.com/blogs/kerry-root-cause-terrorism-poverty_774682.html.

27. AFP, "Eradicating Poverty Will Defeat Extremists: John Kerry," *Times of India*, September 20, 2014, http://timesofindia.indiatimes.com/world/us/Eradicating-poverty-will-defeat-extremists-John-Kerry/articleshow/42941803.cms.

28. Michelle McPhee and Bryan Ross, "Official: American May Be Key in ISIS Social Media Blitz," *ABC News*, September 3, 2014, http://abcnews.go.com/blogs/headlines/2014/09/official-american-may-be-key-in-isis-social-media-blitz/.

29. Denise Lavoie, "FBI Offers $50,000 Reward in Search for Suspected Terrorist from Mansfield," CBS Boston, October 3, 2012, http://boston.cbslocal.com/2012/10/03/fbi-offers-50000-reward-for-suspected-terrorist-from-mansfield/.

30. McPhee and Ross, "Official: American May Be Key."

31. Josh Kovensky, "ISIS's New Mag Looks like a New York Glossy—with Pictures of Mutilated Bodies," *New Republic*, August 25, 2014, http://www.newrepublic.com/article/119203/isiss-dabiq-vs-al-qaedas-inspire-comparing-two-extremist-magazines.

32. Reuters, "Al-Qaeda Sympathizers Battle 'Infidels' with Rap," *Sydney Morning Herald*, February 11, 2004, http://www.smh.com.au/articles/2004/02/10/1076388363442.html.

33. Sudarsan Raghavan, "American Jihadist Believed to Be Killed in Somalia," *Washington Post*, September 12, 2013, http://www.washingtonpost.com/world/africa/american-jihadist-abu-mansoor-al-amriki-believed-killed-in-somalia/2013/09/12/3230f8ee-1bba-11e3-80ac-96205cacb45a_story.html.

34. J. Dana Stuster, "9 Disturbingly Good Jihadi Raps: OK, Maybe Not So 'Good,'" *Foreign Policy*, April 29, 2013, http://www.foreignpolicy.com/articles/2013/04/29/9_disturbingly_good_jihadi_raps.

35. Miranda Frum, "Bad Rap: An ISIS Killer in His Own Awful Words," *Daily Beast*, September 3, 2014, http://www.thedailybeast.com/articles/2014/09/03/an-isis-killer-in-his-own-awful-words.html.

36. Souad Mekhennet, "German Officials Alarmed by Ex-Rapper's New Message: Jihad," *New York Times*, August 21, 2011, http://www.nytimes.com/2011/09/01/world/europe/01jihadi.html?pagewanted=all&_r=1&.

37. AFP, "German Rapper-Turned-Jihadist Reported Dead in Syria," Al Arabiya News, April 22, 2014, http://english.alarabiya.net/en/News/middle-east/2014/04/22/German-rapper-turned-jihadist-reported-dead-in-Syria-.html.

38. Mekhennet, "German Officials Alarmed."

39. Richard Spencer and Ragdy Samaan, "Islamic State's New Icon Is a Hipster Jihadi: Sword-Wielding Supporter of the Caliphate Is a University Graduate from a Well-Off Cairo Family, Say Friends," *Telegraph*, August 6, 2014, http://www.telegraph.co.uk/news/worldnews/middleeast/11011634/Islamic-States-new-icon-is-a-hipster-jihadi.html.

40. Rajia Aboulkheir, "Meet Islam Yaken, a Cosmopolitan Egyptian Who Turned into ISIS Fighter," Al Arabiya News, August 3, 2014, http://english.alarabiya.net/en/variety/2014/08/03/Meet-Islam-Yaken-a-cosmopolitan-Egyptian-who-turned-into-ISIS-fighter-.html.

41. Spencer and Samaan, "Islamic State's New Icon."

42. Doug Stanglin, "'Rolling Stone' Defends Tsarnaev Glam Cover Amid Outcry: Magazine Says Negative Response Is Similar to Cover 43 Years Ago on Mass Murderer Charles Manson," *USA Today*, July 17, 2013, http://www.usatoday.com/story/news/nation/2013/07/17/dzhokhar-tsarnaev-boston-marathon-bombing-rolling-stone/2523891/.

43. Dylan Stableford, "Rolling Stone's Newsstand Sales Double for Tsarnaev Issue," Yahoo! News, August 1, 2013, http://news.yahoo.com/rolling-stone-s-newsstand-sales-double-for-tsarnaev-issue-171449116.html.

CHAPTER SIX: LONDON FALLING: THE BATTLE FOR BRITAIN

1.   "Group Hails 9/11 'Magnificent 19,'" CNN, September 10, 2003, http:// www.cnn.com/2003/WORLD/europe/09/10/sept.11.ukposter/.

2.   Erick Stakelbeck, "The Watchman Show: The ISIS Caliphate," CBN News, September 24, 2014, http://blogs.cbn.com/stakelbeckonterror/ archive/2014/09/24/the-watchman-show-the-isis-caliphate.aspx.

3.   Simon Tomlinson, "'Only Allah Can Judge Me': Muslim Convert Richard Dart Refuses to Stand in Dock as He Is Sentenced to Six Years in Prison for Terrorism Offenses," *Daily Mail*, April 25, 2013, http://www.dailymail. co.uk/news/article-2314594/Muslim-convert-Richard-Dart-refuses-stand-dock-sentenced-years-prison-terrorism-offences.html.

4.   Sophie Jane Evans, "Moment Muslim Extremist Warned There Would Be Terror Attack during William and Kate's Wedding As He's Jailed for 31 Months for Possessing Terror Manuals," *Daily Mail*, August 12, 2014, http://www.dailymail.co.uk/news/article-2723082/Moment-Muslim-extremist-warned-terror-attack-William-Kates-wedding-hes-jailed-31-months-possessing-terror-manuals.html.

5.   Raheem Kassam, "'Very Good Chaps': Anjem Coudary Admits Pro-ISIS Pamphleteers Are His Students," Breitbart London, August 14, 2014, http://www.breitbart.com/Breitbart-London/2014/08/14/Anjem-admits-ISIS-demonstrators-are-his-students.

6.   "Anjem Choudary and the al-Muhajiroun Network," HOPE not hate, no date, http://www.hopenothate.org.uk/al-muhajiroun/summary/.

7.   "Radical Preacher Anjem Choudary Released from Custody," BBC, September 26, 2014, http://www.bbc.com/news/business-29386983.

8.   Kathy Shaidle, "Islamists on Welfare: Paid to Plot the West's Demise," Middle East Forum, April 4, 2011, http://www.meforum.org/2870/ islamists-on-welfare.

9.   Erica Ritz, "Prominent Muslim Cleric: Collect Gov't Welfare as a 'Jihad Seeker's Allowance,'" TheBlaze, February 18, 2013, http://www.theblaze. com/stories/2013/02/18/prominent-muslim-cleric-collect-govt-welfare-as-a-jihad-seekers-allowance/.

10.   Raheem Kassam, "In Pictures: Pro-ISIS Agitators Take to the Heart of London's Tourist District," Breitbart London, August 12, 2014, http:// www.breitbart.com/Breitbart-London/2014/08/12/ISIS-agitators-London;

Dina al-Shibeeb, "Pro-ISIS Leaflets Target London Shoppers," Al Arabiya News, August 14, 2014, http://english.alarabiya.net/en/News/2014/08/14/Pro-ISIS-leaflets-target-shoppers-on-London-s-Oxford-St-.html.

11. Raheem Kassam, "'Very Good Chaps': Anjem Choudary Admits Pro-ISIS Pamphleteers Are His Students," Breitbart London, August 14, 2014, http://www.breitbart.com/Breitbart-London/2014/08/14/Anjem-admits-ISIS-demonstrators-are-his-students.

12. Steven Stalinsky and R. Sosnow, "On Twitter, British Pro-Jihad Islamist Anjem Choudary—Whose Network Is Regarded as 'Single Biggest Gateway to Terrorism' for European Fighters in Syria—Incites to Violence and Jihad, Calls for Conquest of West; in Tweet, He Defends Opinion Expressed by Accused Islamist During His Trial That U.K. Is 'a Theoretic & Practical Battlefield,'" MEMRI, December 13, 2013, http://www.memri.org/report/en/0/0/0/0/0/0/857/7665.htm#_ednref5.

13. Dominik Lemanski and Neil Doyle, "New Links Found between ISIS Fighters and Preacher Anjem Choudary: We Can Today Reveal New Links between Young Muslims Fighting for the ISIS Group and Preacher Anjem Choudary," *Daily Star* (UK), June 15, 2014, http://www.dailystar.co.uk/news/latest-news/383905/New-links-found-between-Isis-fighters-and-preacher-Anjem-Choudary.

14. Stakelbeck, "The Watchman Show: The ISIS Caliphate."

15. Ibid.

16. Ibid.

17. Madeline Grant and Damien Sharkov, "'Twice As Many' British Muslims Fighting for ISIS than in UK Armed Forces," *Newsweek*, August 20, 2014, http://www.newsweek.com/twice-many-british-muslims-fighting-isis-armed-forces-265865.

18. Kim Hjelmgaard and John Bacon, "More British Muslims Fight for Islamic State than Britain," *USA Today*, August 21, 2014, http://www.usatoday.com/story/news/world/2014/08/21/islamic-state-americans-british/14384045/.

19. Jonathan Owen, "Islamic State: British Fighters Make Up a Quarter of Foreign Jihadists," *Independent* (UK), August 20, 2014, http://www.independent.co.uk/news/world/middle-east/islamic-state-backgrounder-british-fighters-make-up-a-quarter-of-foreign-jihadists-9681547.html.

20. Grant and Sharkov, "'Twice As Many' British Muslims."

21. Mail Foreign Service, "Held by ISIS, Five Jihadi Brits Who Want to Go Home: Wantaway Fighters Stripped of Weapons and Marched to 'Punishment Centre,'" *Daily Mail*, September 12, 2014, http://www.dailymail.co.uk/news/article-2754241/Held-IS-five-jihadi-Brits-want-home-Wantaway-fighters-stripped-weapons-marched-punishment-centre.html.

22. Glen Owen and William Lowther, "Obama Sends CIA to UK to Probe Terrorist 'Breeding Ground': President in Pointed Snub to MI5 over 'Lone Wolf' Mission to Interrogate British Security Experts," *Daily Mail*, June 28, 2014, http://www.dailymail.co.uk/news/article-2673511/Obama-sends-CIA-UK-probe-terrorist-breeding-ground-President-pointed-snub-MI5-lone-wolf-mission-interrogate-British-security-experts.html.

23. Erick Stakelbeck, *The Terrorist Next Door: How the Government Is Deceiving You about the Islamist Threat* (Washington, DC: Regnery Publishing, 2011), 44–45.

24. Chris Pleasance and Tom McTague, "How Muhammad Is Now the Most Popular Name for Baby Boys in England and Wales…but It Doesn't Top Official List because There Are So Many Ways to Spell It," *Daily Mail*, updated August 16, 2014, http://www.dailymail.co.uk/news/article-2725724/How-Muhammad-popular-baby-boys-England-Wales-doesn-t-official-list-ways-spell-it.html.

25. Soeren Kern, "Britain's Sharia Courts: 'You Cannot Go against What Islam Says,'" Gatestone Institute, April 23, 2013, http://www.gatestoneinstitute.org/3682/uk-sharia-courts.

26. Erick Stakelbeck, *The Brotherhood: America's Next Great Enemy* (Washington, DC: Regnery Publishing, 2013), 238–39.

27. Ibid.

28. "Brighton Teenager Abdullah Deghayes Killed in Syria," BBC News, April 18, 2014, http://www.bbc.com/news/uk-england-sussex-27076266.

29. Andrew Malone and David Williams, "Torture Hell of Princes' Hostage Friend: How British Journalist Held by 'Jihadi John' Was Waterboarded, Given Electric Shocks, Tasered and Forced to Fight Other Prisoners to Entertain Barbaric IS Fanatics," *Daily Mail*, updated September 21, 2014,

http://www.dailymail.co.uk/news/article-2762901/John-Cantlie-Briton-ISIS-video-close-William-Harry.html.

30. Daniel Pipes, "Britain's New Export: Islamist Carnage," National Review Online, August 3, 2010, available on DanielPipes.org, http://www.danielpipes.org/8706/britain-export-islamist-terrorism.

31. Sohrab Ahmari, "Inside the Mind of the Western Jihadist: Shiraz Maher, a British Citizen Who Lived the Experience, Describes the Allure of the Islamic State for Young Westerners and the Deadly Peril It Poses," *Wall Street Journal*, August 29, 2014, http://online.wsj.com/articles/sohrab-ahmari-inside-the-mind-of-the-western-jihadist-1409352541.

32. Gordon Rayner and Martin Evans, "'British' Jihadist Who Beheaded Journalist Is Londoner Called John," *Telegraph*, August 20, 2014, http://www.telegraph.co.uk/news/worldnews/middleeast/iraq/11047109/British-jihadist-who-beheaded-journalist-is-Londoner-called-John.html.

33. Larry McShane, "British Doctor May Be Key to Identifying James Foley's ISIS Executioner: Report," *New York Daily News*, August 23, 2014, http://www.nydailynews.com/news/world/uk-doctor-key-iding-james-foley-killer-report-article-1.1913265.

34. John Hall, "'British Banker' Reveals He Has Quit to Join ISIS in Iraq because He Hated 'Being Ruled by Laws Other than Allah's' and 'the Self-Indulgence of the Rich,'" *Daily Mail*, September 17, 2014, http://www.dailymail.co.uk/news/article-2759535/British-banker-reveals-quit-join-ISIS-Iraq-hated-ruled-laws-Allah-s-self-indulgence-rich.html.

35. Soeren Kern, "Britain's Female Jihadists," Gatestone Institute, September 21, 2014, http://www.gatestoneinstitute.org/4714/britain-female-jihadists.

36. Ibid.

37. Jeremy Hodges, "U.K. Terror Police Ask Families to Out Home-Grown Jihadis," Bloomberg, August 26, 2014, http://www.bloomberg.com/news/2014-08-26/u-k-terror-police-ask-families-to-out-home-grown-jihadis.html.

38. Shiv Malik and Sandra Laville, "ISIS Recruitment Moves from Online Networks to British Mosques: Growing Evidence That Britain Is a Specific Target for Jihadis Looking to Exploit Fundamentalist Islam," *Guardian*, September 5, 2014, http://www.theguardian.com/world/2014/sep/05/isis-recruitment-moves-to-radical-network-and-mosques.

39. Abul Taher and Nic North, "'Infidels Must Wear Red Collars and Shave Heads': 'Nazi' Vision of Muslim Britain from Imam Who Ran 'ISIS' Barbecue in Cardiff Park," *Daily Mail*, June 28, 2014, http://www.dailymail.co.uk/news/article-2673493/Infidels-wear-red-collars-shave-heads-Nazi-vision-Muslim-Britain-Imam-ran-Isis-barbecue-Welsh-park.html.

40. "British Islamist Abu Waleed: Muslims Should Humiliate Christians in Order to Make Them Convert to Islam," MEMRI, January 16, 2014, http://www.memri.org/clip_transcript/en/4263.htm.

41. Taher and North, "'Infidels Must Wear Red Collars.'"

42. Anthony Bond, "ISIS: Watch British Student Boast of Joining 'Golden Era of Jihad' in Shocking New Video," *Daily Mirror*, August 28, 2014, http://www.mirror.co.uk/news/uk-news/isis-watch-student-urge-fellow-4126249.

43. Lee Ferran, Rym Momtaz, and James Gordon Meek via *Good Morning America*, "British PM on New ISIS Beheading: 'They're Not Muslims, [but] Monsters,'" ABC News, September 14, 2014, http://abcnews.go.com/International/british-pm-isis-beheading-theyre-muslims-monsters/story?id=25491141.

44. Simon Hooper, "UK Aims to Become Centre for Islamic Finance: Global Islamic Finance Market Is Valued at $1.3tn and Is Growing Faster than the Conventional Banking Sector," Al Jazeera, November 1, 2013, http://www.aljazeera.com/indepth/features/2013/10/uk-aims-become-centre-islamic-finance-201310319840639385.html.

CHAPTER SEVEN: AMSTERDAMNED: ISIS OVER EUROPE

1. Soeren Kern, "The Islamization of Belgium and the Netherlands in 2013," Gatestone Institute, January 13, 2014, http://www.gatestone institute.org/4129/islamization-belgium-netherlands.

2. Damien Sharkov, "Pro-ISIS Demonstrators Call for 'Death to Jews' in the Netherlands," *Newsweek*, July 30, 2014, http://www.newsweek.com/pro-isis-demonstrators-call-death-jews-hague-262064.

3. Abigail R. Esman, "Dutch Mayor Cancels Anti-ISIS Rally as 'Too Provocative,'" Investigative Project on Terrorism, August 14, 2014,

http://www.investigativeproject.org/4518/dutch-mayor-cancels-anti-isis-rally-as-too.

4. "Summery [sic] of Report 'Transformation of Jihadism in the Netherlands,'" Algemene Inlichtingen- en Veiligheidsdienst, no date, click on the hyperlink "The transformation of jihadism in the Netherlands; swarm dynamics and new strength" to accesss the report, https://www.aivd.nl/english/publications-press/@3114/transformation/.

5. Soeren Kern, "Dutch Jihadists in Syria Pose Threat to the Netherlands," Soeren Kern.com, May 15, 2014, http://soerenkern.com/2014/05/15/dutch-jihadists-syria-pose-threat-netherlands/.

6. Soeren Kern, "Moroccan Crime in the Netherlands & the Myths of Multiculturalism: 'Because They Do Not Want To,'" Gatestone Institute, November 28, 2011, http://www.gatestoneinstitute.org/2624/moroccan-crime-netherlands.

7. Jim Hoft, "Dutch Welfare Recipient and Jihadi Poses with Five Severed Heads in Syria," Gateway Pundit, March 18, 2014, http://www.thegatewaypundit.com/2014/03/dutch-welfare-recipient-and-jihadi-poses-with-five-severed-heads-in-syria/.

8. Sophie Jane Evans, "The Dutch Jihadi Fighter (and Artist) Training British Teenagers How to Kill in Syria (and When He's Not Doing That He's Taking Pictures of Cats)," *Daily Mail*, July 9, 2014, http://www.dailymail.co.uk/news/article-2685648/Syria-fighter.html.

9. "Dutch Mum Rescues Daughter from Islamic State in Syria," BBC, November 19, 2014, http://www.bbc.com/news/world-europe-30111040.

10. "Summery [sic] of Report 'Transformation of Jihadism in the Netherlands.'"

11. Kern, "The Islamization of Belgium and the Netherlands."

12. Abigail R. Esman, "Guest Column: The Disturbing Heroes of Dutch Muslim Youth," Investigative Project on Terrorism, November 25, 2014, http://www.investigativeproject.org/4664/the-disturbing-heroes-of-dutch-muslim-youth#; and see "Nederlandse Moslimjongeren en de Arabische Herfst," Forum Verkenning, November 2014, http://www.forum.nl/Portals/0/publicaties/FORUM%20-%20Verkenning%20Nederlandse%20moslimjongeren%20en%20de%20Arabische%20Herfst.pdf.

13. Janene Van Jaarsveldt, "Mayor's Remarks on Jews and Jihadists Sparks [sic] Outrage," NL Times, October 23, 2014, http://www.nltimes.nl/2014/10/23/twitter-uproar-hilversum-mayors-comment/.

14. Evelyn Marcus, "Dutch Official Calls ISIS 'a Zionist Plot,'" Gatestone Institute, August 23, 2014, http://www.gatestoneinstitute.org/4641/isis-zionist-plot; Timon Dias, "Dutch Security Official Haifi Champions Libelous 'Protocols of Zion,'" Gatestone Institute, September 8, 2014, http://www.gatestoneinstitute.org/4678/yasmina-haifi-protocols.

15. Christopher Caldwell, "Islamic Europe?," *Weekly Standard*, October 4, 2004, http://www.weeklystandard.com/Content/Public/Articles/000/000/004/685ozxcq.asp.

16. "The Future of the Global Muslim Population," Pew Research Religion & Public Life Project, January 27, 2011, http://www.pewforum.org/2011/01/27/the-future-of-the-global-muslim-population/.

17. Ibid.

18. "International Religious Freedom Report for 2013," U.S. State Department Bureau of Democracy, Human Rights and Labor, no date, http://www.state.gov/j/drl/rls/irf/religiousfreedom/index.htm#wrapper.

19. "Islamic State Crisis: '3,000 European Jihadists Join Fight,'" BBC, September 26, 2014, http://www.bbc.com/news/world-middle-east-29372494.

20. Greg Miller, "Airstrikes against Islamic State Do Not Seen [sic] to Have Affected Flow of Fighters to Syria," *Washington Post*, October 30, 2014, http://www.washingtonpost.com/world/national-security/airstrikes-against-the-islamic-state-have-not-affected-flow-of-foreign-fighters-to-syria/2014/10/30/aa1f124a-603e-11e4-91f7-5d89b5e8c251_story.html.

21. Richard Barrett, "Foreign Fighters in Syria," Soufan Group, June 2014, http://soufangroup.com/wp-content/uploads/2014/06/TSG-Foreign-Fighters-in-Syria.pdf.

22. Agence France-Presse, "France: 60 Women among Residents Involved 'in Jihad,'" Al Arabiya News, September 14, 2014, http://english.alarabiya.net/en/News/middle-east/2014/09/14/France-says-930-citizens-or-residents-involved-in-jihad-.html.

23. AFP, "60 Germans Died Fighting for IS—Intelligence Chief," Times of Israel, November 23, 2014, http://www.timesofisrael.com/60-germans-died-fighting-for-is-security-chief/.

24. "Summery [sic] of Report 'Transformation of Jihadism in the Netherlands.'"

25. Michael Shields and Toby Chopra, "Islamist Militants on Rise in Austria: Government," Reuters, August 22, 2014, http://www.reuters.com/article/ 2014/08/22/us-austria-militants-syria-iraq-idUSKBN0GM19R2 0140822.

26. Rosie Scammell, "Most Italian Jihadis with ISIS Aren't Immigrants," The Local, August 25, 2014, http://www.thelocal.it/20140825/50-italians-join-isis-in-iraq-and-syria.

27. "Canada's Foreign Fighters: And Don't Come Back," *Economist*, September 23, 2014, http://www.economist.com/blogs/americasview/ 2014/09/canadas-foreign-fighters.

28. Brendan de Beer, "Portugal's Jihadists," *Portugal News*, April 9, 2014, http://theportugalnews.com/news/portugals-jihadists/32641.

29. Barrett, "Foreign Fighters in Syria."

30. Michael McCaul, "Europe Has a Jihadi Superhighway Problem," *Time*, November 11, 2014, http://time.com/3578462/european-union-security-gap-foreign-fighters-terrorists/?utm_source=feedburner&utm_ medium=feed&utm_campaign=Feed%3A+time%2Ftopstories+%28TI ME%3A+Top+Stories%29.

31. "Yusuf al-Qaradawi," Investigative Project on Terrorism, July 9, 2008, http://www.investigativeproject.org/profile/167.

32. Anna Momigliano, "Young European Converts Are Swelling the Ranks of Islamic State: Flocking of Foreigners to Syria and Iraq Is Unprecedented, Expert Tells Haaretz," *Haaretz*, September 2, 2014, http://www.haaretz.com/news/middle-east/.premium-1.613705.

33. Ibid.

34. Madeline Grant, "16% of French Citizens Support ISIS, Poll Finds," *Newsweek*, August 26, 2014, http://www.newsweek.com/16-french-citizens-support-isis-poll-finds-266795.

35. "French-Speaking ISIS Fighters in Al-Raqqa, Including Former French Paratrooper Who Converted to Islam, Urge Fellow Muslims to Join the Jihad," MEMRI, April 22, 2014, http://www.memrijttm.org/french-speaking-isis-fighters-in-al-raqqa-including-former-french-paratrooper -who-converted-to-islam-urge-fellow-muslims-to-join-the-jihad.html.

36. Dan Bilefsky and Maïa de la Baume, "In a Video, ISIS Fighters Call for Attacks in France," *New York Times*, November 20, 2014, http://www.nytimes.com/2014/11/21/world/europe/video-shows-french-isis-fighters-calling-for-attacks-in-france.html?_r=2.

37. Ian Traynor, "Major Terrorist Attack Is 'Inevitable' As ISIS Fighters Return, Say EU Officials," *Guardian*, September 25, 2014, http://www.theguardian.com/world/2014/sep/25/major-terrorist-attack-inevitable-isis-eu.

38. Reuters, "Another Attack in France: Van Rams into Christmas Market, Hits 10 Pedestrians," *Haaretz*, December 22, 2014, http://www.haaretz.com/news/world/.premium-1.633265.

39. Griff Witte and Anthony Faiola, "France Sends 10,000 Troops Across Country, Protecting Hundreds of Jewish Sites," *Washington Post*, January 12, 2015, http://www.washingtonpost.com/world/hollande-calls-crisis-meeting-10000-extra-forces-sent-to-protect-people-of-france/2015/01/12/63610982-9a34-11e4-a7ee-526210d665b4_story.html.

40. Alexandra Hudson and Sabine Siebold, "Germany Warns Security Situation 'Critical' Due to Radical Islam," Reuters, October 28, 2014, http://www.reuters.com/article/2014/10/28/us-mideast-crisis-germany-idUSKBN0IH0PL20141028.

41. Joel Stonington, "On Patrol with the Man behind Germany's 'Sharia Police,'" Vocativ, October 31, 2014, http://www.vocativ.com/world/germany-world/germanys-sharia-police/.

42. A. K. "German Hooligans: Of Riots to Come," *Economist*, October 29, 2014, http://www.economist.com/blogs/charlemagne/2014/10/german-hooligans.

43. Rose Troup Buchanan, "ISIS Riots Spreading across Europe as Islamists Clash with Kurdish Supporters in Germany," *Independent* (UK), October 8, 2014, http://www.independent.co.uk/news/world/europe/dozens-injured-in-prokurdish-protests-in-germany-over-isis-encroachment-9782042.html.

44. "Anti-Islamization PEGIDA Demonstrations in Dresden Draw 15,000," DW, December 12, 2014, http://www.dw.de/anti-islamization-pegida-demonstrations-in-dresden-draw-15000/a-18133601; "Survey Finds One in Three Germans Supports PEGIDA 'Anti-Islamization' Marches," DW,

January 1, 2015, http://www.dw.de/survey-finds-one-in-three-germans-supports-pegida-anti-islamization-marches/a-18166667.

45. "Merkel Criticizes Anti-Islam PEGIDA Movement in New Year's Speech," DW, December 31, 2014, http://www.dw.de/merkel-criticizes-anti-islam-pegida-movement-in-new-years-speech/a-18164445.

46. "Survey Finds One in Three Germans Supports PEGIDA."

47. Reuters, "300 ISIS Supporters Facing Trial in Germany," *Jerusalem Post*, November 30, 2014, http://www.jpost.com/Middle-East/300-ISIS-supporters-facing-trial-in-Germany-383255.

48. News from Elsewhere, "Norway: Mohammed Most Common Men's Name in Oslo," BBC, August 29, 2014, http://www.bbc.com/news/blogs-news-from-elsewhere-28982803.

49. Andrew C. McCarthy, "Losing Malmo: And Brussels, and Rome, and Amsterdam…," National Review Online, August 27, 2011, http://www.nationalreview.com/articles/275686/losing-malmo-andrew-c-mccarthy.

50. AFP, "Danish Jihadists 'on Benefits while Fighting for ISIS,'" Al Arabiya News, November 28, 2014, http://english.alarabiya.net/en/News/world/2014/11/28/Danish-jihadists-on-benefits-while-fighting-for-ISIS-.html.

51. Anthony Faiola and Souad Mekhennet, "Denmark Tries a Soft-Handed Approach to Returned Islamist Fighters," *Washington Post*, October 19, 2014, http://www.washingtonpost.com/world/europe/denmark-tries-a-soft-handed-approach-to-returned-islamist-fighters/2014/10/19/3516e8f3-515e-4adc-a2cb-c0261dd7dd4a_story.html.

52. Natalie Ilsley, "Three Arrested in Copenhagen after Danish Mosque Declares Its Support of ISIS," *Newsweek*, September 4, 2014, http://www.newsweek.com/three-arrested-copenhagen-after-danish-mosque-declares-its-support-isis-268464.

53. Paul Miller, "Reports: Massive New Year's Terrorist Invasion of Israel Thwarted by Security Forces," Breitbart, July 25, 2014, http://www.breitbart.com/Big-Peace/2014/07/25/Reports-Massive-Terrorist-Invasion-of-Israel-Thwarted-by-Security-Forces.

54. *Haaretz* and Reuters, "U.K. Deputy PM: Israel Strikes on Gaza 'Deliberately Disproportionate,'" *Haaretz*, July 17, 2014, http://www.haaretz.com/news/diplomacy-defense/1.605735.

55. Lahav Harkov, "Former British Commander in Afghanistan: No Army Acts with as Much Discretion as IDF Does," *Jerusalem Post*, September 4, 2014, http://www.jpost.com/Arab-Israeli-Conflict/Former-British-commander-in-Afghanistan-No-army-acts-with-as-much-discretion-as-IDF-does-374382.

56. Ben Cohen, "Israeli Think-Tank: Majority of Identified Gaza War Casualties Were Terrorists," *Algemeiner*, December 2, 2014, http://www.algemeiner.com/2014/12/02/israeli-think-tank-52-percent-of-identified-gaza-war-casualties-were-terrorists/.

57. Luke Lewis, "45,000 March in London's Biggest Pro-Palestine Rally Yet," BuzzFeed, July 26, 2014, http://www.buzzfeed.com/lukelewis/londons-biggest-pro-palestinian-protest-yet-draws-45000.

58. Chris Greenwood, "Rising Tide of Anti-Semitism in Britain as Jewish People Face Backlash over Bloodshed in Gaza," *Daily Mail*, July 27, 2014, http://www.dailymail.co.uk/news/article-2707421/Rising-tide-anti-semitism-Britain-Jewish-people-face-backlash-bloodshed-Gaza.html.

59. Ibid.

60. Jessica Elgot, "France's Jews Flee as Rioters Burn Paris Shops, Attack Synagogue," Huffington Post, updated July 23, 2014, http://www.huffingtonpost.co.uk/2014/07/22/france-jewish-shops-riot_n_5608612.html.

61. Jon Henley, "Antisemitism on Rise across Europe 'in Worst Times Since the Nazis,'" *Guardian*, August 7, 2014, http://www.theguardian.com/society/2014/aug/07/antisemitism-rise-europe-worst-since-nazis.

62. Ibid.

63. Liam Hoare, "Brazen Anti-Semitism Sends French Jews Racing to Leave in Record Numbers," *Jewish Daily Forward*, July 16, 2014, http://forward.com/articles/202126/brazen-anti-semitism-sends-french-jews-racing-to-l/.

64. Micki Weinberg, "Wave of Anti-Semitic Rallies Hits Cities across Germany," Times of Israel, July 21, 2014, http://www.timesofisrael.com/wave-of-anti-semitic-rallies-hits-cities-across-germany/; Henley, "Antisemitism on Rise."

65. Henley, "Antisemitism on Rise."

CHAPTER EIGHT: AMERICA FIDDLES AND THE WORLD BURNS

1. Niv Elis and Lahav Harkov, "El Al Says There Is 'No Chance' It Will Cancel Flights to, from Israel," *Jerusalem Post*, July 22, 2014, http://www.jpost.com/Operation-Protective-Edge/Report-US-considering-grounding-flights-to-Israel-amid-rocket-threat-368492.

2. J. E. Dyer, "Finally, Obama Leads from the Front: The Hamas-FAA Move against Ben Gurion," Liberty Unyielding, July 23, 2014, http://libertyunyielding.com/2014/07/23/finally-obama-leads-front-hamas-faa-move-ben-gurion/.

3. Amie Parnes, "Israel Flight Ban 'Prudent,' Obama Says," The Hill, July 24, 2014, http://thehill.com/policy/transportation/213288-obama-defends-israel-flight-ban.

4. Tom Curry, "Ted Cruz Sees Obama 'Economic Boycott' of Israel as FAA Extends Tel Aviv Flight Ban," *Roll Call*, July 23, 2014, http://blogs.rollcall.com/the-container/ted-cruz-sees-obama-economic-boycott-of-israel/.

5. "FAA Lifts Ban on U.S. Airlines Flying into and out of Israel," CBS News, July 24, 2014, http://www.cbsnews.com/news/faa-lifts-ban-on-u-s-airlines-flying-into-and-out-of-israel/; Pete Kasperowicz, "State Goes after Ted Cruz on FAA's Ban on Flights to Israel, TheBlaze, July 23, 2014, http://www.theblaze.com/blog/2014/07/23/state-goes-after-ted-cruz-on-israel/.

6. Aryeh Savir, "Hamas' Mega-Attack through Gaza Terror Tunnels Exposed," Ynetnews, July 27, 2014, http://www.ynetnews.com/articles/0,7340,L-4550733,00.html.

7. Stuart Winer, "Video Warns 'Zionists' More Car Attacks Are Coming," Times of Israel, November 19, 2014, http://www.timesofisrael.com/video-warns-zionists-that-car-attacks-are-coming/.

8. Ibid.

9. Ibid.

10. Elior Levy, "Terrorist Known Hamas Member, Brother of Terrorist Freed in Shalit Deal," Ynetnews, November 5, 2014, http://www.ynetnews.com/articles/0,7340,L-4588477,00.html.

11. Winer, "Video Warns 'Zionists.'"

12. Maayan Lubell, "Palestinians Kill Five in Jerusalem Synagogue Attack," Reuters, November 19, 2014, http://www.reuters.com/article/2014/11/19/us-mideast-palestinians-israel-idUSKCN0J20E220141119.

13. "Hamas: 25 Years of Terror," American Israel Public Affairs Committee, December 10, 2012, http://www.aipac.org/~/media/Publications/Policy%20and%20Politics/AIPAC%20Analyses/Issue%20Memos/2012/12/AIPAC%20Memo%20-%20Hamas%20-%2025%20Years%20of%20Terror.pdf.

14. Ari Yashar, "Hundreds of Hamas Terrorists in Israel Switching to ISIS," *Arutz Sheva*, January 8, 2015, http://www.israelnationalnews.com/News/News.aspx/189706#.VLHaDifQlJk.

15. Amos Harel, "Spreading Out in Syria, ISIS Approaches Israel's Golan Border," *Haaretz*, December 18, 2014, http://www.haaretz.com/news/diplomacy-defense/.premium-1.632498.

16. AFP, "Rebels Seize Most of Syria's Golan Truce Line," Al Arabiya News, September 13, 2014, http://english.alarabiya.net/en/News/middle-east/2014/09/13/NGO-Rebels-seize-most-of-Syrian-side-of-Golan-truce-line.html.

17. Yaakov Lappin and Yonah Jeremy Bob, "Israel Arrests ISIS-Affiliated Cell in West Bank," *Jerusalem Post*, January 4, 2015, http://www.jpost.com/Arab-Israeli-Conflict/Cleared-for-publication-Islamic-State-cell-members-arrested-in-Hebron-386620.

18. Lazar Berman, "Three More Israeli Arabs Join Islamic State," Times of Israel, October 12, 2014, http://www.timesofisrael.com/three-more-israeli-arabs-join-islamic-state/.

19. Eitan Arom, "Spanish Parliament Easily Passes Measure Recognizing Palestinian State," *Jerusalem Post*, November 18, 2014, http://www.jpost.com/International/Spanish-lawmakers-pass-symbolic-motion-on-eventual-recognition-of-Palestine-382189.

20. Tovah Lazaroff, "European Parliament Urges EU Foreign Ministers to Support Palestinian Statehood," *Jerusalem Post*, December 18, 2014, http://www.jpost.com/Arab-Israeli-Conflict/European-Parliament-urges-EU-foreign-ministers-to-support-Palestinian-statehood-385012.

21. Adam Kredo, "Reports: Obama Mulling Sanctions on Israel," Washington Free Beacon, December 4, 2014, http://freebeacon.com/national-security/reports-obama-mulling-sanctions-on-israel/.

22. Robert Tait, "'Solve the Israel-Palestine Issue to Slow ISIL Recruitment,' Says John Kerry," *Telegraph*, October 19, 2014, http://www.telegraph. co.uk/news/worldnews/middleeast/israel/11172550/Solve-the-Israel-Palestine-issue-to-slow-Isil-recruitment-says-John-Kerry.html.

23. Thomas Joscelyn, "Obama Adviser: Jihadists' Caliphate 'Absurd,'" *Weekly Standard*, August 12, 2014, http://www.weeklystandard.com/ blogs/obama-adviser-jihadists-caliphate-absurd_802853.html#.

24. Eric Schmitt, "In Battle to Defang ISIS, U.S. Targets Its Psychology," *New York Times*, December 28, 2014, http://www.nytimes.com/2014/12/29/ us/politics/in-battle-to-defang-isis-us-targets-its-psychology-.html.

25. Michael W. Chapman, "Howard Dean on Paris Attacks: They're Not 'Muslim Terrorists,'" CNS News, January 9, 2015, http://cnsnews.com/ blog/michael-w-chapman/howard-dean-paris-attacks-they-re-not-muslim-terrorists.

26. Jodi Wilgoren, "The Vermont Governor: Dean Narrowing His Separation of Church and Stump," *New York Times*, January 4, 2004, http://www.nytimes.com/2004/01/04/politics/campaigns/04DEAN.htm l?ei=5062&en=1a78968b2fd09908&ex=1073797200&partner=GOOGL E&pagewanted=print&position=.

27. Fran Blandy and Richard Carter, "France Seeks Security Answers after Paris Attacks," Yahoo! News, January 12, 2014, http://news.yahoo.com/ world-leaders-join-paris-march-millions-attack-victims-053608792. html.

28. Dan Friedman, Adam Edelman, and Ginger Adams Otis, "Eric Holder, Top U.S. Officials No-Shows at Paris Unity Rally," *New York Daily News*, updated January 12, 2015, http://www.nydailynews.com/news/politics/ eric-holder-u-s-dignitaries-no-shows-paris-unity-rally-article -1.2073821.

29. Noah Rothman, "Obama Declares World 'Less Violent' than Ever," Hot Air, June 12, 2014, http://hotair.com/archives/2014/06/12/obama-declares-world-less-violent-than-ever/; Ben Wolfgang, "Obama Tells Troops: 'The World Is Better, Safer, More Peaceful,'" *Washington Times*, December 26, 2014, http://www.washingtontimes.com/news/2014/ dec/26/obama-tells-troops-world-better-safer-more-peacefu/.

30. Paul D. Shinkman, "Obama: 'Global War on Terror' Is Over," *U.S. News & World Report*, May 23, 2013, http://www.usnews.com/news/articles/2013/05/23/obama-global-war-on-terror-is-over.

31. Victor Davis Hanson, "Obama: Transforming America," National Review Online, October 1, 2013, http://www.nationalreview.com/article/359967/obama-transforming-america-victor-davis-hanson.

32. Raymond Ibrahim, "Egypt's Sisi: Islamic 'Thinking' Is 'Antagonizing the Entire World,'" Raymond Ibrahim: Islam Translated, January 1, 2015, http://www.raymondibrahim.com/from-the-arab-world/egypts-sisi-islamic-thinking-is-antagonizing-the-entire-world/.

33. Raymond Ibrahim, "A New Year in Egypt: The Significance of President Sisi's Speech," *American Spectator*, January 9, 2015, http://spectator.org/articles/61428/new-year-egypt-significance-president-sisis-speech.

34. Ariel Ben Solomon, "Sisi Becomes First Egyptian Leader to Attend Mass at Coptic Church," *Jerusalem Post*, January 7, 2015, http://www.jpost.com/Middle-East/Sisi-becomes-first-Egyptian-leader-to-attend-mass-at-Coptic-church-387041.

35. Elise Labott, "U.S. Suspends Significant Military Aid to Egypt," CNN, October 9, 2013, http://www.cnn.com/2013/10/09/world/meast/us-egypt-aid/.

36. Julian Pecquet, "Congress Allows Obama to Reopen Military Aid to Egypt," Al Monitor, December 10, 2014, http://www.al-monitor.com/pulse/originals/2014/12/egypt-military-aid-obama-congress-human-rights.html.

37. "What's Become of Egypt's Morsi?," BBC, September 6, 2014, http://www.bbc.com/news/world-middle-east-24772806.

38. "Federal Judge Agrees: CAIR Tied to Hamas," Investigative Project on Terrorism, November 22, 2010, http://www.investigativeproject.org/2340/federal-judge-agrees-cair-tied-to-hamas.

39. Ryan Mauro, "UAE Doubles Down on Designation of CAIR as Terrorists," Clarion Project, November 26, 2014, http://www.clarionproject.org/analysis/uae-doubles-down-designation-cair-terrorists.

40. Patrick Howley, "Obama Admin Spends Christmas Trying to Get Islamist Groups off Terror List [Video]," Daily Caller, December 25, 2014, http://dailycaller.com/2014/12/25/obama-admin-spends-christmas-trying-to-get-islamist-groups-off-terror-list-video/.

41. Steve Emerson and John Rossomando, "A Red Carpet for Radicals at the White House," Investigative Project on Terrorism, October 21, 2012, http://www.investigativeproject.org/3777/a-red-carpet-for-radicals-at-the-white-house.

42. Soner Cagaptay, "Erdogan's Empathy for Morsi," Washington Institute, September 14, 2013, http://www.washingtoninstitute.org/policy-analysis/view/erdogans-empathy-for-morsi.

43. Erick Stakelbeck, "Shady Ally? Qatar Accused of Sponsoring Terror," CBN News, October 15, 2014, http://www.cbn.com/cbnnews/world/2014/October/Shady-Ally-Qatar-Accused-of-Sponsoring-Terror/.

44. "Turkey Denies Allowing Hamas to Operate in Its Territory," Times of Israel, November 28, 2014, http://www.timesofisrael.com/turkey-denies-allowing-hamas-to-operate-in-its-territory/.

45. Jonathan Spyer, "Amid Rumors of Mashaal's Expulsion, Doha Trying to Regain Alliance with Egypt, Saudi Arabia," *Jerusalem Post*, January 11, 2015, http://www.jpost.com/International/Amid-rumors-of-Mashaals-expulsion-Doha-trying-to-regain-alliance-with-Egypt-Saudi-Arabia-387335.

46. "US Condemns Turkey-Hamas Ties," *Jerusalem Post*, January 9, 2015, http://www.jpost.com/Middle-East/US-condemns-Turkey-Hamas-ties-387226.

47. Ryan Mauro, "Call in Congress to Sanction Turkey, Qatar for Terror Support," Clarion Project, December 11, 2014, http://www.clarionproject.org/analysis/members-congress-sanction-turkey-qatar-terror-support.

48. Jay Solomon, "U.S.-Qatar Alliance Strains Coalition against Islamic State," *Wall Street Journal*, October 10, 2014, http://www.wsj.com/articles/u-s-qatar-alliance-strains-coalition-against-islamic-state-1412983181.

49. Ibid.

50. Ibid.

51. "Kerry under Fire in Israel for Negotiating with Qatar, Turkey, Not Egypt, Israel," Times of Israel, July 26, 2014, http://www.timesofisrael.com/kerry-under-fire-in-israel-for-negotiating-with-qatar-turkey-not-egypt-israel/.

52. Jonathan Schanzer and Merve Tahiroglu, "Bordering on Terrorism: Turkey's Syria Policy and the Rise of the Islamic State," Foundation for

Notes

262

Notes

262

Defense of Democracies, November 2014, http://defenddemocracy.org/content/uploads/publications/bordering-on-terrorism.pdf.

53. Thomas Joscelyn, "State Department: Iran Supports Al Qaeda, Taliban," *Weekly Standard*, July 31, 2012, http://www.weeklystandard.com/blogs/state-department-iran-supports-al-qaeda-taliban_649167.html.

54. Reza Kahlili, "Iran General: Our Ultimate Goal Is the Destruction of America and Israel," Daily Caller, January 5, 2015, http://dailycaller.com/2015/01/05/iran-general-our-ultimate-goal-is-the-destruction-of-america-and-israel/.

55. Raphael Ahren, "With Iran Secure as a Threshold State, Has Israel Failed?" Times of Israel, November 24, 2014, http://www.timesofisrael.com/since-iran-is-and-will-remain-a-threshold-state-has-netanyahu-failed/.

56. Krishnadev Calamur, "Obama's Iran Remarks Labeled Conciliatory, Naive," NPR, December 31, 2014, http://www.npr.org/blogs/thetwo-way/2014/12/31/374197687/obamas-iran-remarks-labeled-conciliatory-naive.

57. Missy Ryan and Loveday Morris, "The U.S. and Iran Are Aligned in Iraq against the Islamic State—for Now," *Washington Post*, December 27, 2014, http://www.washingtonpost.com/world/national-security/the-us-and-iran-are-aligned-in-iraq-against-the-islamic-state—for-now/2014/12/27/353a748c-8d0d-11e4-a085-34e9b9f09a58_story.html.

58. "Iran Hits Back at Criticism over Executions," Al Jazeera, November 1, 2014, http://www.aljazeera.com/news/middleeast/2014/11/iran-hits-back-at-criticism-over-executions-2014111111452853492.html.

59. Rowan Scarborough, "Islamic State Launches Social Media Campaign to Unleash 'City Wolves,'" *Washington Times*, January 13, 2015, http://www.washingtontimes.com/news/2015/jan/13/islamic-state-launches-new-jihad-kill-westerners-h/.

60. Mary Grace Lucas, "ISIS Nearly Made It to Baghdad Airport, Top U.S. Military Leader Says," CNN, October 13, 2014, http://www.cnn.com/2014/10/12/politics/isis-baghdad-martin-dempsey/.

61. Damien Sharkov, "ISIS Use Video of Captured Pilot to Force Jordan to Halt Airstrikes," *Newsweek*, January 8, 2015, http://www.newsweek.com/isis-use-video-captured-pilot-force-jordan-halt-airstrikes-297827.

62. Saud Mehsud, "Pakistani Soldier Beheaded by Afghan, Pakistani IS Supporters: Video," Yahoo! News, January 11, 2015, http://news.yahoo.com/pakistani-soldier-beheaded-afghan-pakistani-supporters-video-133821178.html.

63. Adam Withnall, "Syria, Iraq...and Now Afghanistan: ISIS Advance Enters Helmand Province for the First Time, Afghan Officials Confirm," *Independent* (UK), January 13, 2015, http://www.independent.co.uk/news/world/middle-east/syria-iraq-and-now-afghanistan-isis-advance-enters-helmand-province-for-the-first-time-afghan-officials-confirm-9974304.html.

64. Dan Lamothe, "U.S. Military Social Media Accounts Apparently Hacked by Islamic State Sympathizers," *Washington Post*, January 12, 2015, http://www.washingtonpost.com/news/checkpoint/wp/2015/01/12/centcom-twitter-account-apparently-hacked-by-islamic-state-sympathizers/.

65. Aminu Abubakar and Faith Karimi, "2,000 Feared Killed in 'Deadliest' Boko Haram Attack in Nigeria," CNN, January 12, 2015, http://www.cnn.com/2015/01/09/africa/boko-haram-violence/.

INDEX